D0890181

A JEWISH BAKER'S
Pastry Secrets

A JEWISH BAKER'S
Pastry Secrets

RECIPES FROM A NEW YORK BAKING LEGEND
for Strudel, Stollen, Danishes,
Puff Pastry, and More

George Greenstein
with Elaine Greenstein,
Julia Greenstein, and Isaac Bleicher

TEN SPEED PRESS
BERKELEY

All rights reserved.
Published in the United States by Ten Speed Press,
an imprint of the Crown Publishing Group, a division
of Penguin Random House LLC, New York.
www.crownpublishing.com
www.tenspeed.com

Ten Speed Press and the Ten Speed Press colophon are
registered trademarks of Penguin Random House LLC.

Library of Congress Cataloging-in-Publication Data
is on file with the publisher.

Hardcover ISBN: 978-1-60774-673-7
eBook ISBN: 978-1-60774-674-4

Printed in the United States of America

Design by Kara Plikaitis

10 9 8 7 6 5 4 3 2 1

First Edition

CONTENTS

In memory of George and Adele, who are not here to see these wonderful pages.

Front row, from left, Adele Greenstein and George Greenstein. Back row, from left, Shira Bleicher, Julia Greenstein, Jose Medina, Isaac Bleicher, Julia Greenstein, and Paul Bleicher.

Introduction

Elaine and Julia Greenstein, daughters of George Greenstein

Our early childhood memories are of our parents spending more time in the bakery than they did at home. After school and on weekends, we often played in the back of the bakery, drawing pictures, reading books, folding and assembling cake boxes, or running small errands. In fact, before we were even tolerated at the bakery, we folded cake boxes while parked in front of the TV set at home!

When we were tall enough to look over the counter, we started waiting on customers and helping with various jobs in the production areas. We were most often assigned jobs forming dough into pastries such as crumb buns and rugelach. We longed to get our hands on the icing and finishing equipment or to mix the batters, but the answer was always, "no." Sometimes we felt like elves in a production line: standing on milk crates, assembling one tray after another of pastries from enormous batches of dough.

Even though we could eat anything we wanted in the bakery, as young girls we had a secret pleasure. We collected the glass bottles left by the workers in the bakery and returned them for their deposit to the deli next door. Instead of taking the cash, we traded it for a factory-produced, plastic-wrapped, squishy chocolate cupcake or pink coconut mound. We always made sure to eat the evidence before returning to our parents in the bakery. The brothers who ran the deli must have had many a chuckle after the baker's daughters left the deli.

It was not until college and graduate school, well away from our childhood bakery responsibilities, that we started to appreciate the bakery treats and welcomed the care packages sent from home. Our circle of friends really appreciated them, too! One of us, Julia, remembers her PhD advisor claiming that she added the benefits of these care packages to her recommendation letters. Who knows how much of her career was based on the contents of the packages?

Once we moved away from home, we began to become bakers in our own right, finally allowed to take on mixing and decorating duties outside of the bakery. Our dad showed great joy and pride seeing our results. When dividing jobs for our annual Thanksgiving family meal, there was always a negotiation because everyone wanted to make the desserts. Even though our father was always ready with specific comments on the quality of the results, it did not stop the competitive baking, which has continued with the next generation of bakers in our family.

George began this book about 15 years ago, after *Secrets of a Jewish Baker* was published. He worked on it off and on, but for one reason or another, it never made it to publication. George passed away on July 20, 2012. The next day, our family gathered at our mother's house. We all kept busy in our own ways to deal with our grief. Some of us cooked, while others started going through papers. When Paul, Julia's husband, found this manuscript, we, Julia and Elaine, and his grandson, Isaac, made a pact to get the book published. The three of us are the ones who always plan the meals and get excited over food. (It is a good thing we each have our own kitchen. We all inherited being the boss from our dad.) Julia has an amazing ability to create spectacular dinners for large numbers of guests, and Elaine dallied with being a pastry chef. Isaac caught the bug early, astounding us all with his amazing bread and pastries.

Finishing our dad's project has been a way to honor and mourn him. Sometimes as Elaine tested recipes, the image of him dressed in his white pants and apron, his big, floury hands gripping a huge rolling pin, rolling massive lumps of dough, kept her company in her kitchen. For Julia, going through the recipes and trying to see his vision brought back the hours Dad spent in his consistent search for the perfect baked goods, both at his own bakery and in our family travels. Isaac remembered standing on a high stool to see above the counter, watching his grandfather teach him how to roll rugelach, a family favorite. We hope this recipe, as well as the others in the book, bring as much joy and sweetness to your life as our dad did to ours.

Apricot Rugelach

The rugelach we made in the bakery does not fit in any of the chapters. But we love it so much we are including it. The last project our dad did every Sunday would be to roll out a huge sheet of the dough, and we would roll up each pastry. It seemed like it took forever to complete. Don't worry—the recipe below does not make the amount we made in the bakery.

Rugelach Dough

12 ounces (340 grams) cream cheese, at room temperature

2 cups (8.5 ounces / 241 grams) unbleached all-purpose flour

1 cup (8 ounces / 227 grams) cake flour

1½ cups (12 ounces / 340 grams) unsalted butter, cut into ½-inch dice

⅓ cup (2.3 ounces / 65 grams) sugar

¼ teaspoon baking powder

¼ teaspoon kosher salt

2 eggs

½ teaspoon pure vanilla extract

Apricot Filling

1 cup (10.5 ounces / 298 grams) Apricot Butter (page 33)

1½ cups (9 ounces / 255 grams) raisins, preferably golden

2 cups (8 ounces / 227 grams) walnuts, chopped, preferably toasted (page 31)

1½ cups (5.4 ounces / 120 grams) cake crumbs (see page 42) or bread crumbs, preferably fresh

1 cup (7.2 ounces / 200 grams) Cinnamon Sugar (page 40), half reserved for topping

¼ cup (2 ounces / 57 grams) unsalted butter, melted

Line a 12 by 18-inch sheet pan with parchment paper or greased waxed paper. Flour a second 12 x 18-inch baking pan.

To make the dough, in the mixing bowl of a stand mixer fitted with a flat paddle, combine the cream cheese, all-purpose and cake flours, butter, sugar, baking powder, salt, eggs, and vanilla. Pulse with the on/off switch until blended, making sure that the flour does not fly out of the bowl. Mix at low speed until the dough becomes smooth. It's okay if small lumps of butter remain; they will be absorbed into the dough as it is rolled out.

Tip the dough out onto the floured baking pan and press out or roll until the dough is level and fills the entire pan. Cover with parchment paper or plastic wrap. Refrigerate for several hours or overnight, until well chilled. Rugelach are best rolled while partially chilled.

Cut the dough in half and work with one part at a time, keeping the other half refrigerated or frozen until ready to use. (This dough freezes well, tightly wrapped, for up to several months. It is best when thawed slowly in the refrigerator overnight.) Allow the dough to rest until soft enough to roll: fingertips pressed into the dough will leave an indentation.

> ℬ **Baker's Secret:** *Bakers often soften dough that is still quite hard from being chilled by pounding the dough with a heavy rolling pin. First pound lengthwise, and then, crosswise.*

Roll the dough out on a heavily floured surface into a ½-inch-thick rectangle measuring about 20 by 12 inches. Lift the dough and dust with additional flour underneath. This dough tends to stick to the surface when fully rolled out. Brush away any excess flour from the top.

Spread a generous layer of apricot butter over the entire dough, from edge to edge. Cover heavily with layers of half of the raisins, half of the walnuts, half of the cake crumbs, and half of the cinnamon sugar. Press down with your hands or roll lightly to make the filling adhere. Roll the pastry in both length and width until it is about ⅛-inch-thick measuring about 36 by 20 inches. The filling will be compressed right into the dough; it will be almost translucent.

Trim the edges with a 4-inch wheel or pizza cutter, or a sharp knife. Using a thumb or a ruler as a gauge, cut strips along the short side of the rectangle about 1 inch wide. This should yield 30 or more strips. Beginning at the bottom left, roll the strip until it is about 1 inch high, like a snail shell. Tear the pastry free and roll over a half turn so the seam is centered on the bottom. Repeat with the remainder of the first strip, lining up the finished rugelach on the work surface in rows, letting them touch each other. Scrape or brush any crumbs aside with a bench knife, or brush as you work. When you arrive at the end of a strip, attach it to the bottom of the next row by pressing a ½-inch edge onto the strip. Continue rolling as if it is all one piece.

> **৪০ Baker's Secret:** *Press dough scraps and bits of filling that fall out into the strips as you roll them up.*

Continue rolling until all of the dough has been used. Brush the tops with melted butter. Place in even rows, spaced a finger width apart, on the prepared baking sheet. Repeat with the remaining dough and filling ingredients. Brush the tops with butter. (At this point the rugelach can be frozen for use another time or refrigerated to be baked later or the following day. Frozen rugelach can be baked—directly from the freezer to oven—without thawing.)

Preheat the oven to 350°F/175°C with a rack in the center of the oven.

Bake for about 35 minutes, or until lightly and evenly browned. Carefully lift an edge to see if the bottoms have begun to brown.

Remove from the oven and immediately brush the tops with butter. Drizzle a thin line of cinnamon sugar down the length of the rows. Cool on the pan on a wire rack. Serve when completely cool. Rugelach keeps well tightly covered or wrapped at room temperature for about a week. They can be frozen for several months wrapped tightly in plastic.

Yield: About 3 pounds (about 75 pieces)

> **৪০ Baker's Secret:** *Rugelach dough is very tender and tends to overbake on the bottom before the tops are done. Try nesting two baking pans inside the other. This creates an air space between the pans, insulating the pastries just enough to prevent burning on the bottom. Toward the last 5 to 10 minutes of baking time, the bottom pan can be removed if the bottoms are found to be lagging behind the tops in color. Adapt this method to the personality and quirks of your oven.*

Variations

Raspberry Rugelach

Substitute thickened raspberry jam (page 37) (preferably with seeds) for the apricot butter. Omit the raisins.

Chocolate Rugelach

Prepare the dough as above. Roll the dough out to a thickness of ⅛ inch. Melt together 8 ounces (227 grams) semisweet chocolate and 2 tablespoons butter. Spread on the dough instead of the apricot jam. Omit the raisins but use the nuts, if desired. Replace the crumbs with chocolate cake crumbs, if desired. Instead of rolling the filling into the dough, press down with your hands before cutting into strips. Substitute 1 cup sugar mixed with 2 tablespoons Dutch-process cocoa powder for the cinnamon sugar.

Other Variations

Sprinkle a cup or so of your favorite chopped dried fruit or nut over the jam or chocolate layer before cutting into strips. Try dried cranberries or cherries, candied orange peel, pistachios, pecans, or peanuts.

CHAPTER 1

Equipment, Tools, and Ingredients

You could be the most talented baker out there, but without ingredients like the best-quality butter, an accurate oven, and durable pans, it doesn't matter. The proper tools, equipment, and ingredients elevate any baking endeavor, making it easier for the final product to shine. This chapter explores what you'll need so you can tackle the recipes in this book to the best of your ability.

Equipment and Tools

In this section, you'll find all of the tools and equipment that the professional baker finds indispensable, along with tips for buying and using them if you're a home baker.

Some items will be familiar but perhaps used in new ways. Other items might be something new for you to discover. Often the best tools a baker uses are free—his or her hands. But when that isn't enough, the following tools and equipment will see you through most projects as a home baker. Many of them are inexpensive and easy to find; others are investments that will pay off for years to come.

Appliances

OVEN

Ovens are often like divas or temperamental bakers, and each has its own personality. In the trade, ovens are defined as either "baking even," "having top heat" (the top of the bread or cake tends to bake before the bottom is finished), or having excessive "bottom heat" (the bottom burns before the top is done). In most instances, the bottoms lag behind.

In the home oven, when baking heavy or tall breads and cakes that require longer baking time, the problem can become serious. If your oven bakes unevenly, turn the baked goods 180 degrees when half the baking time has elapsed. To counteract excess top heat, bakery ovens have various controls to help compensate. If your own oven consistently tends to leave the bottom of your baked goods underbaked (too light in color or raw), lower the oven rack one space. Often this will concentrate additional heat at the bottom. Alternatively, form a tent out of a sheet of aluminum foil or by cutting a sheet from a brown paper bag. After the first 10 to 15 minutes in the oven, or as the top begins to brown, place the tent over the top to

IN THE OLDEN DAYS

Years ago, bakeries had huge brick and tile ovens fueled with wood or coal. The ovens were cavernous; some were 18 to 20 feet long and 12 feet wide. Working at these ovens required brute strength and was often dangerous.

A flat wooden tongue of at least 18 by 24 inches, called a *peel*, was bolted to a wooden pole long enough to reach to the back of the oven. The baker would shovel breads, cakes, and pastries into the oven using the long poles. Heat was uneven inside, and the oven had hot spots. The bakers were expert at moving the baked goods around so everything would bake evenly. The hottest part of the oven was in the rear; consequently the baked goods in the rear always had to be lifted out over the ones in front. It was heavy work.

Picture this: the oven person positions a weighty pan of baked goods on the peel. He slides the peel and pan to the rear of the oven, some 18 feet away. Then, with one smooth motion, the baker snaps the pole back like a magician snatching a tablecloth out from under all of the tableware. The pan of baked goods remains at rest while peel and pole come flying out of the oven. The space behind the baker is a virtual "no man's land." Should the baker be unaware that someone is behind him, the pole flying backward through his hands is a missile that could cause great injury, even a fatality.

Consequently no one walked within the range of that pole without letting the oven person know of their presence.

NOWADAYS

Modern bakery ovens have rotating shelves (Ferris-wheel style), or rack ovens with turntables that constantly rotate removable racks of baked goods to allow even baking. Deck ovens with individual thermostats and controls for each deck allow variety baking with ease.

Deck ovens and rack ovens are available as convection ovens with blowers that gently circulate the heat inside of the oven while baking. It is claimed that the convection ovens reduce baking time or allow baking at lower temperatures. My own experience leads me to believe that they do not afford any appreciable difference in time or temperature, but they do indeed offer even baking, especially for baked goods.

Some serious cooks and bakers install professional and semiprofessional ovens and ranges in the home. Real restaurant ovens often require building permits and are subject to safety-code adherence and inspection. Extremely hot oven surfaces radiate heat throughout the room and can be dangerous with children about. I do not especially recommend these ovens for home use.

There are professional ovens available that are manufactured to standards for safe home use, allowing them to be placed close to normal walls and next to kitchen cabinets. Keep in mind that they can still radiate lots of heat into the kitchen and require professional venting systems.

Semiprofessional ovens and ranges are now available in sizes as small as 30 inches wide and can replace ordinary kitchen stoves. These are manufactured for heavy-duty use. They bake exceptionally well, doors and surfaces are generally cool to the touch, and they have many professional features, especially on the cook tops. The best burner grates are made from cast iron or enameled cast iron, built for endurance and high heat transfer. The grates are one- or two-piece affairs that cover several burners or the entire range. This makes it easy to slide a heavy pot without lifting, or to offset a pan so that it covers only a portion of a burner for better heat control.

keep it from coloring excessively. Remove the tent during the last 5 to 10 minutes of baking to allow additional browning, if necessary.

To counter excessive bottom heat, try double panning. For cookies and miniature pastries, the pros bake on double pans, two baking sheets nested together, creating a cushion of air to insulate the bottom just enough to allow even baking. Convection baking is an option on many new stoves. If using convection, lower the temperature 25 degrees.

I prefer radiant gas heat for baked goods. Professional bakers generally agree that gas heat is preferable, it creates more steam, and it is easier to adjust for temperature. One helpful hint, regardless of which fuel you use, line the oven shelf with quarry tile or a baking stone. This adds radiant heat to the interior of the oven, producing a better loaf of bread or yeast-raised pastry. (The same applies when baking large roasts, fowl, or casseroles.)

In the United States, most ovens use the Fahrenheit scale to measure temperature. I learned to bake in New York and am accustomed to using Fahrenheit temperatures, so temperatures will be provided in Fahrenheit throughout this book. However, in other countries, the Celcius scale is more prevalent, so I have included Celcius as well as a conversion table for common temperatures here.

Fahrenheit	Celsius
0°F	-18°C
35°F	20°C
325°F	165°C
350°F	175°C
375°F	190°C
400°F	200°C
425°F	220°C
450°F	230°C
475°F	245°C
500°F	260°C

FREEZER

The freezer lets you prepare large batches of dough to be put aside for future baking, with little or no extra time or labor required. Four loaves, for example, can be prepared from one batch of dough, one loaf to be baked immediately, another, perhaps, to be refrigerated unbaked for use within 24 hours, and the others frozen to be freshly baked at your convenience. An entire batch of dough can be mixed, raised, and then frozen either in its entirety or in portions to be thawed as required.

Although frozen dough can be stored for several months when well wrapped, the action of the yeast is never completely stopped, so the dough does age, but very slowly. In the bakery, the storage of unbaked dough was limited to 7 to 10 days so that there was no discernable difference in quality. At home, most dough can be frozen for 1 to 2 months, as long as the freezer keeps a consistent temperature of 0°F/-17°C or below. Dough should be double wrapped tightly with plastic wrap. Thaw dough overnight in the refrigerator.

Most pastries and cakes freeze well for up to 8 weeks, double wrapped tightly in plastic. Thaw in the refrigerator. Baked puff pastry does not freeze well, so it is better to eat it a day or two after baking.

REFRIGERATOR

Your refrigerator is more than just a space to chill and store perishable food. The baker employs refrigeration to retard the growth of yeast dough, allowing it to be prepared in advance and used as desired, within limits.

You can mix, cover, and allow any dough to rise overnight in the refrigerator for use within 24 hours. You can also let the dough rise the first time as usual and then mold it, pan it, and put it in the refrigerator overnight before baking. Keep the dough on the lowest, coldest shelf in the refrigerator.

THE 10-CENT WOODEN WEDGE CONVECTION OVEN

Modern bakery ovens have mechanical means that either allow the baked goods to revolve inside of the oven or have convection capability, a means by which air is constantly circulated in the oven with the use of fans or blowers.

Convection ovens for home use contain a fan that circulates air throughout the baking chamber. The air flow creates a constant, even temperature for baking or roasting.

Here's a trick if there is too much top heat in a regular home oven: if after half to three-quarters of the baking time has elapsed, it becomes apparent that the tops will burn or become overly browned before the interior or bottom is completely baked, prop open the oven door a crack, siphoning off some of the heat at the top of the oven. In baker's jargon, this causes the oven "to blow" or "to draw," meaning it forces the burners to stay on constantly, providing additional heat at the bottom while drawing air off at the top. This way you set up a natural convection flow, the same as if a fan were blowing. This effect can be accomplished at home using a small wooden wedge, cut from a piece of scrap lumber, to prop open the door an inch or less. Keep a cautious eye on the oven when doing this.

A chef's instant-read thermometer works very well for testing refrigerator temperatures; the best temperature is between 33°F/0°C and 38°F/3°C. Do not refrigerate yeast dough for more than 24 hours.

Mixing Tools

MIXING MACHINES

Stand Mixers: Stand mixers, like the Kitchen-Aid, can be used for mixing everything from heavy bread and yeast dough to delicate cookie batter. They come equipped with an all-purpose flat paddle, a dough hook for kneading, and a wire whip for airy batters and for whipping egg whites and cream. Many additional attachments are available for the cook and baker. I prefer to use the larger 5-quart capacity mixer with the more powerful motor, easily worth the extra cost when used for dough mixing.

Food Processor: Food processors such as the Cuisinart are quick for small doughs and batters. There is a Cuisinart processor with 14-cup capacity that is excellent for larger batches of dough. The 14-cup machine is large enough for nearly all of the mixing machine recipes in this book.

All food processors have blades for grating, chopping, and slicing. Processors grind fresh nuts into nut butter, mix all kinds of fillings, and process cake or bread crumbs in seconds. They work with unmatched speed and are good for large batches. Small grating jobs, however, do not warrant the disassembly and cleaning of the large machine. There are mini-processors available for small chores, but the same disassembly and cleaning time is required.

Handheld Beaters: Both hand-operated and electric beaters are good for light batters and general whipping.

WIRE WHISK

You can purchase an entire set of chef's wire whisks in varying sizes. They're good for innumerable uses in the kitchen. A balloon whisk easily whips up egg whites and whipping cream.

SPATULAS

It's helpful to have a set of rubber or silicone spatulas for all kinds of scraping and scooping chores, like scraping down the sides of a bowl and scooping ingredients out of a can or jar into a measuring cup or onto a scale. An extra-large spatula is the ideal tool for folding in egg whites or whipped cream.

SPOONS

An inexpensive set of large wooden spoons can be used for mixing dough and batter and for stirring icings and custards.

MIXING BOWLS

I prefer heavy stoneware for mixing doughs by hand and for letting them rise. The weight keeps the bowl from moving around on the work surface, and it maintains even heat, which aids in the speedier rising of yeast dough.

Stainless steel is virtually unbreakable, and it's good when refrigerating dough or batters. Dough can rise in stainless steel bowls and be moved directly from mixer to storage in the refrigerator, which means less cleaning. Plastic is generally too light for mixing and may retain odors as it ages and the surfaces become scratched.

SCRAPERS (PLASTIC SCOOPS)

The pros find an inexpensive plastic scraper indispensable for scraping or scooping out dough, batter, meringue, or cream from pots or bowls. It can substitute for a bench knife for light cutting and scraping chores. It also is useful as an aid in kneading difficult-to-manage soft dough. When held in one hand, it allows the baker to get underneath the dough and lift it, bottom to top, for kneading with the other hand. Most bakers always keep one at hand. The best shape to use is a rectangle with a curve along the top edge. You can also use a rubber spatula without the handle.

Inexpensive plastic scrapers can be purchased in cookware shops. Look for the kind that has a straight-edged bottom and a curved top. The curved top serves for scraping out dough from mixing bowls and scooping batters into baking pans or for filling pastry bags.

Measuring Tools

Pastries appeal to the eye and palate when they are of even size and are evenly baked. To maintain consistency, they must have an even texture. "Even" is a key word to successful baking at home.

Bakers always measure the length, width, and thickness of the pastry dough they roll and the size of the individual pieces that they cut. In pastry baking, everything one does is either measured or weighed, whether with a ruler, a scale, a clock, or, as the pros do, by adapting certain tools that are always at hand as measuring devices. What follows are some tricks of the trade.

MEASURING CUPS AND SPOONS

I suggest having two sets of measuring cups and spoons, one for dry ingredients and the second for liquids. For your dry set, look for stainless steel cups with rounded edges on the bottom for easy cleanup. For measuring liquids, Pyrex cups give an accurate reading. I like stainless steel measuring spoons.

YOUR HAND

When cutting strips of dough for ropes or twists, for example, bakers can use their thumbs, from the tip of the finger to the fold at the knuckle, as a ruler for measuring even strips about an inch in width. Measure from your knuckle to the tip of your thumb, then cut. Or run your knuckle down the strip while cutting with a pizza wheel or blade held in the other hand, the side of the blade just touching the end of your thumb.

The width of one or more fingers or of the hand is often referred to in a recipe as a gauge for even spacing. For example, to place pastries on a baking sheet in even rows, put them a finger width apart.

YARDSTICK

Sometimes the simplest and least expensive tools are the most useful for the home baker. The yardstick is a perfect example. You can use it to measure length, of course, but use its thickness, too, which is perfect for gauging proper thickness when rolling thin sheets of dough (about ⅛ inch). Use your yardstick for measuring, marking, or scoring, and as a straightedge for cutting long, straight lines of dough. This works best when used with the pizza wheel.

SCALE

I strongly recommend using a scale for accurate measuring. Food scales can be found in chef's supply and cookware shops. Many of the recipes in this book use weights to measure the dough; if no scale is available, estimate.

THERMOMETERS

Chef's Thermometer: A chef's instant-read thermometer has a long, thin probe with a round dial set on top. It comes in a protective sheath that clips onto an apron or shirt pocket. Some have a spring clip that allows you to clip the thermometer to the side of a saucepan. You can use the thermometer for everything from testing dough temperature to checking freezer temperature, as well as for icings and as a substitute for a candy thermometer. It should not be left in the oven.

Oven Thermometer: An oven thermometer is essential. As ovens age, thermostats tend to become inaccurate. In the bakery, the oven thermostats are tested and calibrated regularly. At home, it is essential to check oven temperatures with a good thermometer. Purchase the kind with a glass gauge filled with mercury. If the thermostat is regularly off by the same amount after preheating for 15 to 20 minutes, simply allow for the difference. For instance, if the thermometer shows the oven to be 375°F/190°C when it is set at 350°F/175°C, always set the oven 25°F/15°C cooler (325°F/165°C to maintain a temperature of 350°F/175°C).

Tools for Rolling Dough

BOARDS

Hardwood boards for cutting jobs and rolling dough make the best work surfaces. When well cared for, they will last several lifetimes. Plastic boards are inferior to wood—they scratch easily and are tough on knives. Studies also show that clean hardwood surfaces discourage bacteria growth, while hand-scrubbed but scratched-up plastic boards may actually encourage it.

PASTRY CLOTH

A good pastry cloth is made from smooth cloth, preferably cotton canvas or sailcloth, ideally 18 by 24 inches, or slightly larger than your largest cookie or baking sheet. When rubbed with flour, it allows many types of dough to be rolled quickly and without sticking. A pastry cloth eases the transfer of cutouts and cookie dough onto baking pans and can also be used for rolling up, jelly-roll style, yeast or phyllo dough. Smooth cotton or linen toweling can be substituted, but plain inexpensive cotton canvas, available in most fabric stores, works best. I never use a cloth cover for a rolling pin; it's unnecessary when pastry dough is properly dusted with flour.

ROLLING PINS AND STICKS

French rolling pins are made of hardwood and taper from the center toward each end to make it easier to roll dough evenly. The design overcomes the tendency to roll the ends thinner than the center, which is why I recommend this shape as an all-around rolling pin for kitchen use. It offers good value and improved control.

A fat wooden dowel, 2 to 3 inches in diameter, can suffice for most kitchen jobs. Many bakers cut an ordinary broom handle for use as a rolling pin. It's most useful to have two dowels, 1 or 2 inches in diameter: Cut the first to fit the inside length of your baking sheet. Cut the second to fit the width. Each can be used for rolling and as a measuring tool. The logic for using two rolling pins is that they can be used to roll or even out a sheet of dough after it has been placed inside a baking sheet. These same rolling pins can be used as rulers for measuring the length and width of rolled dough. Any lengths an inch or two longer or shorter than the rolling pins are easy to gauge by eye.

A ridged wooden rolling pin is available for rolling Danish and puff pastry. It eases the rolling in of butter between layers of dough, allowing it to be done in an even manner. It is a great tool if available.

In the bakery, I used heavy wooden or aluminum rolling pins equipped with ball bearings for heavy-duty rolling. In the home kitchen, a wooden rolling pin that rolls while the handles are held stationary is a nice item but certainly not imperative to have. However, it is worth purchasing if you do a lot of pastry baking.

Cutting Tools

KNIVES AND CUTTERS

Good knives are a lifelong investment. I prefer those that have wooden handles and rivets. They should be well balanced and feel good in the hand, with neither end feeling heavier than the other. The best ones are made of high-carbon stainless steel.

Bench Knife: The bench knife is used to cut dough into individual pieces. As an aid in kneading soft dough, it is used to reach under sticky dough and bring it up over the top. Bakers keep one on hand to scrape dough and flour accumulations off wooden and plastic work surfaces. Available in any restaurant supply house, they're inexpensive and will last a lifetime if you keep the blade clean and dry. Purchase one made from ordinary steel with a 6-inch blade. (I prefer wooden handles, but they have become more difficult to find.)

The bench knife can be used for measuring as well as cutting. The length of the cutting edge (6 inches) is the perfect size for large apple turnovers and other puff pastry squares. Use the length of the blade to mark off lines or squares before cutting. Cut with the bench knife by pressing the blade straight down through the dough. To cut a long strip, use a straightedge such as a yardstick as a guide for the bench cutter or pizza wheel.

Bread Knife: An 8- to 16-inch serrated, stainless steel knife is indispensable for slicing loaves and cakes.

Chef's Knife: Use this knife for cutting, slicing, and chopping. I like the 10-inch size.

Paring Knife: Use this helpful knife for general cutting and peeling.

Pizza Wheel: This knife, with its rotary blade 4 inches in diameter and a wooden or plastic handle, can be purchased at a restaurant supply house. Look for one that has a comfortable grip. It is an inexpensive, heavy-duty tool that will last a lifetime. When cutting, hold the blade of the wheel knife at a slight angle away from you so that when you cut along a line you can see where the blade is cutting.

Cookie Cutters: These come plain and fluted, and in graduated sizes for cutting cookies, biscuits, tarts, and puff-pastry rounds. They should have sharp edges on the bottom so they don't require much muscle when cutting. Many novelty shapes are also available.

GRATERS, GRINDERS, AND SKEWERS
Box Grater: The chunky old-fashioned four-sided grater will perform most jobs.

Coffee Grinder: In an electric grinder, a small rotary blade grinds or chops small batches of nuts, seeds, and spices. I keep one with my baking utensils, separate from my regular coffee grinder. In the bakery, I dedicated a meat grinder for chopping large batches of nuts—a coffee grinder is a relatively inexpensive alternative for home kitchens.

Rotary Grater: This handheld grater has a hopper on top and a crank that turns removable rotary blades to grind everything from cheese to nuts. It allows nuts to be ground without releasing their oils. It is perfect for small jobs and disassembles quickly for easy washing.

Skewers: Use a metal or wooden skewer or ice pick to punch holes in yeast dough before baking. This allows excess gas to escape so that the baked goods do not burst in the oven.

Piping and Portioning Tools
PASTRY BAG
Inexpensive disposable plastic pastry bags are available in cooking stores. Also available are canvas cones that can be reused. In a pinch, use a ziplock bag, fill the bag, seal it, and cut one of the corners. I like to use metal #8 star or French star tips and #4 or #6 plain round tips. The tips give more uniform portions and results. Tips are also made of plastic. If not available, pastry bags can be used without tips.

PARCHMENT PAPER CONE (DECORATING BAG)
The parchment cone is used for piping or "dropping out" (see page 36) small dots or lines of cream or fillings. It can also be used for decorating, for delicate writing on cakes, and for making stripes, scallops, and even drawings on cake.

Pans and Pan Liners
PANS
Invest in heavy pans that will last a lifetime and allow even baking. Purchase them in restaurant and bakery supply houses and better cookery shops.

Baking Sheets (Cookie Sheets): Heavy pans bake best. Two or more heavy aluminum baking sheets are a wise investment. Extras are useful to have on hand to freeze extra dough. Inexpensive, professional half-sheet pans (18 by 12 inches) are available in restaurant supply houses, gourmet cookery shops, by mail order, and in some warehouse clubs. Professional baking sheets have rolled edges. With normal use, these pans will last a lifetime. If possible, avoid using thin, lightweight pans.

Heavy steel pans (15 by 12 inches with 1 inch sides), sometimes called jelly roll pans, also work well, and two pans can often fit side by side on a single oven shelf in the average 30-inch oven. Cookie sheets insulated with a cushion of air between two layers of aluminum are effective for baking cookies and miniature pastries, which tend to overbake on the bottom. Although fine for cookie baking, they are not best for general baking.

Bundt Pan: This round, high-sided pan with a tube in the center is popular for yeast cakes, tea rings, and angel food cake.

Coffee Ring Pans: Excellent for baking high, evenly shaped coffee rings, these aluminum rings, 8 to 10 inches in diameter and 2 inches high, have flat bottoms and a 2½- to 3-inch tube rising from the center. They are also available in disposable aluminum foil, which, with care, can be reused a number of times.

Gugelhopf Pans: These embossed, curved tube pans are designed for fancy Hungarian and Austrian yeast cakes; the 7-inch and 9-inch sizes work well for the home baker.

Layer Cake Pans: These pans are available in round and square sizes from 1 inch to 4 inches high; some wedding cake forms are higher. In the bakery, I generally used pans made of heavy aluminum. Useful sizes to have at home are 7, 9, and 10 inch.

Savarin Pans: Used for baking savarins and babas, French savarin pans have a rounded bottom and a 4-inch tube rising in the center. They usually have a diameter of 10 inches with 2-inch sides; individual serving sizes are also available. The pans also can be used for some coffee cake rings, such as pecan and streusel or similar rings, when the toppings are scattered over the bottom of the pan and the cake is inverted after baking.

Springform Pans: Made with a removable bottom and a rim that snaps open and closed, these versatile pans ease the removal of the baked product. I highly recommend them. The sizes needed for this book are 9 inch and 10 inch.

Aluminum Foil Pans: Generally considered throwaways, in reality they can be used many times if handled with care. Widely available in many sizes and shapes, they are convenient to use when a form is required that is not often called for or is of an odd size or shape. Cakes baked in these forms store well, are transported easily and safely, and work well when baking for gift giving.

PAN HANDLERS

Oven mitts and pot holders are a must for the baker. The best are heavy mitts or pads available in chef's or baker's supply houses and some gourmet shops. If you use towels, be careful because dangling ends can dip into open flames. Never use wet mitts or pot holders, which can generate steam and cause a nasty burn.

PAN LINERS

Parchment Paper: For many years, the primary choice of professional bakers for lining baking pans was heavy silicone-treated parchment paper. Bakers were able to reuse the paper many times. It was also rolled to make decorating tubes, which could be refilled a number of times. As the cost of parchment paper rose, technology was developed for thinner substitutes. The thinner kind is what you will find available in most supermarkets and cookware shops. Although, as with all paper goods, the prices in recent years have gone up considerably, parchment paper still makes the best pan liner. Often a great part of the cost can be offset by reusing the same baking sheet several times. When the paper begins to brown, discard it. Parchment paper releases baked goods and cookies without the need for greasing. Even when it is necessary to grease the sheets, they will only need a light coating, which is still a big advantage over other papers.

Silicone Sheets: These state-of-the-art pan liners are designed for cookie and miniature pastry baking. The nonstick, removable, reusable sheets are textured and feel rubbery to the touch. Found in restaurant and chef's supply houses, they are available in full sheets (18 by 24 inches) that can be cut in half for a standard half-sheet baking pan. They also come in half-sheet sizes, which can be found in cookware shops and mail-order catalogs. They are expensive but warranted if you do a good deal of cookie baking.

Aluminum Foil: Though expensive, foil can be reused and is easy to cut and shape. It is also handy in an emergency when you find yourself ready to bake without your usual pan liner on hand.

Waxed Paper: A staple before the advent of plastic wrap, this versatile household aid still enjoys a useful function in the modern kitchen. It can be greased and used by the frugal baker as an economical baking sheet. Always grease waxed paper for oven use or it will burn. Exposed edges may char while baking, but this will not have any adverse effect on the baked goods. Waxed paper tends to stick to the baked goods but can always be removed with a bit of care or the blade of a knife.

Brown Paper: Cut from a paper grocery bag, brown paper makes an excellent pan liner. Recycling is environmentally desirable, and the price is right. These liners should always be greased.

Additional Tools

METAL SPATULAS

Bakers call them icing spatulas and use them to scrape down dough and batter from the sides and bottom of the mixing bowl, move pastries, and for cake decorating and spreading icings, toppings, and batters. Offset spatulas are exceptionally good for spreading batters and fillings. The blade is bent an inch or more below the handle (like a trowel) so that a batter or filling can be spread evenly. Look for high-quality stainless steel spatulas with thin blades, 6 to 10 inches long and 1½ inches wide. Test several for flexibility before purchasing. Ideally, one short, one offset, and one long spatula should suffice for any baking task.

WATER FILTER

There was a time when I scoffed at advocates of filtered water. Today we have filtered water on tap in our kitchen. When baking away from home, I use bottled or filtered water whenever I can.

I resorted to filtered water because where I live, the amount of chlorine in the water made it unpalatable. I discovered by accident that using filtered water recipes for yeast-raised baked goods resulted in dough that rose noticeably quicker. I also detect a brighter flavor overall in the finished baked goods.

For people who take cooking and baking seriously, I strongly recommend a good filter system.

Ingredients

Without the proper ingredients, you can't achieve the best results. Chocolate needs to be the best quality you can afford, cream is preferably not ultra-pasteurized, and vanilla extract should be pure. In this section, you'll find hints for buying the best ingredients possible and tips for making at home what you may not be able to buy, such as apricot butter.

ACIDULATED WATER

Acidulated water is used to prevent apples and other light-colored cut fruit from discoloring. Mix 4 cups water with the juice of half a lemon. If you just need a small amount, mix 1 teaspoon lemon juice to 1 cup water. As you cut slices or chop pieces of fruit, put them in the bowl of acidulated water; drain before using.

ALMOND PASTE

A very important ingredient in fine baking, almond paste is expensive and may be difficult to obtain. It is available in many markets packed in 8-ounce cans. Buy pure almond paste, not almond filling.

CHOCOLATE

There is an entire world of fine chocolate available to you. For outstanding pastry, always use the best chocolate. Over the years, I have come to prefer imported chocolate, including Callebaut (Belgium), Lindt (Switzerland), Nestlé bulk chocolate (Switzerland), and Valrhona (France), to name just a few.

Most of the recipes in this book call for semisweet, bittersweet, or, occasionally, white chocolate. Milk chocolate is used mainly in candy making and not used for these recipes.

The difference between semisweet and bittersweet chocolate is basically in the sugar content. The best way to select your own favorite is to taste not only the semisweet and bittersweet versions but also the various brands.

White chocolate should be made from cocoa butter, which is expensive. It will have an off-white or creamy appearance. Read the label to be sure the brand contains cocoa butter.

Chocolate chips, drops, and bits are hardened so as not to melt when baked in cookies. I use them for fillings and toppings in some of the pastries where I would like to have the chocolate crunch.

Chocolate wafers, generally used for molding or dipping chocolate, are compound chocolates containing additives that aid in hardening when dry, so they are not as rich tasting.

COCOA

Dutch-process cocoa powder is preferred for baking. It is alkalized so that it has a neutral pH, a less bitter flavor, and a richer color. Cocoa is manufactured with as little as 10 percent butterfat content. Available in light or dark blends, the best imported cocoa has a butterfat content of at least 16 to 18 percent and goes as high as 22 to 24 percent. In the bakery, I used Royal Bensdorp 22 to 24 percent dark cocoa powder imported from Holland. Using the best imported cocoa makes a marked difference in taste. The better cocoas are available in gourmet shops and mail-order catalogs. Read labels carefully. Do not use sweetened cocoa or so-called hot chocolate preparations for baking.

CREAM

Cream or whipping cream, when referred to in this book and unless otherwise stated, is heavy cream with a butterfat content of 38 to 40 percent. Most of the cream found in local markets is ultra-pasteurized. Pasteurization is a heat-based process. Basically the milk or cream is brought to a temperature of 160°F/71°C and held there for a defined amount of time. Ultra-pasteurization is sterilization, and chemicals may even be added to the cream. Read the label. Sterilization imparts a long shelf life to cream, which is nice for the manufacturer and the retailer, less so for the consumer. The cream loses some of its wonderful depth and richness. It also loses some of its better whipping qualities. Seek out a source for fresh whipping cream that hasn't been ultra-pasteurized. It's worth the effort.

> ➄ **Baker's Secret:** *Bakers prefer to use cream that is at least 2 to 3 days old. Many claim that it whips up both thicker and with extra volume. When cream has stood in the refrigerator for several days, shake it before using.*

EGGS

Use eggs that are as fresh as possible. There is no difference in quality or taste between white eggs and brown. For uniformity in measuring, the eggs required in the recipes are always assumed to be large eggs. Never use an egg that is cracked or crazed.

For uncooked creams and meringue, I suggest using powdered albumen (egg white powder) or meringue powder, available in gourmet shops and by mail order. I recommend avoiding eating raw eggs: they can be a source of foodborne illness.

FATS AND OILS

Both animal and vegetable fats, when used in cooking and baking, impart the foundation for rich flavor. What we consider to be rich food is generally synonymous with high fat content. Although we strive to limit its use in our daily diet, a certain percentage of fat is necessary to sustain normal nutrition. The prudent person consumes food with high-fat content in moderation. The basis for any healthy diet is moderation and variety.

Butter: Butter is one of the most important ingredients in fine baking. I remember my mother sending me out for milk or butter as a child. Money was not needed at the corner grocery shop. One merely told the grocer to "mark it down," and the bill was usually settled on payday. The grocery had a walk-in "icebox," which formed a wall behind the service counter. The contents were revealed through oak-framed double-hung windows with polished brass hardware. Behind two of the windows stood two tubs, turned sideways, each containing 64 pounds of golden yellow butter. Turned on their sides so that the contents were exposed to the viewer, one tub contained what my mother called "fresh butter," or "sweet butter," and the other "storage butter," or "salt butter," which cost a few pennies less per pound. Butter was cut from the block with a huge knife.

I don't remember having salted butter until I was at least 12 years old. When I was sent to the grocery, my mother always admonished, "Now make sure you ask for the fresh butter." In those times, it really was sweet and dairy fresh. Refrigeration was not readily available, and butter was perishable. It had to be moved quickly from farm to market to consumer. Foods such as butter and meat, as is still the case in many parts of the world, were often preserved by salting, but the fresh unsalted butter had a subtle penetrating flavor and aroma that we generally do not enjoy today. Recipes in this book all use unsalted butter.

Vegetable Oil: This liquid shortening is polyunsaturated or monounsaturated fat. Nutritionally it is more desirable than hard fats, but keep in mind it still has the same number of calories from fat as all of the above. In baking, vegetable oil often cannot be substituted for hard fats. Use vegetable or canola oil in the recipes where oil is specified.

Vegetable Shortening: Hydrogenated vegetable oil that is hardened and aerated produces a solid fat that has a long shelf life and does not require refrigeration. It works well in baking, producing cakes with a very light and tender crumb. Some vegetable shortenings are emulsified to further expand these qualities by allowing a greater ratio of sugar to fat to be absorbed into the batter. These shortenings are bland and add no taste or flavor of their own, although some are available with butter flavor. When using vegetable shortening, do not use the flavored variety.

FLOURS

All-Purpose Flour: All-purpose flour is a combination of different flours milled for the home baker. It is also used by many restaurant chefs, but it is not used in the bakery. Bakers have other flour available when a lower protein content is desirable. All-purpose flour has a gluten content of about 12 grams per cup. Unbleached all-purpose flour, which I prefer, contains about 13 grams of gluten per cup. Many of the recipes in this book require all-purpose flour. It can generally be used as a substitute for bread flour—unbleached is better—but it will not produce the same results.

Bread Flour: In the bakery, this flour is called high-gluten flour. Gluten is the protein found in flour, and the best high-gluten flour contains about 14 grams of gluten in each cup. Today it can be found in most supermarkets.

Bread flour is milled from hard wheat. The best, which may be difficult to obtain, comes from Montana and North Dakota and is usually packaged for professional bakers. A friendly local bake shop or mail-order sources are your best bet. You may want to try several locally available bread flours to determine which one you prefer.

When used for preparing yeast goods, high-gluten flour produces higher, lighter, and a more tender bread or yeast cake. Until recently, bread flour was difficult for the home baker to obtain. Consequently recipes were written using all-purpose flour or cake and pastry flour. Experienced home bakers will be surprised at the difference when preparing their favorite yeast-raised recipes with high-gluten flour. Those new to yeast baking can expect noteworthy results from the very beginning.

Bread flour sometimes produces a texture too light for some breads and pastry. In those instances, the texture is changed by adding flour with lower gluten content or by using pastry flour or soft cake flour. Pastry prepared without leavening or with baking powder or baking soda becomes too tough if you make it with bread flour. For pie crust and certain cookies, use soft flour with a lower gluten content.

Cake Flour: This soft flour is the most refined and is milled for light, airy batters and cookies. In the bakery, it is labeled "high-ratio" cake flour because it is milled to allow a higher sugar-to-fat ratio to be absorbed in a cake batter. SoftasSilk and Swans Down are two popular brands of cake flour.

Pastry Flour: A soft flour with a lower gluten content, use pastry flour for pies, short pastry dough, and cookies.

JAMS AND JELLIES

For quality baking, commercial jams and jellies are generally too thin, meaning diluted in flavor and likely to become runny when baked in the oven. Look for a product that emits the true flavor of the fruit and hasn't been overwhelmed by too much sweetener or excess added citric acid. Raspberry jam is available in cans specially for baking in some supermarkets and specialty grocers. Try apricot jam purchased in a Middle Eastern market. In domestic jams, I like Smucker's brand, both the raspberry and apricot jam.

LEKVAR

This Hungarian fruit butter is made from pureed, cooked dried fruits, such as prune and apricot. Poppy butter, made from ground poppy seed, is often included in this group (see page 38, for making lekvar).

NUTS

Use nuts that are as fresh as possible because flavor is lost as nuts age. Buy from a busy source that sells nuts by the pound and has a large turnover. Keeping nuts refrigerated extends their life, or they can be frozen and kept for up to 6 months. In baking, when nuts are to be mixed into the dough or batter, better bakers always toast them. Toasting brings out full flavor and refreshes stale nuts.

Almonds: Shelled almonds can be purchased raw (with the skins on) or blanched (skins removed). They are available as whole almonds, sliced whole almonds, blanched whole almonds, or blanched sliced almonds. They vary in price as well as in use. The recipes always specify which kind of almond to use.

When using shelled almonds, whole almonds are the most economical and versatile to purchase. These can be blanched, toasted, or ground as necessary. Their shelf life can be extended by refrigerating the nuts in a tightly closed container. Freezing will keep almonds for up to 6 months. Although nuts tend to lose flavor the longer they are stored, toasting or baking generally brings back most of the original flavor.

SALT

Salt has several functions in baked goods, the most obvious being flavor. When salt is omitted from bread, the result is often flat and tasteless. A secondary function of salt is its ability, when added in minute quantities, to enhance other flavors present in food. In the bakery, a pinch of salt is often added to fruits, puddings, creams, and custards to stimulate the taste buds, intensifying and bringing forth the sweet flavor already in the food.

In yeast baking, salt serves another important function. It controls the action of the yeast. Salt works as the opposite of a catalyst, allowing the baker to control the rise of the dough. When salt is not present, yeast dough rises with uncontrolled speed, and the dough quickly collapses, essential ingredients having been devoured by the yeast. The recipe measures in this book are based on using kosher salt, which has a larger crystal structure than regular table salt.

Sea Salt: Modern chefs and bakers use many varieties of sea salt, gathered the world over, for cooking and baking. Some can add exotic flavor and are very expensive, such as Guatemalan sea salt. All contain minute quantities of minerals, which add their own subtle and complex flavors to food, while at the same time finely honing the tang of the salt itself. Sea salt can be purchased loose, in health food stores, at very reasonable cost. It is available in fine and course grinds.

SOUR CREAM

Hungarian bakers often add sour cream to yeast dough. Sour cream aids in the fermentation, producing a lighter cake. It adds its own flavor while acting as a natural emulsifier to develop a moister and more tender crumb.

SUGARS AND SWEETENERS

Sugar fills an entire shelf in my cupboard. Jars of white, confectioners', turbinado, and light and dark brown sugar compete for space. The next shelf contains a few types of honey, molasses, and corn syrup. Each has its own special use and characteristics.

Brown Sugar: Brown sugar is sugar with molasses added. Light and dark varieties contain different percentages of molasses. Keep brown sugar tightly wrapped to prevent hardening. If it has hardened, brown sugar can be softened in the microwave. Measure brown sugar by firmly packing it into the measuring utensil. In the recipes, "brown sugar" always refers to light brown sugar unless otherwise specified. Light and dark brown are usually interchangeable if only one kind is on hand. The dark will have a stronger molasses taste.

Coarse Sugar: This sugar is used for topping on pastry and cookies. Look for coarse sugar in gourmet shops and mail-order catalogs. It may be called standard sugar, medium sugar, sanding sugar, or crystal sugar. These specialty sugars vary in coarseness. Any one of them will do.

Confectioners' Sugar: Powdered sugar (10X is the finest) contains a small percentage of cornstarch to prevent caking. It is used for icings and toppings. If lumpy, sift before using.

Granulated Sugar: Unless stated otherwise in the recipe, "sugar" refers to granulated or fine granulated sugar. For home use, I find no appreciable difference between brands. Try to buy sugar that is fresh and not lumpy.

Honey: Honey is produced worldwide. Each type of honey has its own flavor derived from the flowers from which the nectar is gathered. Honey is sweeter than sugar, although for ease of use it can generally replace sugar cup for cup. When replacing sugar with honey in a recipe, bakers like to use half honey, half sugar.

In the bakery, I used clover honey for its light color and taste, and buckwheat honey when dark color and strong assertive flavor was desired. The old-time Austrian and Hungarian bakers insisted on aging the honey. In my bakeries, as in my father's time, honey was stored for a minimum of 6 months and preferably for a year before we used it. We purchased it twice a year, in the winter for use during the spring holidays and then in spring for winter use.

YEAST

Yeast is the fundamental component in any leavened bread or pastry. The home baker has several choices available when selecting yeast. I have indicated my personal preferences.

Active Dry Yeast: The recipes in this book are formulated to use active dry yeast, the kind available in ¼-ounce packets and sold in your local market. Activate the yeast by softening it in a small amount of warm liquid, 95°F to 115°F/35°F to 46°F. You can purchase active dry yeast in bulk, available in sealed 1- or 2-pound bags in restaurant supply houses, warehouse clubs, and by mail order. This brings the cost down significantly. Once the bag is opened, the granules will keep well for 6 months in the refrigerator or indefinitely in the freezer. There's no need to thaw yeast, just measure

In my dad's time, when refrigeration was not always available and iceboxes were often in use, the bakers always proofed, or tested, the yeast before using it. They dissolved the yeast in a portion of warm water deducted from the liquid in the recipe, added a pinch of sugar, and allowed the mixture to stand for 5 or 10 minutes while they prepared the rest of the recipe. If the yeast was viable, it would bubble up and foam. If not, it was discarded. You will find many current cookbook recipes still making use of this procedure. If the yeast is not outdated or has been stored properly as outlined above, proofing is not necessary. Only if the yeast is suspect would I take the time to proof. When proofing yeast, the addition of sugar can be omitted; a pinch of flour works just as well.

(a scant tablespoon is equivalent to one ¼-ounce packet) and use in the recipe.

Fresh Compressed Yeast: In the bakery, we used fresh, compressed cakes of yeast. Bakers feel, with some justification, that dough made with fresh yeast has more spring and aroma. Genuinely fresh yeast is difficult for the home baker to obtain. In the bakery, we never used yeast more than 1 week old. Yeast generally comes in 2-pound cakes. To use up that much product is impractical in the home kitchen, though I have cut fresh yeast into 1-ounce or teaspoon-size portions and kept them frozen until needed. This works but it is difficult to manage, and you can never be assured as to how fresh the yeast was when first obtained.

If you still want to use fresh yeast, use 1 part fresh yeast in place of 2 parts active dry yeast. I do not recommend using the small squares found in local markets because they are easily mishandled.

Instant Dry Yeast: Developed in Europe, instant dry yeast is formulated to dissolve and become activated when mixed with the dry ingredients. There is no need to dissolve it in warm water. It is becoming more popular with professional bakers.

In my father's day, bakers always dissolved fresh compressed yeast in warm water before adding it to the dough. Bakers now mix fresh yeast by crumbling it atop the flour in the mixing machine. Instant dry yeast is supposed to work in the same manner. This is fine when mixing by machine, which develops enough heat to dissolve the instant yeast. When mixing by hand, its use becomes questionable because no appreciable heat is developed while kneading.

Rapid-Rise Yeast: I do not recommend using so-called rapid-rise yeast because its use requires high heat in the recipe. The best yeast-baked goods are prepared by the slow, nurturing, controlled rise, or fermentation, of the dough. The ideal temperature is 78°F to 82°F/26°C to 28°C for the finished dough. Rapid rising causes the yeast cells to feed voraciously upon the starch and sugar in the dough, literally consuming the ingredients necessary for baked goods to be moist, tender, and tasty.

CHAPTER 2

Basic Techniques and Recipes

You'll find everything you need to know about techniques and basic recipes here, including baker's secrets for handling dough and ingredients, as well as recipes for preparing fillings, icings, and glazes. Although it's helpful to glance through this chapter before starting work, individual recipes will also refer to the correct page in this section as needed.

Pan Preparation

There are many ways to grease a pan. In the bakery we brushed solid vegetable shortening in the pan. For home use I recommend softened butter applied with a piece of wax paper or a brush. A convenient alternative is a spray of canola oil from an aerosol can or pump.

Cutting Parchment Paper

Parchment or silicone-treated papers of various sizes and shapes are in constant use in the bakery. Types of liners range from those cut to fit the bottoms of tube pans (they have a hole in the center to fit over the tube) to circles that fit the bottom of round pans to full liners for loaf pans and deep layer pans.

It is impractical and expensive to attempt to keep paper parchment sheets in a variety of sizes in the home kitchen. Here are directions for cutting out liners from a roll of parchment paper available in supermarkets and cookware shops to use as pan liners. Also included are directions to make paper cones for piping or bagging out.

Loaf Pan Liner: Lay the parchment down with the long edge facing you. Place the pan on its side, the open end toward you. Place the long edge of the pan along the bottom edge of the paper, centering the pan so that is equidistant from both ends. Carefully, so as not to change its position, slowly tip the pan away from you so that it lies bottom down on the parchment. With a pencil, draw four lines marking off the bottom of the pan on the paper. Set the pan aside. With pencil and ruler, draw four lines extending the sides and ends of the rectangle to the ends of the paper. You will have a long, exaggerated tic-tac-toe design. Cut the paper from the roll along the last pencil line.

Fold the short ends in toward the center at the lines marking the end of the pan. With scissors, cut through the 2 lines you have drawn from the short end of the paper in toward the center rectangle that represents the bottom of the loaf pan. Do not cut into the rectangle. This forms a center tab on the short side. Do the same on the opposite end. Fold the long sides over and crease them along the edges of the rectangle. Place in the loaf pan with the short ends to the inside. Trim any edges that come over the rim.

In the bakery, we would set this liner aside and keep it to be used as a template for measuring a new liner each time we needed one for that size. You might want to make a liner on heavier paper and keep it as a template.

Parchment Paper Circle: To cut a circle to fit the bottom of a round pan (such as a layer pan), start with a square of parchment cut slightly larger than the pan you wish to use. Fold it in half into a triangle. Fold the triangle in half once more, it should look like a piece of pie. Fold the pie shape in half into a thinner slice. Turn over the pan you wish to line. Place the tip of the triangle in the center of the pan. Fold the opposite end over at the edge or rim. With scissors, cut through the paper at the crease. When opened, you will have a paper circle that fits the bottom of the pan.

Parchment Paper Cone: To make a parchment paper cone, prepare an 8- to 12-inch square of parchment paper. Fold diagonally in half from opposite corners, into a triangular shape. Cut in half at the fold into 2 triangles, setting one aside. Hold with the base (the long end) of the triangle away from you, as in an upside-down triangle. Grasp the right end between your thumb and forefinger. Bring the right end over until above the bottom tip of the triangle. Do not release your hold. Your thumb should be on top, your index finger underneath. Twist slightly, counterclockwise so that your thumb is on the bottom, forming the beginning of the cone shape. At the same time, with your left hand grasp the tip of the cone between your thumb and your first two fingers. Grip the open end of the cone in the same manner, thumb on top.

Using your left hand as a pivot, continue rolling the cone to the end. Fold the protruding ends inward and crease the edges to prevent the cone from opening, or use a little tape if needed. With a teaspoon, fill the bag until one-half to three-quarters full. Press the open end to close. Seal by folding each end over into a dog-ear meeting at the center. Fold the top down, one or two turns to ensure the seal. With scissors or a sharp blade, snip off ⅛ to ¼ inch from the tip.

To use, hold the cone straight up and down in your fist, thumb on top. Apply gentle, even pressure with your fingers and the ball of your hand. Use the index finger of your other hand to guide or help hold the tip.

Measuring for Recipes

A prime measure of a baker is how a baker measures. A German expression, *"Mit Hand gewiegt und Auge gemessen"* or "With hand weighed and eye measured," derides the careless or inaccurate baker. In baking, a professional measures ingredients carefully and accurately. Indifference to the formulation of baked goods can lead to poor results. Why bother preparing your own baked goods, using the best of ingredients, and expending all of your effort, only to have a mediocre result, when you can produce dazzling cakes and pastries? Always follow recipes carefully and measure accurately.

Professional bakers generally measure liquids by volume: cups, quarts, and so on. Dry ingredients, however, are almost always weighed. I encourage the reader to do the same. Small amounts of ingredients, such as salt and most spices (those that weigh less than an ounce) are often best measured by the spoonful.

Measuring

FLOUR

Unless specifically stated otherwise, flour measurements in this book are always for unsifted flour. Measure the flour by dipping and scooping. Dip the measuring cup into unsifted flour and then level off with a quick pass over the top using a straight-edged tool, such as the back of a knife. Measuring by the spoonful is done the same way. Scoop out the flour so that the spoon is overfull. Level it off with a quick pass of the straight edge, as above.

The weight of a cup of flour can vary, depending on the amount of moisture in the flour, which is affected by humidity, storage, the age of the flour, the season, temperature, and even altitude. The recipes will always offer a guide for the baker to follow. For yeast dough, begin with less flour rather than more. Often the recipes give a range, such as 1 to 1½ cups flour. Begin with the lesser amount. As the flour is absorbed, more can be added as necessary. Adjust for moisture by adding small amounts of additional flour as necessary, not by adding more liquid. It is much easier to coax the dough to absorb additional flour than it is to absorb water. The most frequent mistake made when preparing dough for a yeast cake is making the dough too stiff. Too much additional flour results in a stiff dough more suitable for bread. Excess flour in the dough reduces the ratio of the rich ingredients, such as butter, sugar, and eggs, that make the cake tasty and tender.

After baking a number of yeast cakes, you will develop a feel for the dough and will easily make your own adjustments. Fortunately, yeast doughs are very forgiving in this matter, so do not worry about failure.

> **∽ Baker's Secret:** *A keen observer watching yeast dough being mixed might notice that as the kneading process approaches completion, the baker always stops the machine, reaches in, and touches and presses the dough with his or her hand. Often the baker will then run the machine at slow speed, adding small dustings of flour until the dough feels just right to the practiced touch. This feel for the dough can easily be mastered in the kitchen by making it a habit of touching and squeezing every dough. After a while, without thought, you will be endowed with the touch.*

Mixing

All mixing can be done with an electric stand mixer, in a food processor, or by hand-powered tools.

USING AN ELECTRIC STAND MIXER

Assume the recipes require use of the paddle attachment with a stand mixer for mixing. The recipe will specify if a dough hook or whip is required.

USING A FOOD PROCESSOR

If you want to mix the dough in a food processor, soften the yeast in a ¼ to ½ cup of the water in a small bowl. Add the dry ingredients to the bowl of the food processor. Add the yeast mixture on top of the dry ingredients. Then, with the machine running, slowly add any other liquids in the recipe. Pulse until the dough begins to form into a ball and pulls away from the sides of the bowl.

For a nonyeast dough, process in the same manner, but mix or pulse only until the ingredients are combined. Dough heats up quickly in a food processor. Do not process for more than several minutes using short pulses. Keep the dough temperature between 78°F and 82°F/26°C and 28°C.

MIXING BY HAND

The recipes in this book can all be mixed by hand using a bowl and a wooden spoon.

Working with Dough: The Basics

Every dough is unique and needs to be handled in its own special way. Depending on the weather, the temperature of your kitchen, humidity, variations in flour, and your strength and experience, the dough may act a little differently. Remember, yeast is alive. The dough might stick more or be a little more stretchy. Be flexible: maybe you need a little more flour, maybe it needs more time to rest. If the room is cold, it will take longer to rise; if it is hot, it will speed up. Be patient, stop and have a cup of tea; the more you bake, the easier it becomes.

KNEADING DOUGH BY HAND

When kneading by hand, it is important to have the work surface at the proper height so your back is kept almost straight and you can apply pressure from your shoulder, with your arms held fairly straight. This allows pressure to be applied with the least effort and prevents unnecessary strain on your back. To knead, dip your hands in flour, place the dough on a floured work surface, and press and push away with the palms of your hands. Fold an end over, rotate the dough a quarter turn and then press and push away again.

In the beginning, when the dough is wet and sloppy, use a bench knife as an aid to getting under the dough to lift and turn. As you knead, the dough will become elastic and can be worked up into a ball. Squeeze the ball, turn it, squeeze, and turn until the dough is fully kneaded. It may be necessary to dust with additional flour if the dough remains too sticky. Knead the dough for 8 to 10 minutes, until it becomes elastic and silky feeling. When pressed, the dough should push back. It literally takes on life. When properly kneaded, the dough becomes smooth and will not stick to your hands when you press on it with your palm.

Kneading develops strands of gluten, the protein present in flour. These strands form minute pockets or cells that trap the gasses emitted by the growth and reproduction of the yeast cells. This in turn leavens the dough; that is, it causes the dough to rise. Often the dough can be kneaded for as long as 10 to 15 minutes to develop the gluten to the maximum. When a small piece of fully kneaded yeast dough is stretched between your fingers until tissue-paper thin when held up to bright light or a sunny window, the strands of gluten are clearly visible.

When kneading dough that is made without yeast, like short pastry dough or chemically leavened dough (made with baking powder or baking soda), the baker uses softer flour with a lower gluten content and kneads only until the ingredients are combined. The goal is to avoid developing the gluten, keeping the dough short and tender—not elastic. Good examples are pie pastry and cookie dough. These doughs also require as little rolling as possible because the rolling is a kneading action.

KNEADING DOUGH IN A STAND MIXER

When kneading yeast dough in a stand electric mixer, use the dough hook for the best kneading action. A soft dough, like a gugelhoph dough, often requires beginning with the paddle. Knead until the dough comes away from the sides of the bowl. Then replace the paddle with the dough hook.

Kneading dough at a slow speed for a longer period of time is best for developing the protein (gluten) in flour and results in a lighter, higher, and more tender yeast cake. After running the machine for 8 to 10 minutes or more, the dough is considered fully kneaded.

In the bakery, most yeast doughs are kneaded for 15 to 20 minutes to further develop the gluten. The limiting factor is dough temperature. Dough can be kneaded by machine at home for this length of time (15 to 20 minutes), provided the dough is not brought to an excessive temperature by the friction created by the machine. This is accomplished by using only a small amount of warm water to soften and awaken active dry yeast. The rest of the liquids should be at room temperature or cooler. In summer, I often use ice water and keep the ingredients cool.

The nice thing about yeast dough is that it is forgiving of errors and allows leeway for mistakes. If the dough is somewhat overheated, it can often be saved by setting it in the refrigerator to rise, thereby slowing down the rising process so that the yeast remains viable.

REMOVING DOUGH FROM THE MIXING BOWL

To remove sticky yeast dough from the bowl, first remove the dough hook. Have on hand a plastic bowl scraper or a bowl knife. Sprinkle a generous amount of flour on the work surface. Tip the mixing bowl over on its side so that the rim is resting on the floured surface. Quickly sprinkle additional flour along the inside of the bowl to form a nonstick path for the dough to follow as it is dumped out. Lift the bottom of the bowl up at a 45-degree angle and begin to dump. With your tool of choice, free any dough that is stuck. Continue lifting the bowl until the dough begins to spill out onto the work surface. With the plastic scraper, encourage the dough to move forward while slowly pulling the entire bowl backward. All of the dough should pull itself out onto the floured surface without further mess or extra lifting.

PROOFING DOUGH

The term "proofing dough" refers to the volume that yeast dough is allowed to attain when rising. "Full proof" denotes the optimum volume that the dough can attain while still allowing the yeast to remain viable. Underproofing is sometimes desirable, but it generally means the finished product will be smaller with a tighter texture. When overproofed, yeast doughs will either collapse in the oven or end up with a tough, stringy texture. Yeast dough does allow a generous amount of latitude, but following the recipe directions will produce the most positive results.

ROLLING DOUGH

Roll yeast dough as if the dough has a "grain," like wood. Rolling the dough gently from the center outward, roll the length first, with the grain and then the width, against the grain.

If you are rolling tough dough, roll as above—first the length and then the width. Then roll in the width on a diagonal. First roll on a left diagonal and then a right diagonal. This seems to break the elasticity of the dough and makes the dough respond better. If the dough seems tough and resistant to rolling, cover and set aside to rest for a while before continuing.

SHRINKING DOWN DOUGH

Yeast dough and puff pastry dough become tough and develop resistance when rolled out until very thin. When this dough is cut to form individual pieces, the pieces will often shrink upon being cut, sometimes as much as ½ to 1 inch. To avoid this, prior to cutting a sheet of thin dough, allow the dough to shrink a little by gently lifting it away from the work surface.

There are several ways to shrink down the dough. You can grasp the dough by the corners, lift, and give it a quick shake, like smoothing wrinkles out of a tablecloth. Alternatively, fold the dough over in half, flip it back, and repeat from the opposite side.

SHAPING DOUGH

Shaping dough is an important step in making a professional-looking finished product with the proper texture. The dough must be molded correctly and have the appropriate shape to bake correctly. Extra effort spent shaping the dough results in better baked goods always.

Listed are basic shaping instructions. Other techniques will be discussed as needed.

Three-Fold: When rolling in butter for Danish or puff pastry, fold the rolled rectangle of dough in thirds, like folding a letter to be inserted in an envelope, creating a rectangle made up of three layers.

Four-Fold: When rolling in butter for Danish or puff pastry, fold the rolled rectangle of dough by bringing each end in to the center. Then fold the dough in half along the center line creating a rectangle made up of four layers.

Figure Eight: To wind dough into a figure eight, as for babka loaves, elongate a rope of dough or twist it into a spiral as prescribed in a recipe. Lengthen it by working it back and forth between the palms of your hands, working from the center out toward both ends until it is about 18 inches in length.

With a fingertip, press the dough to mark a spot on the rope one-third of the way down from the left end. Bring the right end around, clockwise, into a loop, the end resting over the mark. Press down to seal. Bring the left end over and through the loop, bringing it out again under the bottom of the loop at about the center. While holding onto the left end with the left hand, take hold of the right end of the loop with the right hand—fingers on top, thumb on the bottom—and twist one-half turn to the right, forming a figure 8. Bring the end that is in the left hand over and down through the bottom loop of the figure 8, with the end just about protruding from the bottom of the 8. Press lightly to seal.

Handling Nuts

I like to buy nuts in popular Middle Eastern or health food stores. Freshness is important; they contain concentrated protein and oils that can go rancid over time.

BLANCHING ALMONDS
To blanch almonds, plunge the raw almonds into boiling water, remove the pot from the heat, and let stand for several minutes. Drain and then rinse in cold water. The thin skins will slip off easily when squeezed between your fingers. Air dry thoroughly, preferably overnight, before using.

TOASTING NUTS
Toast nuts on a baking sheet in a preheated 350°F/175°C oven for 10 to 15 minutes. Shake or stir occasionally to prevent burning. Toast the nuts lightly to avoid a burnt taste. I recommend using a timer because nuts burn fast.

SKINNING HAZELNUTS
Toast hazelnuts until the skins start to crack. Rub the nuts in a clean kitchen towel. Most of the skin will be removed. Whatever skin remains is okay to leave.

Fillings, Jams and Jellies, Streusels, Icings, and Other Basics

Fillings, streusels, and icings are the bakers color palette. The canvas is the dough. The final "objet de art" depends on the choices added in the creation. The recipes below are used in the recipes throughout the book. As you gain more experience using this book, I encourage you to used them as building blocks to create your original pastries with your favorite doughs.

ALMOND FILLINGS
Almond fillings, including frangipane and almond pasteola, are the primary fillings for most yeast-raised coffee cakes. Almond fillings can be prepared in advance and kept under refrigeration, but bring to room temperature before using. Almond paste can be purchased or processed in the kitchen according to this recipe, although it is best when purchased.

Almond Paste

This paste gives the filling fresh almond flavor.

> ½ cup water
>
> ¼ cup (2 ounces / 57 grams) sugar
>
> 2 cups (10 ounces / 285 grams) blanched almonds
>
> 2 cups (10 ounces / 285 grams) confectioners' sugar

Heat water and sugar in a small saucepan until sugar dissolves. Set aside to cool. Place almonds and half of the confectioners' sugar in a food processor and process to a powder. Add remaining confectioners' sugar, pulse to combine.

With the machine running gradually add the water and sugar mixture until a paste is formed. Chill 1 hour before use. Store in the refrigerator for up to 2 weeks. Wrapped tightly in plastic the paste may be frozen for up to 12 weeks.

Yield: 2 cups (1½ pounds / 680 grams)

Processed Almond-Paste Filling

This filling is preferable to the pasteola listed below but has a more extensive ingredient list. The final product is well worth the extra effort.

> ½ cup (4 ounces / 114 grams) pure Almond Paste (pages 18, 31)
>
> ½ cup (3.5 ounces / 99 grams) sugar
>
> ¼ cup (2 ounces / 62 grams) unsalted butter (see Note)
>
> ¼ cup (1.8 ounces / 51 grams) vegetable shortening
>
> 1 to 2 cups (3.5 to 7 ounces / 100 to 200 grams) cake crumbs (see page 42)
>
> ½ cup (4 fluid ounces / 118 milliliters) water

Pulse the almond paste in a food processor or beat in the mixing bowl of a stand mixer fitted with a paddle attachment with half of the sugar for about a minute. Cream the almond paste mixture with the remaining sugar, butter, and shortening. Blend in the cake crumbs, using enough crumbs to make a thick filling. Additional crumbs subdue a strong almond flavor. Mix to taste.

With the machine running, add the water, a small amount at a time, until it is absorbed and a thick spreadable paste is formed. Scrape down the sides and bottom with a spatula and mix until smooth.

Refrigerate in a covered container for up to a week or freeze for 3 to 4 weeks. Use it at room temperature. If the paste thickens upon standing, add additional water as necessary to spread.

Yield: About 3 cups (19 to 23 ounces / 540 to 650 grams)

Note: For a nondairy recipe, substitute margarine for butter.

Almond Pasteola

This is an almond butter that can be used as a filling or as a substitute when almond paste is not available. Prepare it in a food processor.

> 1½ cups (6 ounces / 170 grams) blanched almonds, lightly toasted (page 31)
>
> 6 tablespoons (2.6 ounces / 75 grams) sugar
>
> 2 tablespoons (1.5 ounces / 43 grams) honey
>
> 4 teaspoons (0.7 ounces / 19 grams) vegetable oil
>
> Water (optional)

Place the nuts in the bowl of a food processor fitted with a steel blade. Process until the nuts release their oil and begin to form a paste. Almonds release less oil than other nuts and will not easily form a nut butter. When processed long enough, however, they will have a paste-like consistency when pressed between the fingers. With the machine running, add the sugar and honey until absorbed. Continue running and slowly add vegetable oil. The mixture can be thinned lightly with water if needed for spreading.

Yield: About 2 cups (11 ounces / 310 grams)

Apple Filling

Use tart apples like Granny Smith, or New York State Greenings. For variety, combine apples like Granny Smith and Rome, the Grannies for tart flavor and Rome for good baking quality.

> 12 medium-sized tart apples (about 4 pounds / 2 kilos), cored and peeled
>
> 1 cup (7 ounces / 198 grams) sugar
>
> 2 tablespoons cornstarch
>
> 1 tablespoon ground cinnamon
>
> ¼ teaspoon ground nutmeg, preferably freshly ground
>
> Juice and finely grated zest of 1 lemon

Cut the apples into ½-inch slices and place them in a large bowl. Add the sugar, cornstarch, cinnamon, nutmeg, and lemon juice and zest. Toss gently to combine. This can be prepared a day in advance; keep chilled.

Yield: Approximately 6 cups (1½ pounds / 680 grams)

Apricot Butter

Authentic Hungarian apricot butter is made from dried apricots. Apricot jam can be used as a substitute, but it will not taste as rich, and it tends to run when baked. Apricot butter can be purchased in gourmet or specialty food shops and from some mail-order sources. Here's an easy recipe that works well.

> 2 cups (10 to 12 ounces / 300 to 340 grams) dried apricots
>
> ½ cup (3.5 ounces / 99 grams) sugar

Put the apricots in a nonreactive saucepan with an inch of water to cover. Bring to a boil over medium-high heat. Reduce the heat and simmer, uncovered, stirring occasionally until tender. Check after 15 minutes—time will vary depending on apricots. Drain. While they are still warm, puree by pressing through a sieve, process in a food processor fitted with a steel blade, or puree in small batches in a blender. Return the puree to the saucepan. Add the sugar and bring to a simmer, stirring constantly. Simmer until the sugar is dissolved. Cool before using. It keeps well in the refrigerator for several weeks.

Yield: About 2½ cups (17.5 to 19.5 ounces / 500 to 550 grams)

Cannoli Filling

Italian bakeries in New York are frequently judged by the quality of their cannolis, and a particular one stands out. In Italy, several bakers told me that even in Rome they know about this bakery. I'll share a secret with you. In the olden days, the bakery was purchased to be operated as a front for bookmaking. Immigrant bakers from Italy were employed. The cannolis were outstanding, and people thronged to the bakery in such numbers that the business became immensely lucrative. There was neither time nor room for bookmaking activities. A simple little pastry brought honesty and acclaim. Citron or candied orange peel can be used in this recipe. I prefer orange peel.

> 2 cups (1 pound / 454 grams) ricotta cheese, drained (see Note)
>
> ½ cup (4 ounces / 113 grams) cream cheese (optional), room temperature
>
> ½ cup plus 2 tablespoons (4.4 ounces / 125 grams) sugar
>
> 2 to 3 drops oil of cinnamon (optional)
>
> 1½ teaspoons pure vanilla extract
>
> ½ ounce (14 grams) semisweet chocolate, chopped
>
> 1 tablespoon citron or candied orange peel, finely diced

Mix the ricotta, cream cheese, sugar, oil of cinnamon, and vanilla. Fold in the chocolate and citron. Chill. The filling can be prepared 1 or 2 days in advance.

Yield: About 2½ cups (1.6 pounds / 725 grams

Note: To drain the ricotta cheese, wrap it in a double layer of cheesecloth, place in a sieve or colander over a bowl, and drain overnight in the refrigerator. Squeeze out any additional water before using. Baker's ricotta is called "impastata," and is processed to make it dry. Impastata will make a thicker, richer cannoli filling. Purchase it in a friendly Italian bakery.

> ℬ **Baker's Secret:** *In the bakery, I found that the somewhat unorthodox inclusion of cream cheese in the filling helps stabilize the cannoli cream and adds additional body. I have since learned that in Italy it is not unknown to add another cheese to the ricotta to make it flavor specific.*
>
> *Surprisingly, knowledgeable old-time Italian bakers with whom I worked claimed that granulated sugar is best in cannoli cream, not the usual confectioners' sugar called for in most recipes.*

> ℬ **Baker's Secret:** *Another secret: oil of cinnamon is necessary for true cannoli flavor. You can substitute ¼ teaspoon of ground cinnamon, but it will never taste the same. Use caution with oil of cinnamon. It is very powerful. Do not add directly it to the cheese. Measure off to one side—measure with a medicine dropper, if possible—then add. Do not get any on your tongue or lips. You will regret it. It can cause a serious burn to the skin.*

Variations

Chocolate Cannoli Filling

Make the cannoli filling as above. Melt 2 to 4 ounces (56 to 113 grams) semisweet chocolate, and then cool. Stir ½ cup of the cannoli cream into the chocolate, a small amount at a time. Then add back into the cannoli cream, mixing until blended. The chocolate is added to taste.

Yield: About 2½ cups (1.75 pounds / 790 grams)

Cheese Filling

Customers in the bakery often wanted to know the secret in our cheese Danish and coffee cakes. Here is the recipe: make sure to use fresh cheese and a heavy hand.

> 3 tablespoons (1.2 ounces / 42 grams) unsalted butter, at room temperature
>
> ½ cup plus 2 tablespoons (4.4 ounces / 125 grams) sugar
>
> 1½ cups (12 ounces / 340 grams) pot cheese or farmer cheese (see Note)
>
> 1 egg yolk
>
> ½ cup (2.2 ounces / 62 grams) unbleached all-purpose flour
>
> Pinch of kosher salt
>
> ¼ cup (2 ounces / 57 grams) canned crushed pineapple, drained (optional) (see Note)

In a stand mixer fitted with a paddle or with a hand-held electric beater, mix the butter with the sugar until blended; do not cream. Add the cheese; mix lightly. Add the egg yolk, flour, salt, and pineapple. Mix at slow speed until blended. With a large rubber spatula, scrape the beaters and the sides and bottom of the bowl, bringing the ingredients up to the top. Mix to blend.

Yield: About 3 cups (22.5 ounces / 640 grams)

Note: Pot cheese or farmer cheese will produce a smooth, dry filling, but if unavailable, substitute dry-curd cottage cheese. Drain excess liquid from the cottage cheese by placing it in a double layer of cheesecloth and twisting to squeeze out as much liquid as possible.

In the bakery, I used a specially formulated baker's cheese that is processed with rennet to make it dry. You might try to cajole your friendly neighborhood baker into selling you some.

The pineapple, if used, disappears into the cheese and adds to the flavor. This recipe can be doubled and kept for a week or more. It can be frozen for 3 to 4 weeks, but there will be some change in taste.

Cream Cheese Filling

Creamiest of the cheese fillings, we used this as a substitute for the cheese filling, above.

> 1 cup (8 ounces / 227 grams) cream cheese, at room temperature
>
> ½ cup plus 2 tablespoons (4.4 ounces / 125 grams) sugar
>
> 2 cups (1 pound / 454 grams) small-curd cottage cheese (or ricotta cheese), drained (see Note)
>
> 3 tablespoons (1.5 ounces / 42 grams) unsalted butter, at room temperature
>
> ¼ teaspoon kosher salt
>
> 1 egg yolk
>
> ½ cup (2.2 ounces / 62 grams) unbleached all-purpose flour
>
> ⅛ teaspoon pure vanilla extract

In the bowl of a stand mixer fitted with the paddle attachment or in a mixing bowl with a handheld electric beater, mix the cream cheese with 2 tablespoons of the sugar to soften. Add the cottage cheese and the remaining sugar. Mix lightly; do not cream. Add the butter, salt, egg yolk, flour, and vanilla. Mix at slow speed until blended. With a large rubber spatula, scrape the beaters and the sides and bottom of the bowl, bringing the ingredients up to the top. Mix at slow speed to ensure that all of the ingredients are blended but avoid aerating. Covered and refrigerated, the filling keeps for up to a week.

Yield: About 3 cups (1.9 pounds / 860 grams)

Note: Drain cottage or ricotta cheese overnight in the refrigerator in a sieve lined with two layers of cheesecloth placed over a bowl. Or put in a double layer of cheesecloth and twist the ends to squeeze out excess liquid.

Frangipane

Frangipane is a rich almond cream filling. Eggs and flour make it perishable. It can be prepared 1 to 2 days in advance and refrigerated.

> 1 (8 ounces / 227 grams) can almond paste (page 18)
>
> ¼ cup (2 ounces / 57 grams) sugar
>
> ½ cup (4 ounces / 113 grams) unsalted butter, at room temperature
>
> 2 eggs
>
> 2 teaspoons unbleached all-purpose flour

Pulse the almond paste in a food processor fitted with a steel blade or beat with an electric mixer with half of the sugar. Then cream the almond paste mixture with the remainder of the sugar and the butter. Add the eggs, one at a time, mixing until blended. Beat in the flour until absorbed. Keep tightly covered and refrigerated for up to 2 days. Any excess can be kept frozen for up to 4 weeks.

Yield: 1½ cups (18 ounces / 510 grams)

> ℘ **Baker's Secret:** *The technique of rapidly distributing filling onto pieces of dough is worth learning if you work with fillings often. Bakers call it "dropping out." With clean hands, drop out filling by enclosing a handful in your fist (left hand if you are right-handed) and squeezing progressively from the pinkie upward (like the reverse of milking a cow) until a small dollop appears at the top of your fist. With the index finger of the opposite hand, flick this off onto the center of a square of dough. The speed with which this can be done increases with experience. Some bakers can perform this with bullet-like rapidity and amazing accuracy. When mastered, filling by "dropping out" can be done more rapidly than by "bagging out" (using a pastry bag), and cleanup is effortless.*

Hazelnut Filling
(Filbert Filling, Praline Filling)

This filling also works with walnuts and pecans.

> 2 cups (about 11 ounces / 312 grams) hazelnuts, toasted and skinned (page 31)
>
> ¼ cup plus 2 tablespoons (2.6 ounces / 75 grams) sugar
>
> 2 tablespoons (1.5 ounces / 42 grams) honey
>
> 2 tablespoons (1 ounce / 27 grams) vegetable oil, plus more if needed

Process the nuts in a food processor fitted with a steel blade until the nuts release their oil and form a paste. With the machine running, slowly add the sugar, honey, and oil until absorbed. If filling has not formed into a paste, add 1 or 2 more tablespoons of oil. Store refrigerated for up to 4 weeks.

Yield: About 3 cups (1 pound / 450 grams)

a jewish baker's pastry secrets

JAMS AND JELLIES

In the bakery, I used specially prepared, oven-proof jam. This jam will not leak out of the pastry in the oven. To thicken jam for oven baking in the home kitchen, heat it in a small saucepan over low to medium-low heat. Stir slowly with a wooden spoon. To avoid aerating, do not use a whisk. Simmer slowly, stirring occasionally, until thickened.

Apricot jam is strained to make it smooth unless it is to be baked in a filling. In a filling, it adds additional flavor when not strained.

Raspberry jam should be passed through a sieve if you want a seedless jam. Heat the jam slightly before straining. My own preference is to leave the seeds in. A good domestic brand of raspberry jam is Smucker's.

Pastry Cream

Pastry cream, sometimes referred to as custard, is easy to make. Many pastry chefs and most Italian bakers thicken pastry cream with flour instead of cornstarch. I find that the taste of flour is present in the finished product, so I prefer cornstarch, which is bland and easier to work with. Prepare and measure the ingredients before beginning.

> 2 cups (16 fluid ounces / 473 milliliters) milk
>
> ¼ cup (1 ounce / 28 grams) cornstarch
>
> 4 egg yolks, lightly beaten
>
> ½ cup (3.5 ounces / 99 grams) sugar
>
> Pinch of kosher salt
>
> 1 tablespoon (0.5 ounces / 14 grams) unsalted butter
>
> ¼ teaspoon pure vanilla extract

Pour 1½ cups of the milk into a heavy saucepan over medium heat and heat until bubbles begin to form around the edge. Meanwhile, in a separate bowl, combine the remaining ½ cup milk and cornstarch and stir with a wire whisk until combined. Stir eggs, ¼ cup of the sugar, and salt into the cornstarch mixture.

When the heated milk is about to boil, mix about ½ cup of the hot milk mixture into the cold mixture and then slowly add it all back into the hot milk, stirring constantly. Stir thoroughly along the sides and bottom to prevent scorching. As the mixture begins to thicken, reduce the heat to medium low and continue cooking until you see the first sign of boiling. Cook for an additional minute, stirring all of the time.

Remove from the heat. Immediately add the remaining ¼ cup of sugar and the butter, mixing until dissolved. Stir in the vanilla. Cover and cool with plastic wrap touching the surface so that a skin does not form. Chill thoroughly. The pastry cream can be prepared 1 day in advance. Keep well chilled and covered. When cool, stir with a wire whisk to fluff it up before using.

Yield: 3 cups (22.3 ounces / 630 grams)

> ℬ **Baker's Secret:** *To chill pastry cream and custards quickly for immediate use, pour the hot mixture onto a clean, buttered rimmed baking sheet. Cover with plastic wrap as above. Cool for 5 to 10 minutes on a wire rack, then place in the coldest part of the refrigerator until chilled (30 to 60 minutes). Remove the plastic wrap and stir thoroughly with a wire whip.*

Variation

Chocolate Custard

Add ½ cup (4 ounces / 113 grams) or more to taste, bittersweet or semisweet chocolate, chopped or grated, to the hot custard. Stir until melted.

Yield: About 3¼ cups (26.3 ounces / 743 grams)

Poppy Butter
(Mohn)

Poppy butter can be purchased in specialty and gourmet shops, in some ethnic markets (such as Hungarian or Polish), and by mail order. Homemade is better. In the bakery, I added pure tart raspberry jam to offset what some people feel is the bitter tang of poppy seed. The raspberry jam binds with the poppy seeds to make the taste of the poppy butter softer and somewhat mysterious to the sensitive palate. Use the best-quality, thick raspberry jam, preferably with seeds. For the poppy seeds, I prefer Dutch blue poppy seeds. Grind the poppy seeds in small batches in a blender, clean coffee grinder, or nut grinder. In the coffee grinder, grind the seeds until the sound of the motor changes pitch. The seeds will have been ground into a semipaste.

½ cup (4 fluid ounces / 118 milliliters) milk

1 cup (6 ounces / 170 grams) poppy seeds, ground

¼ cup (1.75 ounces / 50 grams) sugar

1 tablespoon (0.75 ounces / 21 grams) honey

1 tablespoon (0.5 ounces / 14 grams) unsalted butter or margarine

½ teaspoon ground cinnamon

⅛ teaspoon ground cloves, preferably freshly ground

¼ cup thickened raspberry jam (2.8 ounces / 80 grams) (see Note)

Juice plus finely grated zest of ½ lemon (0.75 ounces / 21 grams)

In a 1-quart saucepan, combine the milk, ground poppy seeds, and sugar over medium-high heat. Stir constantly until bubbles appear around the sides. Add the honey, butter, cinnamon, and cloves. Stir until the sugar dissolves and the butter melts. Reduce the heat and continue stirring until thick, about 5 to 10 minutes. Remove from the heat. Add the raspberry jam and the lemon juice and zest.

Poppy butter is best when stored, tightly covered, in the refrigerator for 3 to 4 days to allow the flavors to ripen. It can be refrigerated for up to 2 weeks or frozen for 2 to 6 weeks. Use it at room temperature. If the mixture becomes too thick to spread, soften with water, added 1 tablespoon at a time.

Yield: About 1½ cups (16.5 ounces / 470 grams)

Note: If a nondairy recipe is desired, substitute water for the milk and use margarine, not butter.

Prune Lekvar
(Prune Butter)

Hungarian-style lekvar, commercially made, is almost always used in the bakery. It is easy to make at home. Pure lekvar is made using only prunes. Most of the commercial products available today have apples mixed in. Apple can add some flavor, but its inclusion is primarily a function of cost. Lekvar can often be found in supermarkets. Some ethnic markets have it labeled as "plum butter," and it is sold as a spread. Use sour prunes, if possible. The best come from Oregon.

> 2 cups (10 ounces / 284 grams) pitted prunes
>
> ¼ cup (1.75 ounces / 50 grams) sugar
>
> 1 teaspoon finely grated lemon zest
>
> 1 teaspoon finely grated orange zest
>
> Pinch of ground nutmeg, preferably freshly ground

Put the prunes in a nonreactive saucepan and add water to cover. Bring to a boil over medium heat. Reduce the heat and simmer for 5 minutes, uncovered. Drain and puree in small batches in a blender or in a food processor. While still warm, mix in the sugar, lemon zest, orange zest, and nutmeg. Return to saucepan over low heat and simmer, stirring constantly, for about 5 minutes, or until thickened.

Cool. Refrigerate overnight before using. Lekvar is best when allowed to ripen, tightly covered in the refrigerator, for several days. It keeps well and can be frozen for up to 8 weeks.

Yield: 2½ cups (12 ounces / 340 grams)

Walnut Filling
(Walnut Butter)

Walnut filling was more common in my dad's day as a baker. It reminds me of Eastern European fields and forests. Enjoy.

> 2 cups (8 ounces / 227 grams) walnuts, lightly toasted (page 31)

> ¼ cup plus 2 tablespoons (2.6 ounces / 74 grams) sugar
>
> 2 tablespoons (1.5 ounces / 42 grams) honey
>
> Water (optional)

Put the nuts in the bowl of a food processor fitted with the steel blade. Process until the nuts release their oil and form a paste. With the machine running, slowly add the sugar and honey until absorbed. Thin with water as needed for a spreading consistency. Store, tightly covered, in the refrigerator for up to 2 weeks, or freeze for 2 to 6 weeks.

Yield: About 2 cups (12 ounces / 340 grams)

STREUSEL AND FLAVORED SUGARS
Customers often asked why our products tasted so great. I like to think it was our love for baking, but perhaps these flavored sugars and rich streusels added that special something.

Almond Sugar

A small handheld rotary nut grinder works best for small batches. When using a food processor or blender, grind the almonds with the confectioners' sugar so that the nuts do not become oily. If using a blender, grind in small batches. Grind by pulsing until very fine. Alternatively, using a food grinder (fine holes), grind three times together with the confectioners' sugar so that they do not become oily. In a pinch, almond sugar can be used in place of almond filling.

> 1 cup (4 ounces / 113 grams) blanched almonds (page 31)
>
> ¾ cup (3.2 ounces / 91 grams) confectioners' sugar

Grind the almonds until very fine and then blend the ground nuts with the confectioners' sugar. Store at room temperature for up to 3 weeks.

Yield: About 1¾ cups (7.2 ounces / 204 grams)

Variation

Walnut Sugar or Hazelnut Sugar
Replace the almonds with walnuts or skinned hazelnuts.

Butter Streusel

Streusel is often treated with a certain reverence. Aficionados can be overtaken with passion from the first whiff of its aroma as it emerges from the oven, followed by the burst of taste as it clings to the lips and falls upon tongue and palate. Confirmed streusel lovers are like so-called chocoholics and can never be satiated.

Apply as a topping by rubbing through your fingertips and allowing the streusel to fall lightly over the dough or batter. Do not press down. Sprinkle delicately with your fingers, if necessary to cover.

> ½ cup (3.9 ounces / 110 grams) firmly packed brown sugar
>
> ½ cup (3.5 ounces / 99 grams) granulated sugar
>
> 1 cup (8 ounces / 227 grams) unsalted butter, cubed
>
> 2 to 2½ cups (8.5 to 10.5 ounces / 240 to 300 grams) unbleached all-purpose flour
>
> ⅛ teaspoon kosher salt

> 1 teaspoon ground cinnamon
>
> ⅛ teaspoon ground nutmeg, preferably freshly ground
>
> 1 teaspoon pure vanilla extract

Using a stand mixer with the paddle attachment, a handheld beater, or a food processor fitted with the steel blade, mix together the brown sugar, granulated sugar, butter, 2 cups of the flour, salt, cinnamon, nutmeg, and vanilla. Mix with short pulses only until combined; do not cream. (If mixing by hand, rub the brown and granulated sugars and butter between your fingers, until it resembles coarse grain, and then add the 2 cups of the flour, salt, cinnamon, ground nutmeg, and vanilla.) Add the additional flour, 1 tablespoon at a time, if a small amount of streusel does not clump together when pinched and rolled together. Transfer to a covered container. It keeps well for up to 4 weeks in the refrigerator or for up to 6 months in the freezer.

Yield: 2½ cups (24 ounces / 680 grams)

Cinnamon Sugar

Mix 1 cup (7 ounces / 198 grams) sugar with 1 to 2 tablespoons ground cinnamon. Store in a jar at room temperature.

Cocoa Sugar

Mix ¾ cup (5.25 ounces / 149 grams) sugar with ¼ cup (0.75 ounce, / 21 grams) Dutch-process cocoa. Store in a jar at room temperature.

ICINGS AND GLAZES
Gilding the lily, a little decoration adds a look of completion and a little extra sweetness to your

work. Some icings and glazes are spread, others poured; any way they are applied, the extra effort is worth the results.

Apricot Glaze

Warm strained apricot jam with just enough water (added 1 teaspoon at a time) to allow it to be applied with a pastry brush.

Egg Wash

Beat 1 egg lightly with 1 tablespoon water and use to glaze finished pastries before baking to give them a shiny crust. You can add a pinch of salt to the wash to add a little flavor.

Danish Glaze

Immediately upon removing from the oven any yeast-raised pastry that has been baked with egg wash painted on, brush the pastry with a Danish glaze, also known as Danish syrup or Danish wash. This creates an exceptionally high gloss for a professional finish.

Baker's Danish Glaze

The following is the glaze I used in the bakery. If you bake regularly, it's worth keeping a store on hand. It will keep for 1 to 2 weeks in the refrigerator.

1 cup water (8 fluid ounces/ 237 milliliters)

1 cup (7 ounces / 198 grams) granulated sugar

1 cup (7.75 ounces / 20 grams) firmly packed brown sugar

¼ cup (2.5 ounces / 71 grams) apricot jam

Juice and finely grated zest of ½ lemon

In a 1-quart saucepan, combine the water and granulated and brown sugars to a boil over medium-high heat. Add the jam, lemon juice, and zest. Reduce the heat and boil for 5 minutes. Remove from the heat. Use the mixture while warm to glaze pastry. Store glaze in the refrigerator for up to 8 weeks. Reheat slowly on stove or in microware until warm.

Yield: 3 cups (26 ounces / 740 grams)

Quick Danish Glaze

½ cup (5.6 ounces / 160 grams) apricot jam or orange marmalade

½ cup (4.2 ounces / 120 grams) water

Combine apricot jam or orange marmalade and water in a small pan and bring to a simmer over low heat. If necessary, thin with additional water to brushing consistency. Brush over hot pastries immediately upon removal from the oven. Store in the refrigerator for up to 8 weeks.

Yield: 1 cup (9.8 ounces / 280 grams)

Simple Icing
(Bun Dough Icing)

In the bakery I almost always dressed each coffee cake and bun with a drizzle of white icing before it went out into the store. The icing added a little more sweetness and a little pizzaz. You can add it or not.

This is used for icing sweet doughs and coffee cakes. The corn syrup, if used, enhances the shine and helps prevent crystallization.

3½ cups (14 ounces / 396 grams) confectioners' sugar, plus more as needed

5 to 6 tablespoons (2.6 to 3.1 ounces / 74 to 89 grams) water

2 teaspoons (0.5 ounces / 14 grams) light corn syrup (optional)

¼ teaspoon pure vanilla extract

¼ teaspoon finely grated lemon zest (optional)

Fill a nonreactive saucepan about three-quarters full of water. Heat the water over medium-high heat until steaming, but do not boil. Reduce the heat to medium low. Put confectioners' sugar in a metal or heatproof bowl over the saucepan. The bowl should not touch the water.

Slowly whisk 5 to 6 tablespoons water into the confectioners' sugar, stirring constantly until smooth and warm to the touch. The icing should form ribbons for a few seconds before disappearing when drizzled over the surface with the whisk. Heat the mixture only until warm to the touch. Do not overheat the icing, or it will lose its shine and become dull and spotted when dry. Stir in the corn syrup, vanilla, and lemon zest. The icing thickens upon standing; if it remains too thin, add additional confectioners' sugar, 1 tablespoon at a time. Use the icing while warm.

Icing can be stored for a few days in the refrigerator. Float 2 tablespoons of water over the top to prevent a crust from developing. Cover tightly. Reheat before using.

Yield: About 1½ cups (17 ounces / 480 grams)

OTHER BASICS

Even the most organized baker has a few stray tools, ingredients, or recipes that do not fit in a group. Think of this as my "junk drawer." Here are those basic recipes.

CRUMBS

In a bakery, crumbs are used in a frugal and environmentally sound fashion to recycle leftovers and to improve texture. In the artisan bakery, such inventory control can mean the difference between profit and loss.

Crumbs absorb excess moisture (especially from fruit) and bind fillings together, keeping them from running out of the dough in the oven. Also, the use of crumbs allows the dough to soak up additional amounts of butter and sugar, allowing us to further enrich many cakes and pastries. Cake crumbs also contribute their own flavors to the overall taste and are used as the base for apple charlottes and rugelach.

In the bakery, we always kept a healthy supply of cake crumbs on hand. I like to grind fresh crumbs as soon as cake becomes available and keep them in a plastic bag in the freezer where they are ready for immediate use at any time. There's no need to defrost the crumbs.

Sometimes, especially during holidays, we would run out of fresh crumbs in the bakery. At those times, we were forced to bake a quick sheet cake to grind up for crumbs. This was the ultimate insult: to have to bake cakes and expend labor for what in the normal course of business was free.

Bread crumbs can be substituted when cake crumbs are not available, although cake crumbs are preferable in most pastry applications. Occasionally bread crumbs are called for in specific recipes.

To keep fresh cake crumbs on hand, frugal bakers grind trimmings, ends, and leftovers as they become available. In the bakery, leftovers are rubbed through a large coarse sieve. At home, you can rub the cake through a grater or chop in the food processor. Store in a covered container in the refrigerator for several days or freeze in a plastic bag for up to 6 months.

a jewish baker's pastry secrets

Quick Sheet Cake

Here is an easy recipe to use for crumbs.

    1 cup (7 ounces / 198 grams) sugar

    ¾ cup (5.4 ounces / 153 grams) solid
    vegetable shortening

    2½ cups (11 ounces / 312 grams)
    unbleached all-purpose flour

    2 teaspoons baking powder

    1 teaspoon kosher salt

    3 eggs

    1 teaspoon pure vanilla extract

    1 cup (8 fluid ounces / 237 milliliters)
    milk

Position a rack in the center of the oven and preheat to 350°F/175°C. Line a rimmed half-sheet pan with parchment paper.

In the large mixing bowl of a stand mixer using the paddle attachment, cream the sugar and shortening. Add the flour, baking powder, and salt. Lightly sift through the dry ingredients with your fingertips to combine. Add the eggs and vanilla. Mix at slow speed to combine. With the machine running, slowly add the milk until absorbed. Scrape down the sides and bottom of the bowl with a rubber spatula to bring any unmixed ingredients up to the top. Mix at slow speed until smooth.

Turn out into the prepared baking sheet. Spread with a spatula to fill the pan evenly. Bake for 20 to 25 minutes, until lightly browned and the center springs back when gently pressed.

Cool in the pan on a wire rack. Can be frozen or ground into cake crumbs.

Yield: One 12 by 18 by 1-inch cake or about 8 cups crumbs

Note: To use as a sheet cake, bake in a smaller (15 by 10-inch) baking sheet for a little longer.

Sugar Cookie Dough

Bakers call this pastry dough "One-Two-Three Dough" because it is formulated with a ratio of 1 part fat to 2 parts sugar to 3 parts flour.

    ½ cup (4 ounces / 113 grams) unsalted
    butter, softened (see Note)

    1 cup (7 ounces / 198 grams) sugar

    1 egg

    1 tablespoon water

    1 teaspoon pure vanilla extract

    2 cups plus 3 tablespoons (10 ounces /
    284 grams) unbleached all-purpose flour

    1½ teaspoons baking powder

    ½ teaspoon kosher salt

Flour a halfsheet pan.

In a stand mixer fitted with a paddle or in a bowl with a handheld electric beater, cream the butter and sugar. Beat in the egg, water, and vanilla until the sugar dissolves. Add the flour, baking powder, and salt. Sift lightly through the dry ingredients with your fingertips to distribute. Mix at slow speed only until the mixture comes together.

Turn out onto a floured work surface. With floured hands, knead lightly until the flour is fully absorbed. Overmixing or too much kneading makes the dough tough. Transfer to the floured baking sheet. Flatten the dough so that it is fairly even in thickness. Wrap in plastic and refrigerate until chilled, preferably overnight. Refrigerate for up to a week; freeze for up to 8 weeks.

Yield: 4 cups (23.5 ounces / 670 grams)

Note: For a nondairy recipe, substitute margarine or vegetable shortening for the butter.

CHAPTER 3

Bundt

Bundt dough (also called bun dough or Bundt kuchen) is the basic sweet yeast-raised dough. It's the basis of a large and interesting collection of familiar sweet goods and some not-so-familiar ones. Crumb buns are probably the most well-known item made from this dough. Today doughnuts are a popular coffee-break treat. In my day, the more common choice was a bun made of this delicious dough. The usual choices in most shops were crumb, cheese, raisin, and cherry buns. Bundt dough is easy for beginners, but the helpful tips and tricks that follow may surprise even the most experienced bakers.

— Master Recipe —
Bundt Dough

In the bakery, both buns and Danish were big sellers. Customers were often confused when they pointed to a tray of cheese buns and said, "Three cheese Danish, please," and the sales clerk would go to another tray. Danish are made from Danish dough, a dough that is richer in butter and more labor-intensive to make. Danish are also larger and filled with more cheese, so they were the pricier choice. I had many choices of both pastries in the bakery.

Many years back, I worked with Rudi, a German baker, a fellow with a sense of humor who could keep you chuckling all night long. With appropriate hand gestures and facial expressions and, of course, his German accent, Rudi once recounted a tale about his first job in America, working for his uncle.

There was a huge bowl of bundt dough churning away on the mixing machine and the uncle walked over to check on the nephew. He looked, stopped the machine, and pushed the dough with his fingers to test the consistency and elasticity. Like kicking the tires on a new car, it was an act he put on. Uncle really could tell whether he had a dough to his liking with little more than a passing glance and by listening to the pitch of the motor straining while driving the beater that kneaded the dough. Without speaking, he held his hand up, palm out, signaling his nephew to stop the machine and walked away momentarily. Upon returning, he leaned over and dropped a handful of egg shells into the dough and signaled to Rudi to resume running the machine. Rudi looked at the uncle with astonishment and crooked an eyebrow questioningly. Not a word had been spoken to this point. Uncle, nonchalantly, with a slight shrug of the shoulders answered the unspoken query. Rudi mimicked the uncle's heavy accent, "We want to make sure that the customer knows we use plenty fresh eggs in the buns."

The recipe that follows has "plenty fresh eggs." But please omit the eggshells.

½ cup (4 fluid ounces / 115 milliliters) warm water (95°F to 115°F / 35°C to 46°C)

3 scant tablespoons (3 packets / 21 grams) active dry yeast

1 cup (8 fluid ounces / 237 milliliters) milk, at room temperature

¾ cup (5.25 ounces / 149 grams) sugar

¾ cup (6 ounces / 170 grams) unsalted butter, diced, or half butter, half solid vegetable shortening

3 eggs

6 cups (29 ounces / 822 grams) bread flour (preferred) or unbleached all-purpose flour

¼ cup (1 ounce / 28 grams) nonfat dry milk (see Note)

2¼ teaspoons kosher salt

2 teaspoons pure vanilla extract

¼ teaspoon ground cardamom, preferably freshly ground (optional)

In the bowl of a stand mixer fitted with a paddle attachment, or a large mixing bowl, sprinkle the yeast over warm water to soften. Add the milk, sugar, butter, eggs, flour, nonfat dry milk, salt, vanilla, and cardamom. Pulse with the on/off switch until blended, making sure the flour does not fly out of the bowl. You can cover the mixer with a kitchen towel for the first few pulses to keep the flour contained. Then mix at slow speed until the dough comes together. Change to a dough hook, if available. If mixing by hand, stir with a wooden spoon until the dough comes away from the sides of the bowl.

Knead with a dough hook in the stand mixer or turn out onto a floured work surface and knead by hand for 8 to 10 minutes, or more if necessary, until the dough has become elastic and has a silky sheen.

Place the dough in a clean, oiled bowl, turning to coat. Cover with a cloth or plastic wrap and allow to rise until doubled in volume, 45 to 60 minutes (the time will vary with temperature and humidity) or allow to rise slowly overnight in the refrigerator.

Turn the dough out onto a floured work surface. Punch down, fold the ends in toward the center, and roll up into a tight rectangle. Allow to rest for at least 10 and up to 15 minutes.

At this point, the dough can be refrigerated overnight. (All or part of the dough can be frozen at this stage for a week or more, if wrapped tightly in plastic wrap.) I recommend dividing the dough into 8-ounce portions and shaping into balls. Wrap and freeze individually.

Yield: About 4 pounds dough

Note: For a nondairy dough, substitute water for milk, margarine or shortening for butter, and omit the nonfat dry milk.

Streusel Cake
(Crumb Cake)

Streusel cake is probably the most popular and the easiest to make of all yeast-raised cakes. When baked with a rich butter streusel topping and served while warm from the oven, the aroma of butter and cinnamon pervades the room. When I am seated at the table with a steaming mug of coffee in hand and a piece of streusel cake in front of me, I think home and hearth don't get much better than this.

2 (8-ounce / 255-gram) portions Bundt Dough (page 46) (see Note)

½ cup (4 ounces / 113 grams) unsalted butter, melted

2½ cups (24 ounces / 680 grams) Butter Streusel (page 40)

Confectioners' sugar, for topping (optional)

Butter or grease two 10-inch round or 9-inch square layer-cake pans; pans with 1-inch-high sides are best.

Shape each piece of dough into a ball, cover, and allow to rest for about 15 minutes.

Flatten and then roll out each piece on a lightly floured surface until it is about 1 inch wider than the pan. Place in the prepared pans and, with your fingertips, press gently to fit in each pan. With a fork, stipple a series of holes over the entire dough.

Use your fingers to break up the streusel, rubbing until it resembles coarse grain, or squeeze together so that it forms large clumps, depending upon how you like your streusel. Brush the dough with melted butter and then sprinkle with the streusel to cover. Set aside and allow the dough to stand until the dough doubles in volume, 45 to 60 minutes (time will vary depending on temperature and humidity). When touched very gently on the side with a fingertip, the dough should be soft and yield readily.

Position a rack in the center of the oven and preheat to 350°F/175°C.

Bake for 25 to 35 minutes, until browned. The tops should feel firm to the touch and spring back when lightly pressed with the fingers. Be careful when pressing because hot streusel can burn.

Cool on wire racks for 10 to 15 minutes, and then remove from the pans. Serve warm or at room temperature. Sift a light coating of confectioners' sugar over the tops before serving. The cakes keep well in a covered container or plastic bag for several days at room temperature. They can be frozen for a few months if well wrapped.

Yield: Two cakes with 8 servings each

Note: One recipe of Bundt dough yields about 64 ounces. If measuring without a scale, one-quarter of the dough, halved, yields two pieces about 8 ounces each.

Variations

Filled Streusel Cake

Split a thoroughly cooled 9-inch round streusel cake in half horizontally, using a sharp knife with a serrated blade (like cutting a layer cake for filling). Set the top half aside. Place the base on a serving dish. Fit a pastry bag with a #8 star or French star tip and fill with 1½ cups Pastry Cream (page 37). Pipe or "bag out" (squeeze out) a 1-inch spiral border of pastry cream and then fill with concentric circles until completely covered. Or, using a spatula, spread with ½-inch layer of pastry cream, to cover. Lift the top carefully, with a spatula slipped underneath for support, and place on top of the pastry cream. Dust the top half lightly with confectioners' sugar. The filled cake is best served immediately, but it can be refrigerated for several hours. Both the cake and pastry cream can be prepared one day in advance.

Bienerstück

Bienerstück, known as "beehive cake," is a yeast-raised coffee cake topped with caramelized honey and nuts and filled with cream custard. This is a lovely German coffee cake, at one time very popular but unusual now. A delight to old-generation Europeans, it waits its turn to be discovered all over again. The name in the original German suggests "bee sting." Perhaps it was its name that "done it in."

1 (8-ounce / 255-gram) portion Bundt Dough (page 46)

¼ cup (2 ounces / 56 grams) unsalted butter, melted

1½ cups (11.1 ounces / 315 grams) Pastry Cream (page 37)

Honey Beehive Topping

¼ cup (2 ounces / 56 grams) unsalted butter

½ cup (4 ounces / 113 grams) sugar

¼ cup (3 ounces / 85 grams) honey

1½ cups (6 ounces / 170 grams) sliced almonds or chopped walnuts, preferably toasted

½ teaspoon ground cinnamon

⅛ teaspoon nutmeg, preferably freshly ground

Butter or grease a 10-inch round or 9-inch square cake layer pan; pans with 1-inch-high sides are best.

Shape the dough into a ball, cover, and allow to rest for about 15 minutes.

Flatten and then roll out the dough on a flour-dusted work surface until it is about 1-inch wider than the pan. Place in the prepared pans and, with your fingertips, press gently to fit the pan. With a fork, stipple a series of holes over the entire dough. Brush the dough with the melted butter.

Allow the dough to stand until double in volume, 45 to 60 minutes (time will vary depending on temperature and humidity). When touched very gently on the side with a fingertip, the dough should be soft and yield readily.

Meanwhile, prepare the Honey Beehive Topping. Melt the butter in a heavy saucepan over medium-low heat. Add the sugar and honey and stir to dissolve. Remove from the heat; stir in the nuts, cinnamon, and nutmeg.

Position a rack in the center of the oven and preheat to 350°F/175°C.

Bake for about 20 minutes, until lightly browned on top. Remove from the oven and set aside on a wire rack for about 5 minutes. Carefully spread the topping over the cake. Return to the hot oven and bake for an additional 10 minutes, or until the topping bubbles and begins to caramelize. Allow to cool thoroughly on a wire rack.

Carefully, turn the cake out of the pan. Turn right-side up. Split in half horizontally with a sharp serrated knife. Set the top half aside. Place the base on a serving dish. Fit a pastry bag with a #8 star or French star tip and fill with pastry cream Pipe and "bag out" (squeeze out) a 1-inch spiral border of pastry cream and then fill with concentric circles until completely covered. Or, using a spatula, spread with ½-inch layer of pastry cream, to cover. Lift the top carefully, with a spatula slipped underneath for support, and place on top of the pastry cream.

The cake keeps well, unfilled and lightly covered, for up to 24 hours at room temperature. Fill just before serving. The cake can be refrigerated or frozen while unfilled.

Yield: One cake, serving 8

Variation

Bienerstück with Honey Oatmeal Topping

Make the cake as above, but prepare a different topping by melting ¼ cup (2 ounces / 56 grams) unsalted butter in a heavy saucepan over medium-low heat. Add 1 cup (7.76 ounces / 220 grams) firmly packed light brown sugar and ¼ cup (3 ounces / 85 grams) honey and stir to dissolve. Remove from the heat and stir in 1 cup (3 ounces / 85 grams) old-fashioned rolled oats, ½ teaspoon ground cinnamon, and ⅛ teaspoon nutmeg, preferably freshly ground. Bake the cake as above, spreading this topping instead of the Honey Beehive Topping and finishing the cake as above.

Streusel Buns
(Crumb Buns)

In the bakery, I placed a 3- to 3½-pound round disk of dough into a dough divider (also called a dough press), an old hand-operated device that, at the pull of a long handle, presses the dough out so that it is even and cuts the dough into 36 equal pieces. These pieces are then placed, evenly spaced, on a baking sheet and made up into individual buns. Weighing and shaping each piece could become burdensome to do at home, so I resort to the method described below.

1 (1½-pound / 680-gram) portion Bundt Dough (page 46)

2½ cups (24 ounces / 680 grams) Butter Streusel (page 40)

¼ cup (2 ounces / 56 grams) unsalted butter, melted

Confectioners' sugar, for topping (optional)

Line a half-sheet pan with parchment paper or greased waxed paper.

Roll out the dough into a rectangle an inch larger than the baking sheet. Roll the dough, first to the desired length, and then to the desired width. If the dough becomes too tough to roll, allow it to rest, covered, for 5 minutes or more and then continue. Fold the dough in half widthwise and then in half again lengthwise to make lifting easier. Place in one corner of the baking sheet and open to cover the sheet. If the dough has shrunk from the sides, dimple and stretch the dough from the center out, pushing so that it covers from edge to edge. Keep the dough at an even thickness.

Use your fingers to break up the streusel, rubbing until it resembles coarse grain, or squeeze it together so that it forms large clumps, depending upon how you like your streusel. Brush the dough with melted butter and sprinkle with streusel to cover.

a jewish baker's pastry secrets

Let stand, uncovered, until the dough doubles in volume, 45 to 60 minutes; the time will vary with temperature and humidity. When touched very gently on the side with a fingertip, the dough should be soft and yield readily.

Position an oven rack in the center of the oven and preheat the oven to 350°F/175°C.

Bake for 25 to 35 minutes, until browned. The top should feel firm to the touch and spring back when lightly pressed with the fingers. Be careful when pressing because hot streusel can burn. Cool on a wire rack for 10 to 15 minutes and then remove from the pan.

When fully cooled, cut into three rows across and six rows down to make eighteen equal pieces. Sift confectioners' sugar lightly over the top. Store wrapped in plastic at room temperature for up to 4 days. May be frozen, tightly double wrapped in plastic, for up to 6 weeks.

Yield: 18 buns

> ꙮ **Baker's Secret:** *For professional-looking individual buns with slightly rounded tops, after fitting the unbaked dough in the baking sheet, cut into eighteen pieces (six rows by three rows) with a bench knife or chef's knife. The pieces will shrink. Allow to rest for 5 minutes and then press and stretch the pieces with your fingertips from the centers out to the edges. Don't worry if spaces are left. They will be filled in with the streusel. Brush with melted butter or water. Sprinkle with streusel, including the spaces between each cut. Allow to rise and bake and finish as above.*

Variation

Large Streusel Cakes

For two large streusel cakes (each about 9 by 12 inches), cut the dough in half crosswise, brush with butter, cover with streusel, and proceed as for Streusel Buns.

Butter Kuchen with Two Sugars
(Butter Cake)

Butter kuchen, a specialty of German pastry shops where it most likely originated, is a perfect example of a basic cake comprised of simple honest ingredients that has been lifted to an epicurean level. The secret to great butter kuchen is to dust the butter with two sugars before baking.

Many bakers, especially German-American bakers, made a big fuss over this kuchen. They always worked with a smile and easy banter while awaiting its emergence from the oven, surely in anticipation of sampling their wares while still warm. There would be a discernible buzz in the air as the inner clocks of these old pros signaled that the time was near.

This brings to mind the coffee that they prepared. When you labor all night long, the coffee has to be strong and bitter. No problem for these gruff codgers. A stockpot on the candy stove with water at a boil, a pinch of salt, so many handfuls of coffee added along with the "codger's secret": a scattering of eggshells. Reduce the flame, sprinkle cold water over the top, wait a few minutes for the grounds to settle, and then drink. *Ah, ganz gut* (very good).

2 (8-ounce/ 255-gram) portions **Bundt Dough (page 46)**

1 cup (8 ounces / 227 grams) unsalted **butter (or more if desired), softened**

Granulated sugar, for topping

Confectioners' sugar, for topping

Butter or grease two 10-inch round or 9-inch square layer cake pans; 1-inch sides give the best results.

Shape the dough up into two balls, cover, and allow to rest for about 10 minutes. Flatten and then roll out each ball into a 10-inch round on a surface lightly dusted with flour.

Place the dough in the prepared pans and with your fingertips, dimple and press gently to fit the pan. Allow to rise until puffy. Time will vary, depending on temperature and humidity.

Dimple again, pressing your fingertips all the way down into the dough, making little wells in straight lines over the entire surface. Fill a pastry bag fitted with a #4 or #6 plain round tip with the softened butter and squeeze out dots into all of the wells or carefully "drop out" (page 36) small dots by hand. Allow to rise until doubled in volume, 30 minutes or more (time will vary with temperature and humidity).

Sprinkle a light coating of granulated sugar over the top and then dust with confectioners' sugar to cover. In the heat of the oven, the two sugars will melt and weld with the butter, forming a very delicate butter-infused crust.

Position a rack in the center of the oven and preheat to 350°F/175°C.

Bake for 35 to 45 minutes, until browned. The top should feel firm to the touch and spring back when lightly pressed with your fingers.

Remove from the oven and cool on a wire rack for 10 to 15 minutes. Remove from the pan. Serve warm or at room temperature. The cake is best when served fresh, but it keeps well overnight, if covered. The cake can be refrigerated for up to 4 days or frozen, tightly double wrapped in plastic, for up to 6 weeks.

Yield: Two 10-inch cakes, each serving 10 to 12

Sugar Buns
(Cinnamon Rolls)

I once saw a sign in a bakery shop window: "Your Honey Will Be Sweeter When You Feed Her Our Sugar Buns." These are tall, Texas-size, "reach-for-the-sky" cinnamon rolls. You will find them lush, moist, and full of flavor.

1 (1½-pound / 680-gram) portion Bundt Dough (page 46)

¼ cup (2 ounces / 56 grams) unsalted butter, melted

1 cup (9.6 ounces / 272 grams) Butter Streusel (page 40)

1 egg

1 tablespoon water

Filling

1 cup (7 ounces / 198 grams) granulated sugar

1 tablespoon cinnamon, plus more to taste

1 cup (5 ounces / 142 grams) raisins

Simple Icing (page 41), warm

Grease two jumbo 4-inch muffin tins (with 6 muffin cups each) or two 9 by 9 by 2-inch baking pans.

On a floured work surface, roll out the dough into a ¼-inch-thick rectangle measuring 18 to 20 inches long and 14 inches wide; have the long side facing you. While rolling, dust with flour as necessary to prevent sticking. Brush off any excess flour and then paint the dough with the melted butter, leaving a ½-inch border along the top. Rub the streusel through a sieve to resemble coarse grains or break up by hand using your fingers. Sprinkle the streusel evenly over the buttered dough. Lightly beat the egg with the water to make an egg wash.

To make the filling, mix together the sugar, cinnamon, and raisins. Sprinkle over the streusel.

Brush the ½-inch border at the top with egg wash. Starting at the bottom edge, fold over a flap about 1 to 1½ inches wide. Fold over again and press down lightly. Keep folding and pressing until the end is reached. Seal the seam by pressing with your fingertips. Roll the dough over so the seam is centered along the bottom.

Trim the ends. Brush the top with melted butter. Cut into twelve equal pieces. Place in the muffin tins or evenly space 6 on each baking pan, cut side up. Brush the tops with the egg wash. Set aside and allow to rise until over the top of the rim, at least 45 minutes (time will vary with temperature and humidity).

a jewish baker's pastry secrets

Position a rack in the center of the oven and preheat to 350°F/175°C. Bake for about 35 minutes, or until evenly browned. The time varies with the size of the buns and the pan being used. If the top browns too quickly, cover with a tent cut from aluminum foil or a brown paper grocery bag. When done, the top of each bun should feel firm to the touch and spring back when lightly pressed with the fingers.

If you are using baking pans, cool in the pan on a wire rack. If you are using muffin tins, allow the buns to cool for 5 minutes and then remove them from the tins by placing an inverted baking sheet over the top and flipping the muffins over. Use oven mitts or pads to avoid burning your fingers and invert each roll so that the baked top is upright.

Spread or drizzle the warm icing over the top. Serve warm or at room temperature. The buns keep well in a plastic bag for several days at room temperature, or frozen for up to 6 weeks. Thaw overnight in the refrigerator. If you are planning to store them, ice the buns just before serving.

Yield: 12 rolls

℘ Baker's Secret: *Shake a dusting of ground cinnamon over the filling to intensify the flavor.*

Variations

Small Sugar Buns
Cut the filled and rolled dough into eighteen pieces for small sugar buns. Place on a greased 15 by 10-inch baking sheet or place in standard-size muffin tins. Bake for about 30 minutes or until evenly browned.

Rum Buns
These are seen mostly in the South. Add 2 tablespoons of dark rum to the bundt dough recipe with the other liquids. Additionally, replace water in the simple icing with 2 tablespoons of rum.

Hot and Spicy Buns
Grease or butter two 9 by 9 by 2-inch square baking sheets. Prepare the dough as for the sugar bun recipe, but omit the raisins. When the dough is rolled out for filling, top the butter streusel with ¼ cup (2 ounces / 56 grams) spicy red cinnamon candies, crushed or lightly chopped in a blender or food processor. Proceed and bake as for sugar buns.

Sticky Buns

In the bakery, sticky buns were always made from the standard Bundt dough recipe. This sticky bun variation uses a slightly different recipe that surprises the taste buds with a bit of extra zest. Try it both ways. Boysenberry jam, if available, adds a subtle touch of flavor. An abundance of pecans will bring murmurs of approval when the buns are served.

2 scant tablespoons (2 packets / 14 grams) active dry yeast

¼ cup (2 fluid ounces / 59 millimeters) warm water 95°F to 115°F / 35°C to 46°C

½ cup (4 fluid ounces / 118 milliliters) milk, room temperature

¼ cup (1.75 ounces / 50 grams) granulated sugar

¼ cup (1.9 ounces / 54 grams) firmly packed light brown sugar

½ cup (4 ounces / 113 grams) unsalted butter, diced, plus ½ cup (4 ounces / 113 grams) melted, for brushing

2 eggs

4 to 5 cups (18 to 22.4 ounces / 508 to 635 grams) bread flour or unbleached all-purpose flour

¼ cup (1.25 ounces / 35 grams) nonfat dry milk

1½ teaspoons kosher salt

1 tablespoon ground cinnamon

¼ cup (2 fluid ounces / 59 milliliters) orange juice, freshly squeezed, pulp included

1 tablespoon finely grated orange zest

Filling

¼ cup (1.9 ounces / 54 grams) firmly packed brown sugar

¼ cup (1.75 ounces / 50 grams) granulated sugar

2 teaspoons ground cinnamon

1 cup (4 ounces / 113 grams) walnuts or pecans, preferably toasted (page 31) and then chopped

1 cup (5 ounces / 140 grams) raisins, or more to taste (optional)

1 cup (8 ounces / 227 grams) Butter Streusel (page 40)

Topping

½ cup (3.9 ounces / 110 grams) firmly packed brown sugar, plus additional for dusting

½ cup (4 ounces/ 113 grams) solid vegetable shortening

¼ cup (2 ounces / 56 grams) unsalted butter, diced

¼ cup (3 ounces / 85 grams) light corn syrup

¼ cup (3 ounces / 85 grams) honey

¼ cup (2 ounces / 56 grams) boysenberry, raspberry, or red currant jam

1 cup (3.5 ounces / 99 grams) pecan halves or walnut pieces (optional)

½ cup (2.5 ounces / 70 grams) raisins (optional)

Butter or grease a 9 by 9-inch baking pan, two standard 12-hole muffin tins, or two jumbo 4-inch muffin tins.

In the mixing bowl of a stand mixer fitted with a flat paddle, sprinkle yeast over the warm water to soften. Add the milk, granulated sugar, brown sugar, diced butter, eggs, 4 cups of the flour, nonfat dry milk, salt, cinnamon, orange juice, and zest. Pulse with the on/off switch until ingredients are blended. Cover the mixer with a kitchen towel to avoid flying flour! Then mix at slow speed until the dough comes together, adding more flour only if necessary to allow dough to come together. Change to a dough hook if available. Knead for 8 to 10 minutes until the dough becomes elastic with a silky sheen.

Place the dough in a clean, oiled bowl, turning to coat. Cover with a cloth or plastic wrap and allow to rise until doubled in volume, about 60 minutes (time will vary with temperature and humidity) or allow to rise slowly overnight in the refrigerator. While the dough is rising, prepare the filling and the topping.

To make the filling, mix together the brown sugar, granulated sugar, cinnamon, nuts, raisins, and butter streusel and set aside.

To make the topping, mix together the brown sugar, shortening, and butter until blended, but do not cream. Add the corn syrup, 2 tablespoons of the honey, and jam. Mix together until blended. (This mixture will keep for a week or longer at room temperature. Refrigerate for long-term storage. Use at room temperature; it is good as a topping on toast or French toast, too.)

When the dough has risen, turn it out onto a floured work surface. Punch down, fold the ends in toward the center, and roll up into a tight rectangle. Allow to rest for 10 to 15 minutes. At this point, dough can be refrigerated overnight. (All or part of the dough can be frozen at this stage for a week or more if tightly wrapped in plastic wrap.)

> ℘ **Baker's Secret:** *It is easier to work with chilled dough. If your dough gets too soft and sticky, give it 15 to 30 minutes in your refrigerator and the handling will be easier.*

Brush the greased pans generously (heavy on the bottom) with the topping mixture or spread with the fingers. Sprinkle a generous portion of brown sugar over bottom of pans. Cover each pan with a baking sheet, invert, and, while holding them together, shake to distribute the sugar. Place the muffin pan or one baking sheet right side up. With a teaspoon, place a drop of the remaining honey at the bottom of each muffin cup or drizzle over the bottom of the baking pan. Cover the bottom of each muffin cup or the baking pan with the nuts and raisins. Set aside.

On a floured work surface, roll out the bun dough into a ¼-inch-thick rectangle, about 22 inches long by 14 inches wide, with the long side toward you. Brush off any excess flour and then paint the dough with melted butter, leaving a ½-inch border along the top. Distribute the filling over the melted butter. Brush the ½-inch border with water.

Starting at the bottom edge, fold over a flap about 1 to 1½ inches wide. Fold over again, and press down lightly. Keep folding and pressing until the end is reached. Seal the seam by pressing with your fingertips. Roll the dough log over so the seam is centered along the bottom.

Trim the ends. Brush the top with melted butter. If you are using the baking pan or jumbo muffin tins, cut into twelve equal pieces and place, evenly spaced, in the pan or muffin tins. If you are using a standard muffin pan, cut into eighteen to twenty-four pieces and place in the prepared muffin pans. Set aside and allow to rise until over the top of the rim, about 45 minutes or more (time will vary with temperature and humidity).

Position a rack in the center of the oven and preheat the oven to 350°F/175°C.

Bake for about 35 minutes or until evenly browned. The time varies with the size of the buns and the pan being used. If the tops brown too quickly, cover with a tent cut from aluminum foil or a brown paper grocery bag. When done, the top of each bun should feel firm to the touch and spring back when lightly pressed with the fingers.

Remove from the oven and cover with an inverted baking sheet. With oven pads or gloves, flip over and carefully release the buns. Be careful not to get hot sticky bun coating on your fingers. Serve warm or at room temperature. Allow the baking pans to soak in hot water to dissolve any remaining caramelized sugar. Keeps well, wrapped in plastic, at room temperature for about 4 days; may be frozen, double wrapped tightly in plastic, for up to 6 weeks.

Yield: 12 to 24 buns, depending on size

Variations

Plain Sticky Buns
Omit the nuts and/or raisins as desired.

Chocolate-Pecan Sticky Buns
After rolling out the dough, sprinkle 1 cup (8 ounces / 227 grams) semisweet chocolate chips over the melted butter and streusel. Replace the walnuts with 1 cup pecans, preferably toasted. Bake as above.

Lemon–Poppy Seed Buns

The thin wooden dowel you'll need for this recipe can be found in a local hardware store, or you can improvise with a chopstick or even a clean pencil.

1 cup (9.6 ounces / 283 grams) Butter Streusel (page 40)

1 (2-pound / 907-gram) portion Bundt Dough (page 46)

½ cup (5.4 ounces / 152 grams) lemon curd or marmalade, or more, to cover

½ cup (2.5 ounces / 70 grams) poppy seeds, preferably Dutch blue poppy seeds

1 egg

1 tablespoon water

Simple Icing (page 41), warm

Line two half-sheet pans with parchment paper or greased waxed paper.

Rub the butter streusel through your fingers or through a sieve until it resembles coarse grain.

On a floured work surface, roll out the bun dough into a ⅛-inch rectangle about 18 inches long, 12 or more inches wide, with long side toward you. Dust with flour as necessary to prevent sticking.

Brush off any excess flour. Spread a thin layer of lemon curd over the dough, leaving a ½-inch border along the top. Sprinkle the butter streusel on top. Sprinkle the poppy seeds over the streusel.

Starting at the bottom edge of the dough, fold over a flap about 3 inches wide. Fold over again and press down lightly. Keep folding and pressing until the end is reached. Roll over so that the seam is centered along the bottom.

Using a bench knife or chef's knife, cut into eighteen equal pieces, each about 1 inch wide. With a thin dowel held over the center of each piece, with the pieces flat on the counter, press quickly down, squeezing the center of the dough down to the bottom in one quick motion. The cut ends will flare out, forming petals on each side. Place the pieces, evenly spaced, on the prepared baking sheets, three per row.

Lightly beat the egg with the water to make an egg wash.

Brush the tops of the dough with the egg wash, taking care not to let the egg drip down the sides of the dough. Set aside and allow to rise, until doubled in volume, 45 to 60 minutes or more (time depends on temperature and humidity). When pressed very gently on the side with a fingertip, the dough should be soft and yield readily. Carefully brush a second time with egg wash using a delicate touch. Allow to dry for a few minutes.

Position a rack in the center of the oven and preheat the oven to 350°F/175°C.

Bake for 35 to 45 minutes, until browned. The top should feel firm to the touch and spring back when lightly pressed with the fingers. If two sheets cannot fit side by side in your oven, bake one at a time. (Alternately place the racks to divide the oven into thirds. Rotate the baking pans from top to bottom half way into baking time.) Cool in the pan on a wire rack for 10 to 15 minutes. Spread or drizzle with warm icing. Serve warm or at room temperature. The buns keep well in a covered container for up to 24 hours. They can be refrigerated for a few days or frozen for 1 month. Thaw overnight in the refrigerator.

Yield: About 18 buns

Variations

Raspberry–Poppy Seed Buns
Substitute thickened raspberry jam (page 37) for the lemon curd.

Cheese Buns

Over a number of years, I became friendly with a group of Chinese bakers. Years back, the Chinese rarely used dairy products, and when I stopped at their bakery for coffee, they often asked, "Did you bring any cheese buns?" (Actually they called them "cheesy buns.") "Yes," was always my answer, and these buns are good and cheesy.

1 (2-pound / 907-gram) portion Bundt Dough (page 46)

1 egg

1 tablespoon water

1½ cup (15.2 ounces / 430 grams) Cream Cheese Filling (page 35)

Simple Icing (page 41), warm (optional)

Line two half-sheet pans with parchment paper or greased waxed paper.

Cut the dough into eighteen equal pieces, about 1¾ to 2 ounces each. Roll into balls. Place the balls on the prepared pans, equally spaced in staggered rows of nine buns, three to a row. Set aside and allow to rise until the balls are puffed up, not quite doubled in volume, about 45 minutes.

Take a clean, dry glass or plastic jar with a 2-inch bottom (I use an empty vitamin container). Dip the bottom in flour, shake off the excess, and press down into the center of each ball of dough with a twisting motion, jiggling it a little with a circular motion to create a well, flat at the bottom with a well-rounded rim. (Be quick and try to press and twist in one continuous motion.) To keep the dough from sticking, dip the bottom in flour every two or three buns, or as often as necessary.

Lightly beat the egg with the water to make an egg wash. Carefully brush the bun rims with the wash. Avoid letting the egg wash drip onto the pan to prevent burning.

Use a pastry bag with a ¼- to ½-inch opening (no tip is needed in the pastry bag) or a tablespoon to place walnut-sized mounds of the Cream Cheese Filling into the well in each bun. Allow the rim to dry and let the dough rise until the rim is puffy and nicely rounded, about 20 minutes.

Carefully paint the rims a second time with egg wash, using a delicate touch. Allow to dry for a few minutes.

Position a rack in the center of the oven and preheat to 350°F/175°C.

Bake for 25 to 35 minutes, or until well browned. The top of the rim should feel firm to the touch and spring back when lightly pressed with the fingers. If two sheets cannot fit side by side in your oven, bake one at a time. (Alternately, place the racks to divide the oven into thirds. Rotate the baking pans from top to bottom half way into baking time.)

Cool on a wire rack for 10 to 15 minutes before removing the buns from the pan. Drizzle or spread with the simple icing. Serve warm or at room temperature. The buns are best when served immediately but will keep for 1 day. The buns can be refrigerated, wrapped in plastic, for a few days or frozen for up to 6 weeks. Thaw overnight in the refrigerator.

Yield: 18 buns

Variations

Fruit Buns

Prepare as for Cheese Buns. Substitute any fruit filling or thickened jam (page 37) for the cheese.

Coconut Buns

1 cup (3 ounces / 85 grams) sweetened flaked coconut

¼ cup (2 ounces / 57 grams) unsalted butter, melted

1 egg, lightly beaten

1 tablespoon sugar

Pinch of salt, kosher

⅛ teaspoon pure vanilla extract

¼ cup (2 fluid ounces / 59 milliliters) milk or half and half

Prepare the dough as for Cheese Buns (above). Instead of the cheese filling, make a coconut filling by mixing together the coconut, butter, and egg into a moist paste. Add the sugar, salt, vanilla, and enough milk or half and half, 1 tablespoon at a time, to make the mixture pliable. Use in place of the cheese and fill and bake as above.

Hot Cross Buns

The Simple Icing (page 41) should be thicker than usual. It should be fairly stiff so that it does not run too much when piped.

1 cup (5.3 ounces / 150 grams) currants

1 (2-pound / 907-gram) portion Bundt Dough (page 46)

1 cup (6 ounces / 170 grams) diced citron

1 egg

1 tablespoon water

Simple Icing (page 41), warm, made thicker if needed by adding a little more confectioners' sugar

Line a half-sheet pan with parchment paper or greased waxed paper.

Soak the currants in hot water to cover for 10 to 15 minutes and then drain. Turn out the dough onto floured work surface. Knead the currants and citron into the dough. Allow to rest for 10 minutes.

Divide the dough into twenty-four pieces and roll into tight balls. Place the balls on the prepared baking pan in six rows of four buns. Allow to rise until doubled in size, 30 to 45 minutes. It's okay if the buns grow together while rising.

Position a rack in the center of the oven and preheat to 350°F/175°C.

Lightly beat the egg with the water to make an egg wash. Brush the tops of the buns with the wash. Try to avoid dripping down the sides. Cut a cross about ¼ inch deep through the top of each bun.

Bake for 25 to 35 minutes, until evenly browned. Cool in the pan on a wire rack for about 15 minutes.

Spoon the icing into a parchment paper or waxed paper cone and cut off ¼-inch tip (see page 26). Pipe the icing over the crosses cut into each bun. Alternately, spread the Simple Icing over the tops of the buns. The buns can be refrigerated, wrapped in plastic, for a few days or frozen, double wrapped tightly in plastic, for up to 6 weeks. Thaw overnight in the refrigerator.

Yield: 24 buns

Variation

Substitute 1 cup (6 ounces / 170 grams) dried apricots, finely diced, for the citron.

CHAPTER 4

Babka

Spring 1950: I remember customers coming into our bakery asking for "Grandma's Loaf." Grandma's Loaf was babka: a rich, moist, and tender yeast-raised loaf made with nut paste, walnuts, raisins, butter, and cinnamon. Topped with fragrant chunks of crunchy streusel, the loaves were baked in corrugated paper liners. Babka is sliced like bread and served plain, buttered, or toasted.

I figured that the name "Grandma's Loaf" was derived from the words *babba*, *bubbie*, or *babushka*, all of which translate as "grandma." *Babushka* literally refers to a kerchief, the head cover that elderly Russian women wore. Some elderly Russian ladies eventually were fondly referred to as "Babushkas."

Our standard babka choices in the bakery were cinnamon and chocolate baked in yellow corrugated paper pan liners. Customers told me they would scrape the paper after peeling it off their slice so as not to miss a delicious morsel. Babka dough can be used for an assortment of other coffee cakes and individual pastries. This chapter contains recipes for many variations.

Often considered a Polish or Jewish pastry, babka appears to be Slavic in origin. Variations of the pastry extend through Europe to Austria, Hungary, and Northern Italy. Modern babka counterparts exist in Scandinavian Julekake, Russian coffee cake, Austro-Hungarian-German gugelhopf,

Italian panettone, French brioche, and even Portuguese sweet bread. Scandinavians flavor with cardamom, Portuguese with mace, French with butter. Italians add citron to panettone. Many areas in Italy bake their own version with exotic flavors and spices, making each cake representative of a specific city, town, or village. Remarkably, to this very day, most Italian-American bakeries and food shops, rather than bake their own, import panettone from Italy, mainly from Milan.

Russian coffee cake, as made in the American bakery, is baked in huge, high-sided pans and filled with thick, moist fillings. Some cakes weigh in at as much as 20 pounds when baked. You'll find a collection of recipes for these "Russians" later in this chapter.

Although all of these related sweet breads can be thought of as "kissing cousins," babka dough is generally richer in eggs and butter. Make this easy-to-follow recipe your personal best. A long repertoire can be developed from the basic dough, worthy of becoming family treasures to be handed down from "Baba" to grandchild.

Although the recipes that follow the master recipes are for single loaves, I always make two or more with little additional effort. Extra loaves can be frozen for up to 8 weeks, thawed overnight in the refrigerator, and then allowed to rise and bake at your convenience. Pre-baked loaves also freeze well.

Babka Dough

My father immigrated to New York from Budapest with a suitcase full of recipes. This babka dough is one of my favorites.

Sponge

4 scant tablespoons (4 packets / 28 grams) active dry yeast

¼ cup (2 fluid ounces / 59 milliliters) warm water, 95°F to 115°F / 35°C to 46°C

¾ cup (6 fluid ounces / 178 milliliters) milk, room temperature

1½ cups (6.75 ounces / 191 grams) bread flour (see Note)

Mix

4 eggs

2 egg yolks

½ cup (3.5 ounces / 99 grams) sugar

1 tablespoon nonfat dry milk

3⅓ cups (1 pound / 454 grams) bread flour

2¼ teaspoons kosher salt

Finely grated zest of ½ orange

2 tablespoons orange juice

¼ cup (2.5 ounces / 71 grams) orange marmalade

1½ teaspoons pure vanilla extract

¼ teaspoon ground nutmeg, preferably freshly ground

¼ cup (2 ounces / 56 grams) sour cream (or substitute yogurt)

1 cup (8 ounces / 227 grams) unsalted butter, melted and cooled

Flour a half-sheet pan.

To make the sponge, in the mixing bowl of a stand mixer fitted with a flat paddle, sprinkle the yeast over the warm water to soften. Add the milk and flour, pulsing the on/off switch until blended, making sure the flour does not fly out of the bowl. Continue to mix on low speed for 8 to 10 minutes. After a few minutes change to a dough hook, if available. The dough should come away from the sides of the bowl. If not, continue for a few minutes at medium speed. Remove the hook or paddle and cover the bowl with a cloth. Let stand until doubled in volume, 20 to 35 minutes.

To make the mix, beat the sponge down with a few turns of the paddle. Mixing at slow speed, add the eggs and yolks in three additions.

When barely blended (it's easier if the mixture is still a little wet), add the sugar, milk powder, flour, salt, orange zest and juice, marmalade, vanilla, nutmeg, and sour cream. Mix by pulsing the on/off switch until the dry ingredients are absorbed so that the flour does not fly out of the bowl. Switch to the dough hook and knead for 8 to 10 minutes at slow speed. Add the butter in several additions, allowing it to become absorbed after each addition. Mix until fully blended. The dough should remain soft, moist, a little sticky, and have a silky appearance.

Transfer the dough into a clean, oiled bowl, turning to coat. Cover with a cloth or plastic wrap and let rest until puffy, about 30 minutes.

Turn out the dough onto a floured work surface and punch down so that all of the air is released. Cut the dough into 8 equal pieces, about 8 ounces each. (It is easy to knead several pieces together later, if a larger piece of dough is required.) Roll up each piece, jelly-roll style, into a loaf shape. Place on the floured baking sheet and cover lightly.

Refrigerate for several hours or leave refrigerated overnight in the coldest part of the refrigerator before baking the following morning. Double wrap each piece tightly in plastic. May be refrigerated for up to 4 days and frozen for up to 8 weeks. Thaw in the refrigerator.

Yield: About 4 pounds (1.8 kilograms) of dough, enough for 8 babkas

> **ɛɔ Baker's Secret:** *If possible, before refrigerating, place the dough in the freezer for 30 to 45 minutes to quickly retard the initial rise, intensifying flavor and slowing the fermentation process. This makes for a better rise before baking and is especially helpful on warm days. Alternatively, freeze the entire baking sheet. When frozen, wrap each piece with a double layer of plastic wrap. It is best to allow the dough to thaw overnight in the refrigerator.*

Note: You can substitute unbleached all-purpose flour for the bread flour, but the babka will not rise as high and will be a bit less tender.

In the summer, chill all ingredients (except for the warm water used to soften the yeast). Use butter softened at room temperature instead of melted.

Cinnamon Babka Loaf

This is perhaps the most popular babka we made in the bakery. The aroma is amazing, but wait until you taste it!

1 (8-ounce / 227-gram) portion Babka Dough (page 68), at room temperature

1 to 1½ cups (10 ounces / 285 grams) Processed Almond-Paste Filling (page 32)

2 cups (11 ounces / 312 grams) Butter Streusel (page 40)

½ cup (2 ounces / 57 grams) walnuts, toasted and coarsely chopped

½ cup (2.5 ounces / 71 grams) raisins, plumped in warm water for 15 minutes or soaked overnight in rum or brandy, drained

½ cup (3.5 ounces / 100 grams) Cinnamon Sugar (page 40)

Ground cinnamon, for dusting

2 tablespoons unsalted butter, melted

Grease one 8-inch or 9-inch loaf pan or line it with parchment paper. If you are using an aluminum foil loaf pan, grease the pan.

Dust the dough with flour. On a floured work surface, roll out the dough into a 1-inch-thick rectangle that measures about 10 by 7 inches. Brush off any excess flour. Spread the almond filling over the dough, leaving a ½-inch border around the top. Sprinkle with the streusel, walnuts, and raisins. Cover with the cinnamon sugar. Press down lightly using your hands or a rolling pin. Sprinkle a light dusting of cinnamon over the top (a shaker jar works well). Drizzle with melted butter. Brush the ½-inch border lightly with water.

From the bottom edge of the longer side, fold over a 1-inch flap along the length, press down lightly, fold, and press again. Keep folding and pressing until the end is reached. Seal by pressing the seam with your fingertips.

With one hand at each end, twist the strip by rolling with the palms in opposite directions, elongating the twist to about 15 to 18 inches in length. For a simple finish, without lifting, bring the ends around in a circle. Do not be concerned if some of the filling spills out. Insert about 1 inch of one end inside the other. Holding the ring down where the ends are joined, twist both strands together into a double twist. In the bakery, I twisted the babka into the shape of a figure 8. The figure 8 results in a pleasing pattern and an even distribution of the filling when sliced. Place the babka into the prepared loaf pan. If necessary, press down lightly with your fingertips from the center out to fill the pan along the edges.

Brush the top with melted butter or water. If any filling spilled out during the shaping process, scatter it on top. Sprinkle with the streusel to cover. The streusel can be pressed in large clumps for those who like additional crunch. Set the babka aside and let rise until doubled in volume and the top has risen above the pan, 45 to 60 minutes. When touched very gently on the side with a fingertip, the dough should be soft and yield readily.

> හ **Baker's Secret:** *Before baking, some bakers like to drizzle additional streusel over the top, especially where cracks have appeared. Spread gently, to avoid causing the dough to collapse.*

Position a rack in the center of the oven and preheat to 350°F/175°C.

Bake for 35 to 45 minutes, until browned. When done, the top should feel firm to the touch and spring back when lightly pressed with the fingers. Use caution as the hot streusel can cause a burn.

Cool on a wire rack before removing from the pan. Babka is served sliced, either plain or with butter or jam. It's excellent when toasted or grilled in a buttered skillet. It can make a wicked French toast as well! Babka keeps well in a plastic bag for several days at room temperature. It can be refrigerated for 7 days or frozen for up to 8 weeks.

Yield: 1 loaf, serving 8

Babka with Three Chocolates

If you are a chocoholic, this is the babka to try first.

1 (8-ounce / 227-gram) portion
Babka Dough (page 68)

¾ cup (6 ounces / 170 grams) Processed
Almond-Paste Filling (page 32), or more
to cover

¾ cup (6 ounces / 69 grams) semisweet
or bittersweet chocolate chopped or chips

1 tablespoon unsalted butter

½ cup (3.6 ounces / 100 grams)
Cinnamon Sugar (page 40)

2 tablespoons Dutch-process cocoa,
preferably imported, for dusting

½ cup (2 ounces / 56 grams) walnuts,
toasted, coarsely chopped (optional)

1 cup (5.6 ounces / 160 grams) Butter
Streusel (page 40), or more to taste

Grease one 8 or 9-inch loaf pan or line it with parchment paper (page 26). If you are using an aluminum foil loaf pan, grease the pan.

Dust the dough with flour. On a floured work surface, roll out dough into a 1-inch-thick rectangle that measures about 10 by 7 inches. Brush off any excess flour. Spread the almond filling over the dough, leaving a ½-inch border around the top.

Melt ¼ cup (2 ounce / 56 grams) of the chocolate together with the butter. Spread the melted chocolate over the almond filling. Dust with Cinnamon Sugar and cocoa powder. Scatter the chocolate bits and nuts over the top.

Twist the dough, place in the pan, and let rise as in the Cinnamon Babka Loaf recipe (page 70). Top with ¼ cup chocolate chips over the streusel before baking and bake as in the Cinnamon Babka Loaf recipe (page 70) or better still, drizzle the top with the remaining ¼ cup melted chocolate after the baked loaf is cooled. Babka keeps well in a plastic bag for several days at room temperature. It can be refrigerated for 7 days or frozen for up to 8 weeks.

Yield: 1 loaf, serving 8

a jewish baker's pastry secrets

Cheese Babka

Sometimes I can't decide what I want—a crumb bun, a cheese Danish, or a piece of babka. This has a little bit of all three, so there's no need to decide.

1 (8-ounce / 227-gram) portion Babka Dough (page 68)

1 cup (7.8 ounces / 221 grams) Cream Cheese Filling (page 35)

½ cup (3.6 ounces / 100 grams) Cinnamon Sugar (page 40)

Melted butter

1 cup (5.6 ounces / 160 grams) Butter Streusel (page 40), plus more for topping

Line an 8- or 9-inch loaf pan with parchment paper.

Dust the dough with flour. On a floured work surface, roll out the dough into a 1-inch-thick rectangle measuring about 10 by 7 inches. Brush off any excess flour. Spread the Cream Cheese Filling over the dough, leaving a ½-inch border around the top. Cover with the Cinnamon Sugar. Press down lightly with hands or a rolling pin. Brush the ½-inch border lightly with water.

Roll up, twist the dough, and place in the pan as in the Cinnamon Babka Loaf recipe (page 70). Brush the top with melted butter or water. Sprinkle with streusel to cover. Let rise and bake as in the Cinnamon Babka Loaf recipe.

Yield: 1 loaf, serving 8

Variation

Raisin-Cheese Babka
Soak ¼ cup (2.5 ounces / 70 grams) raisins or currants in rum or water for 10 to 15 minutes and then drain. Follow the directions for Cheese Babka. Sprinkle the raisins on the cheese filling before rolling.

Fruit Babka

Dave Goodman was the mixer in the bakery for many years. He kept three huge mixers spinning most of the day, and he made all the doughs and icings we used. He often brought a loaf of this babka home.

1 (8-ounce / 227-gram) portion Babka Dough (page 68), at room temperature

1½ cups (10 ounces / 284 grams) Apple Filling (page 33) or prepared pie filling of your choice, such as pineapple, cherry, or blueberry

2 tablespoons unsalted butter, melted, or water

1 cup (5.6 ounces / 160 grams) Butter Streusel (page 40)

Grease or butter an 8-inch or 9-inch layer cake pan with 1-inch high sides or a pie tin.

Dust the dough with flour. On a floured work surface, roll out the dough into a rectangle about ½ inch thick and measuring 10 by 7 inches. Spread a 1-inch line of filling along the longer bottom edge. Roll up jelly-roll style. Pinch the seam shut with your fingers. With one hand at each end, twist the dough by rolling with the palms of your hands in opposite directions, elongating the twist to about 15 to 18 inches in length. Wind the rope, counterclockwise, into a loose spiral and place in the prepared pan. If necessary, press lightly from the center, outward, to fill the pan. Brush with melted butter or water and cover with streusel.

Set the babka aside and let rise until doubled in volume and the top has risen above the pan, 45 to 60 minutes. When touched very gently on the side with a fingertip, the dough should be soft and yield readily.

Position a rack in the center of the oven and preheat to 350°F/175°C.

Bake for 35 to 45 minutes, until browned. When done, the top should feel firm to the touch and spring back when lightly pressed with the fingers. Use caution as the hot streusel can burn. Remove from the oven. Cool on a wire rack before removing from the pan. Babka keeps well in a plastic bag for several days at room temperature. It can be refrigerated for 7 days or frozen for up to 8 weeks.

Yield: 1 loaf, serving 8

a jewish baker's pastry secrets

Variation

Round Cheese Babka

Follow the directions for Fruit Babka. Substitute 1 to 1½ cups (8 to 12 ounces / 227 to 340 grams) Cream Cheese Filling (page 35) for the pie filling. Leave plain, sprinkle with Cinnamon Sugar (page 40), or spread 1 or 2 tablespoons of fruit filling over the top of the cheese. Roll up, brush with butter or water, and sprinkle with butter streusel. Let it rise and then bake as for Fruit Babka.

Hungarian Walnut Loaf

The distinctive shape and design of this loaf will allow you to bring to the table what I would define as a yeast-raised strudel in a loaf form. I learned how to make these Hungarian loaves from Will Golden, an African-American baker and cake-decorating artist who was accomplished in all phases of Jewish-American baking. Those who worked with him all agreed that he had "golden" hands. In another life, Willie might have been a sculptor or painter.

1 (8-ounce / 227-gram) portion Babka Dough (page 68), chilled

1½ cups (15 ounces / 426 grams) Processed Almond-Paste Filling (page 32)

½ cup (2 ounces / 57 grams) walnuts, chopped, preferably toasted

1 cup (3.6 ounces / 90 grams) cake crumbs (see page 42)

¼ cup (1.8 ounces / 51 grams) Cinnamon Sugar (page 40)

Ground cinnamon, for dusting (optional)

1 egg

1 tablespoon water

Grease an 8- or 9-inch loaf pan.

Dust the dough with flour. On a floured work surface, roll out the dough into a rectangle about 1 inch thick and measuring 8 by 7 inches. Brush off any excess flour. Spread the almond filling over the dough in a layer about ⅛ inch thick, leaving a ½-inch border at the top long end. Sprinkle the walnuts evenly over the filling. Cover with a blanket of cake crumbs. Sprinkle with enough Cinnamon Sugar to cover. Press down lightly with hands or a rolling pin on the crumbs and Cinnamon Sugar.

> ✺ **Baker's Secret:** *A fine dusting of ground cinnamon over the top before proceeding will add a burst of flavor to the finished cake.*

a jewish baker's pastry secrets

Starting from the right side (the short end), roll up jelly-roll style. Stop rolling midway, upon reaching the center of the rectangle. Roll up the opposite end (from left side to center). Place the dough in the prepared loaf pan, scroll side up. With a square-edge metal spatula (a narrow putty knife works just as well), cut straight down with the tip held perpendicular to the center line, making a series of cuts across the center of the scroll, about ½ inch apart and 1 inch deep, down the entire length. Lightly beat the egg and water to make an egg wash. Brush the top with the egg wash, taking care not to let the egg drip down the sides of the dough.

Set aside and let rise until doubled in volume or beginning to rise over the rim of the pan, about 45 minutes. When pressed very gently on the side with a fingertip, the dough should be soft and yield readily. Using a delicate touch, carefully brush a second time with the egg wash. Let dry for a few minutes.

Position a rack in the center of the oven and preheat to 350°F/175°C.

Bake for 35 to 45 minutes, until well browned. The top should feel firm and spring back when lightly pressed with the fingers. Cool for 10 to 15 minutes on a wire rack before removing from the loaf pan. Babka keeps well in a plastic bag for several days at room temperature. It can be refrigerated for 7 days or frozen for up to 8 weeks.

Yield: 1 loaf, serving 8

Variation

Chocolate Hungarian Loaf

Follow the directions for the Hungarian Walnut Loaf, rolling out and spreading on the almond filling. Melt 2 ounces (56 grams) chopped semi-sweet chocolate with 1 tablespoon unsalted butter and spread on top of the almond filling before sprinkling on the walnuts. Finish as above.

Polish Easter Bread

Mr. Blau was an elderly Hungarian gentleman who raised chickens in Manorville, Long Island. He supplied us with fresh eggs. He loved to stop and chat with the bakers whenever he made a delivery. Blau had an ongoing love affair with our huge assortment of cakes and pastries, many of which were Hungarian in origin and not widely available on Long Island. Due to his health, however, he was not allowed to eat them. When offered, he would only accept bread or a few rolls. Always cheerful though, he seemed to enjoy eyeing the sweets and taking in the aroma.

Once, a few days before Easter, he was startled to see a full rack of Polish Easter bread. His eyes wide, he turned toward me, shaking his head from side to side in apparent disbelief, and questioningly called out the Hungarian name for the confection. "Oh my," he uttered softly, with wonder in his voice. "They used to make this with golden raisins when I was a boy in Hungary." I smiled and cut a loaf in half, exposing a rounded yellow dome chock-full of golden raisins. I looked into his tear-filled eyes and watched him being transported back in time. I placed another bread, still warm from the oven, in a box and handed it to him. He looked at me and, without hesitation, said, "This one, I will eat."

1 (1-pound / 454-gram) portion Babka Dough (page 68), chilled

1 cup (5 ounces / 140 grams) raisins, preferably golden

1 egg

1 tablespoon water

Baker's Danish Glaze (page 41), (optional)

Grease an 8-inch or 9-inch layer cake pan with 1-inch-high sides. A pie plate makes an acceptable substitute.

Pinch off a golf ball–sized piece of dough and set aside. Flatten the remaining dough and cover with raisins and knead into a tight ball, seam on the bottom. Lightly beat the egg with the water to make an egg wash. Brush with the egg wash and place in the prepared pan.

To decorate in the traditional manner, roll the reserved piece of dough into a rectangle about 1 inch thick and measuring 8 by 1 inch. Cut two ½-inch strips, 8 inches long. Brush the strips lightly with the egg wash and place them, washed side up, on top of the ball of dough so that they cross one another.

Set aside and let rise until doubled in volume and above the rim of the pan, about 45 minutes. When pressed very gently on the side with a fingertip, the dough should be soft and yield readily. Using a delicate touch, carefully brush a second time with the egg wash. Let dry for a few minutes.

Position a rack in the center of the oven and preheat to 350°F/175°C.

Bake for about 45 minutes, or until well browned. After the first 15 minutes, if the top begins to darken too quickly, cover with a tent cut from aluminum foil or a brown paper grocery bag. The bread is done when the top and sides are firm to the touch and spring back when lightly pressed with your fingers. Remove from the oven and brush with Danish glaze while still hot.

Cool on a wire rack for 10 to 15 minutes before removing from the pan. Serve warm or at room temperature. The bread keeps well in a plastic bag for several days. It can be refrigerated for up to a week or frozen for 1 to 2 months.

Yield: 1 loaf, serving 8 to 10

Polish Cheese Babka

The following babka is the culmination of some 35 years in the bakery. It appears to have a simple taste but is actually rich and quite subtle. If you only make one recipe from this book, this is the one that is worthy of your time.

Polish cheese babka is baked in a distinctive shape that is instantly recognizable. While strolling about the streets of the Polish enclave in the Greenpoint area of Brooklyn, my wife Adele and I used to feel like tourists in another country, enchanted by wonderful sights and smells. We worked our way from restaurant to butcher shop to delicatessen to the bakeries—all of which, without exception, offered look-alike cheese babka that were of one shape, sharing in common an intense flavor and superior quality. A food expert, blindfolded and led from shop to shop in Greenpoint would have had trouble distinguishing between good, better, and best.

Some of the wonderful Polish restaurants toasted this babka on the grill. Mmmm! Lip-smacking good. Try this for a sophisticated breakfast: freshly squeezed orange juice, babka grilled in butter, and a frothy cappuccino.

1 (1½-pound / 680-gram) portion Babka Dough (page 68), chilled

2 cups (15 ounces / 425 grams) Cream Cheese Filling (page 35)

1 egg

1 tablespoon water

Melted butter or vegetable oil, for brushing

Grease a 9-inch layer cake or springform pan with 3-inch sides. Line the bottom with a parchment paper circle or a greased waxed paper circle (see page 26).

Dust the dough with flour. On a floured work surface, roll out the dough into a 1-inch-thick rectangle measuring 18 by 12 inches. Brush off any excess flour. Spread the filling over the dough, leaving a ½-inch border at the top (a long side). Lightly beat the egg with the water to make an egg wash. Brush the edge at the top with egg wash. Starting at the bottom edge, fold over a flap about 2 inches wide. Fold over again; press down lightly. Keep folding and pressing until the end is reached. Seal the seam by pressing with your fingertips. Compress the roll from the ends until it measures about 14 inches. Roll the dough over so that the seam is centered along the bottom. Brush the roll with butter or vegetable oil.

My first teachers were the bakers with whom I worked in Astoria, in Queens, New York. These men took great pride in both their skill and their strength. Boasting about the "good old days," impromptu races were often organized with the participants carrying up cotton sacks of flour from the basement. Each sack weighed 100 pounds and (believe this, I've seen it) a man would lift a sack onto his back and then, while hunched over, someone would place a second bag on top of the first one. Holding onto the bags by the cotton "ears" that protruded on each end, with backs and knees straining, two men, each carrying 200 pounds, would race up the stairs amid hoopla and laughter to see who was quicker. These guys did not give away much, and it was impossible to get a recipe from them without some sort of guile. They did, however, freely teach how to work with finished cakes and pastry dough. This was called "makeup" or "bench work," and it was the first real job an apprentice was allowed to do. The bakers were stern instructors and if you showed any disrespect or did not follow instructions exactly, they refused to teach you anything new for weeks.

Cut into seven equal pieces. Place the first piece, cut side up, in the center of the pan and surround it with the remaining six pieces in an evenly spaced circle. Brush the tops with egg wash, taking care to not let the egg drip down the sides of the dough.

Let rise until doubled in volume, 45 to 60 minutes. When pressed very gently on the side with a fingertip, the dough should be soft and yield readily. Using a delicate touch, carefully brush a second time with the egg wash. Let dry for a few minutes.

Position a rack in the bottom third of the oven and preheat to 350°F/175°C.

Bake for 45 to 60 minutes, until browned. The top should feel firm to the touch and spring back when lightly pressed with the fingers. This is a large cake and tends to darken too much on top while the center has not yet baked. After 15 minutes in the oven, if it appears to be browning too quickly, cover with a tent cut from aluminum foil or a brown paper grocery bag. Uncover for the last 5 to 10 minutes to allow the top to finish browning.

Cool on a wire rack for 10 to 15 minutes and then remove from the springform pan. If you are using a layer cake pan, wait until the babka is just barely warm and invert it onto a flat plate or the back of another pan. Carefully flip it over onto a platter. Serve warm or at room temperature. The babka will keep for a few days in a plastic bag at room temperature, or up to 1 week refrigerated. It freezes well for up to 8 weeks.

Yield: 1 loaf, serving 8 to 10

Cheese Horseshoe

The streusel topping on this pastry horn, presented with a core of rich cheese filling, makes this unassuming yeast cake a favorite.

1 (8-ounce /227-gram) portion
Babka Dough (page 68)

1½ cups (12 ounces / 340 grams)
Cream Cheese Filling (page 35)

2 tablespoons Cinnamon Sugar (page 40)

2 tablespoons unsalted butter, melted

1 cup (5.6 ounces / 160 grams)
Butter Streusel (page 40), for topping

Confectioners' sugar, for dusting
(optional)

Line a half-sheet pan with parchment paper or greased waxed paper.

Dust the dough with flour. On a floured work surface, roll out the dough into a 1-inch-thick rectangle measuring 10 by 5 inches. Brush off any excess flour. Mound the cheese filling along the bottom edge in a line or rope about 1 inch in diameter along the entire length, about an inch from the bottom edge. Sprinkle the cinnamon sugar over the top of the cheese. Brush a ½-inch border along the top edge of the dough with water. Roll up, jelly-roll style, from the bottom up. Pinch the seam shut with your fingers. Roll the dough over so that the seam is centered along the bottom.

Brush the top with butter and sprinkle with a thick layer of streusel. With a bench knife (see page 14) or sharp paring knife, cut a series of ½-inch notches crosswise through the bottom edge, 1-inch apart. The strip should resemble a long cock's comb. Lift gently from each end onto the prepared baking sheet, drawing the ends around into a horseshoe shape (the notches should be along the outer edge) as it is placed on the pan. The ends should be brought around until 2 to 3 inches apart.

Let rise until doubled in volume, about 45 minutes.

Position a rack in the center of the oven and preheat the oven to 350°F/175°C.

Bake for 35 to 45 minutes, until evenly browned. The top should feel firm to the touch and spring back when lightly pressed with the fingers. Use caution as the hot streusel can burn. Remove from the oven.

Cool on a wire rack andthen remove from the pan. When cool, top with a dusting of confectioners' sugar. This is best enjoyed within 24 hours. It keeps well in a plastic wrap for several days at room temperature, or it can be refrigerated for up to a week or frozen for up to 8 weeks.

Yield: 1 loaf, serving 8

Variations

Fruit Horseshoe

In place of the cinnamon sugar, substitute a thin line of 2 tablespoons raisins or currants, or 2 or more tablespoons of fruit filling or preserves, such as pineapple, strawberry, or cherry. Proceed with the recipe above for the Cheese Horseshoe.

Almond Horseshoe

Substitute any almond filling for the cheese filling.

Apple 'n' Cheese Cuts

My Uncle Joe loved to eat this pastry with tea. He always drank his tea dark from a small water glass that he sipped through the sugar cube he held between his front teeth. It fascinated me how he could hold the soggy cube with his teeth without crushing it. When I asked how he did it, Joe answered my question with his own, "Can you keep a secret?" My reply was "Of course!" His comeback was "So can I!"

3 or 4 tart apples (such as Granny Smith), peeled, cored, and cut into ½-inch slices

2 tablespoons cornstarch

¼ cup (2 ounces / 57 grams) Cinnamon Sugar (page 40)

⅛ teaspoon ground nutmeg, preferably freshly ground

Finely grated zest and juice of ½ lemon

1 (8-ounce /227-gram) portion Babka Dough (page 68)

3 to 4 slices of Quick Sheet Cake, each 2½ x 2 x 1 inch thick (see page 43)

1 cup (7.8 ounces / 220 grams) Cream Cheese Filling (page 35)

1 egg

1 tablespoon (2 ounces / 5 grams) water

1 ounce (28 grams) sliced almonds, toasted for garnish (optional)

Baker's Danish Glaze (page 41), (optional)

Grease a half-sheet pan or line with parchment paper or greased waxed paper.

In a mixing bowl, toss the apples, cornstarch, cinnamon sugar, nutmeg, and the lemon zest and juice. Set aside.

On a floured work surface, roll out the dough into a 1-inch-thick rectangle measuring 9 by 8 inches. Turn the dough so that the long side lies vertically in front of you. Place a 1-inch-wide rolling pin across the center line of the dough. Flip the left side of the dough over the pin so that it rests on the right side of the dough with the edges even. With a bench knife or a sharp knife, make a series of 2-inch cuts at a 45-degree angle through the outer edges of both layers of dough, starting ½ inch from the top. Continue every ½ to ¾ inch down to within a ½ inch of the bottom. With the rolling pin, flip the left side of the cut dough back over so that the dough lies flat once more. You should now have a piece of dough that is solid down the middle with symmetrical arms or cuts (pine-tree style) on both sides.

Cut and fit the cake slices into a strip 1 inch thick, about 2½ inches wide, and 8 inches long (trimmed ends from scraps can be saved). Arrange the cake down the center of the dough. It can be pieced together from scraps if you have them. Reserve extra for another use.

Put a handful of the cream cheese filling on a floured work surface. Roll the filling with floured hands from the center out into a rope about ½-inch in diameter. Place this rope so that it encircles the entire layer cake strip. If the rope is too short, simply roll out additional filling and add it in by butting it against the previous strip. Mound the apple mixture on top of the cake and filling. Lightly beat the egg with the water to make an egg wash. Brush all of the cut arms with egg wash; try not to let the egg drip.

Beginning at the top, bring the first strip from the right side over the filling to the left and lightly press the end to seal. If you have to stretch the strip a bit, do it carefully. If it tears, you can mend it by pressing the ends together. Next, bring the top left strip over and to the right and seal. Continue, right over left, left over right, braiding all of the strips in this fashion.

Place the pastry on the greased, lined baking sheet. Brush the top with egg wash, taking care not to let the egg drip down the sides of the dough. Set aside and let rise for about 10 to 15 minutes. Using a delicate touch, carefully brush a second time with egg wash. Sprinkle the top with sliced almonds. Let dry for a few minutes.

Position an oven rack in the center of the oven and preheat the oven to 350°F/175°C.

Bake for 35 to 45 minutes, until well browned. The top should feel firm to the touch and spring back when lightly pressed with your fingers.

Remove the pastry from the oven and brush with the glaze while still hot. Leave the pastry on the baking sheet and cool completely on a wire rack. Serve warm or at room temperature. Wrapped in plastic, it keeps well for 1 or 2 days. It can be refrigerated for up to a week. Freezing is not recommended.

Yield: 1 pastry, serving 6 to 8

Cinnamon-Raisin Russian Coffee Cake

Merely the thought of the weighty amounts of filling in Russian coffee cake, the sweets and spice, nuts and fruits, chocolate and sweet dairy butter, and frangipane, brings forth a Pavlovian surge upon tongue and palate. The long, slow baking of these large pan loaves extracts the essence and full flavor of the ingredients. These "heavenly Russians" are in no way subtle. The aroma is sensual, and whether hoary peasant or haughty Czarina, all are seduced and fling themselves eagerly upon it.

Russian coffee cake is not difficult to make. A beginner, having once prepared a few babka loaves, should have no problem with these cakes. All of the fillings can be prepared in advance. The directions are purposely lengthy to lead you through each stage and are laid out in short easy-to-understand sections describing each step. Your work can be interrupted at any time by placing the dough in the refrigerator or freezer, and continued, unhurried, at your leisure.

The aroma created during the oven bronzing of nuts, butter, and cinnamon can be bewitching. Be warned! Strangers may come "rapping, tap, tap, tapping" upon your door, pleading for entrance. Have fun!

1 (2-pound / 906-gram) portion Babka Dough (page 68)

1 to 1½ cups (10 to 15 ounces / 284 to 426 grams) Processed Almond-Paste Filling (page 32)

Ground cinnamon, for dusting

1½ cups (7.5 ounces / 210 grams) raisins, or more to taste

2 cups (8 ounces / 227 grams) walnuts, toasted and chopped

4 cups (14 ounces / 400 grams) cake crumbs (see page 42) (use bread crumbs, preferably fresh, if cake crumbs are not available)

1¾ cups (14 ounces / 400 grams) Cinnamon Sugar (page 40)

¼ cup (2 ounces / 56 grams) unsalted butter

1 egg

1 tablespoon water

Grease a 9 by 9-inch baking pan with 2-inch sides. Line the bottom and sides with parchment paper or greased waxed paper.

To make the base, cut off an 8-ounce (227-gram) piece of the dough. On a floured work surface, roll out the dough into a square, about 1 inch wider than the baking pan, to allow for shrinkage. Fold the dough into quarters to make lifting easy and transfer to the prepared baking pan. Open the dough so that it covers the pan from edge to edge. If necessary, use your fingers to spread the dough from the center outward to the edges. A tear can be repaired with small bits of dough.

> ℘ **Baker's Secret:** *Set the base aside, preferably in the freezer, or put it in the refrigerator. It is easier to spread the filling without tearing the dough if the dough is frozen.*

To make the twists, roll out the remaining dough into a rectangle. First, roll lengthwise, until the dough is about 12 inches long, then roll the width to about 14 inches; it should be ¼-inch thick. Spread 1 to 1½ cups of the almond filling over the bottom two-thirds of the dough, covering it from edge to edge. Dust with cinnamon. Sprinkle with 1¼ cups of the raisins, then with 1½ cups of the walnuts. Cover with 2 cups of the cake crumbs and 1 cup of cinnamon sugar. Press down lightly with hands or rolling pin. Drizzle 2 tablespoons of melted butter over the cinnamon sugar.

Lightly beat the egg with the water to make an egg wash. Brush the top third of the dough (the uncovered portion) with the egg wash. Proceed as if folding a letter in thirds. Fold the top down, covering a third of the filled portion. Brush off any excess flour, and brush the exposed dough with egg wash. Fold or flip over once more and press to seal.

Dusting with flour as necessary, roll out the folded dough lengthwise to about 12 inches and then roll the width to 10 to 12 inches. If the dough resists rolling, let it rest for 5 to 10 minutes and then continue. With a pizza wheel or sharp blade, cut lengthwise into strips about 1-inch wide. Twist each strip into a rope by rolling with your palms in opposite directions from each end. Line up the twists in the same order as they were cut, and set them aside.

Take the prepared base from the freezer. Spread the remaining almond filling to cover the base. Sprinkle the remaining raisins, walnuts, cake crumbs, and half of the remaining cinnamon sugar over the filling. Drizzle with the remaining 2 tablespoons of melted butter.

If necessary, lengthen the prepared ropes by rolling and twisting from the center out until about 9 inches long. Fit lengthwise on top of the base, one at a time. Snip a piece from the next rope to fill any gaps. Continue with each rope, spacing them so that they fill the entire pan. Gently squeeze the twists together if necessary to fit in all of the pieces. Brush the top with egg wash and sprinkle with the remaining cinnamon sugar to cover.

Let rest, lightly covered, until puffy, about 20 minutes.

Position a rack in the center of the oven and preheat to 325°F/165°C.

Bake for 60 to 80 minutes, or longer if needed, until evenly browned and the top springs back when lightly pressed with your fingertips.

ɞ Baker's Secret: *This cake is best with a tight, compressed texture. If the top rises up over the rim during the first 10 to 15 minutes of baking, when first beginning to brown, invert a baking sheet over the top without removing the pan from the oven. Press down, place a weight on top (such as a brick or use a heavy ovenproof pot, three-quarters full of water), and continue baking. Be careful with the water-filled pan, because the water temperature comes close to boiling. The edges can be trimmed when cool should they become overbaked. It takes time for the center to be done. In the bakery, patrons often begged for the cut trimmings to munch on.*

Cool on a wire rack for several hours while still in the pan, or cover and cool overnight.

Free the sides with a thin bowl knife or blade. The cake can be sliced directly from the pan or flipped over onto a second pan. Shake gently to release, remove the paper lining, and then flip again onto a serving board or platter. The cake can be cut into individual strips for storing. It keeps at room temperature for a week or more when wrapped in plastic. Refrigerate in the summer. The cake freezes well for up to 8 weeks. Serve warm or at room temperature.

Yield: 1 large loaf, serving 20

Note: Raisins can be plumped for 15 minutes in hot water or covered overnight with rum; drain before use.

Variations

Butter Streusel Russian Coffee Cake
In place of the egg wash and cinnamon for the topping, brush with melted butter and cover with Butter Streusel (page 40). Bake as above.

Frangipane Babka
This is the most delicate "Russian" and fit for a connoisseur. Follow the directions for the Cinnamon-Raisin Russian Coffee Cake (page 86). To cover the base, substitute 1 cup (8 ounces / 227 grams) of crème fraîche or sour cream for the almond filling. Replace the almond filling in the twists with Frangipane (page 36). Use chopped or sliced toasted almonds instead of walnuts.

Double Russian Coffee Cake
Proceed as for Cinnamon-Raisin Russian Coffee Cake. The "Double Russian" is made with two different fillings. Draw an imaginary line crosswise through the base and cover each half differently. For example, half cinnamon/raisin and half chocolate (recipe for "Chocolate Russian" follows). Or try half with raisins and nuts and half with the raisins omitted (for my daughter, Julia, who doesn't eat raisins). The combinations are infinite.

Apple Russian Coffee Cake
Follow the instructions for Cinnamon-Raisin Russian Coffee Cake. The raisins are optional. Have ready walnuts or sliced almonds for topping and 6 cups (1½ pounds / 680 grams) of Apple Filling (page 33). Prepare the base and set aside in the freezer. Continue with the rest of the directions for rolling, filling, cutting, and twisting the main body of dough. Take the prepared base from the freezer. Spread from edge to edge with reserved almond filling. Top with the reserved raisins, cake crumbs, and cinnamon sugar. Distribute the apple filling evenly over the base. Drizzle with 2 tablespoons of melted butter. Cover with the twists as above. When the cake is fully assembled, paint the top with egg wash instead of butter; sprinkle with walnuts or sliced almonds for garnish and then bake as directed above.

Fruit Russian Coffee Cake
Follow the instructions for Cinnamon-Raisin Russian Coffee Cake and prepare the base; set aside in the freezer. Continue with the rest of the directions for rolling, filling, cutting, and twisting the main body of dough.

Prepare the fruit for the filling. A variety of fruits can be used: plums, peaches, pears, nectarines, or figs. Slice, peel, and/or core fruit as desired. Alternatively, you can use preserves or canned pie fillings.

Take the prepared base from the freezer. Spread from edge to edge with reserved almond filling. Top with the reserved raisins, cake crumbs, and cinnamon sugar. Arrange the fresh fruit or dot the canned preserves or pie fillings evenly over the base. Drizzle with 2 tablespoons of melted butter. Cover with the twists as above. When the cake is fully assembled, paint the top with egg wash instead of butter; sprinkle with toasted and chopped walnuts or sliced almonds for garnish, and then bake as directed above.

Flying Black Russian Coffee Cake

All you need to know about this cake can be summed up in the phrase "roasted pecans and dripping chocolate."

1 (32-ounce / 906-gram) portion Babka Dough (page 68)

8 ounces (227 grams) semisweet or bittersweet chocolate, chopped

2 tablespoons unsalted butter

¼ cup (2 fluid ounces/ 59 milliliters) Kahlúa or other coffee-flavored liqueur (see Note)

2 cups (1¼ pounds/ 566 grams) Processed Almond-Paste filling (page 32)

2 cups (8 ounces / 227 grams) pecans, chopped and preferably toasted

4 cups (14.4 ounces / 409 grams) cake crumbs (use chocolate cake crumbs if available) (see page 42)

Ground cinnamon, for dusting

1 egg

1 tablespoon water

1 cup (4 ounces / 113 grams) semisweet chocolate mini chips

¾ cup (5.25 ounces / 150 grams) sugar

¼ cup (0.75 ounce/ 25 grams) Dutch-process cocoa

1 cup (4 ounces / 113 grams) pecan halves, or more for topping

Grease a 9 by 9-inch cake pan with 2-inch sides. Line the bottom and sides with parchment paper or greased waxed paper.

To make the base, cut off an 8-ounce piece of the Babka dough. On a floured work surface, roll out the dough into a square about 1 inch wider than the baking pan to allow for shrinkage. Fold the dough into quarters to make lifting easy and transfer it to the prepared baking pan. Open the dough so that it covers the pan from edge to edge. If necessary, use your fingers to spread the dough from the center outward to the edges. A tear can be repaired with small bits of dough.

Set the base aside, preferably in the freezer, but it can be placed the refrigerator. Freezing the dough makes it easier to spread the filling without tearing the dough.

Melt the chocolate with the butter and Kahlúa. Set aside to cool.

Roll out the remaining dough into a rectangle. First, roll lengthwise until the dough is about 12 inches long; then roll the width to about 14 inches. It should be ¼ inch thick, and the longer side should be facing you. Spread three-quarters of the almond filling over the bottom two-thirds of the dough, covering it from edge to edge. On top of the almond filling, spread half of the chocolate-butter-liqueur mixture. (Reserve the rest for topping.) Sprinkle with half of the chopped pecans and half of the chocolate chips. Cover with half of the cake crumbs. Press down lightly with hands or rolling pin. Dust with cinnamon.

Lightly beat the egg with the water to make an egg wash. Brush the uncovered top third of the dough with the egg wash. Proceed as if folding a letter in thirds. Fold the top down, covering a third of the filled portion. Brush off excess flour and brush the exposed dough with egg wash. Fold or flip over once more and press to seal.

Dusting with flour as necessary, roll out the folded dough lengthwise to about 12 inches and then roll the width to about 10 to 12 inches. If the dough resists rolling, let it rest for 5 to 10 minutes and then continue. With a pizza wheel or sharp blade, cut lengthwise into strips about 1-inch wide. Twist each strip into a rope by rolling with your palms in opposite directions from each end. Line up the twists in the same order as they were cut and set aside.

Make cocoa sugar by mixing the sugar and cocoa. Set aside.

Take the prepared base from the freezer. Spread the remaining almond filling to cover the base generously. Sprinkle the remaining chopped pecans, cake crumbs, chocolate chips, and cocoa sugar over the filling.

If necessary, lengthen the prepared ropes by rolling and twisting from the center out until about 9 inches long. Fit lengthwise on top of the base, one at a time. Snip a piece from the next rope to fill any gaps. Continue covering with the ropes, spacing them so that they fill the entire pan. Gently squeeze the twists together if necessary to fit in all of the pieces. Brush the top with egg wash, and then cover completely with a layer of pecan halves. Press down with hands to help the pecans adhere. Let rest for about 10 minutes.

Position a rack in the center of the oven and preheat to 325°F/165°C.

Bake for 60 to 80 minutes, or longer if needed, until evenly browned and the top springs back when lightly pressed with your fingertips.

> ℬ **Baker's Secret:** *This cake is best with a tight, compressed texture. If the top rises up over the rim during the first 10 to 15 minutes of baking, when first beginning to brown, invert a baking sheet over the top without removing pan from the oven. Press down, place a weight on top (such as a brick or use a heavy oven-proof pot, three-quarters full of water), and continue baking. Be careful with the water-filled pan, because the water temperature comes close to boiling. The edges can be trimmed when cool should they become overbaked. It takes time for the center to be done.*

Cool on a wire rack for several hours while still in the pan, or cover and cool overnight.

Turn out of the pan after completely cool. Drizzle the remaining chocolate-butter-liqueur mixture, warmed up if necessary, over the top and let dry. If the chocolate doesn't dry, place in the refrigerator to harden. The cake can be cut into individual strips for storing. Wrapped in plastic, it keeps at room temperature for a week or more. Refrigerate the cake in the summer to store. The cake freezes well for up to 8 weeks. Serve warm or at room temperature.

Yield: 1 cake, serving 20

Note: If desired, substitute 2 tablespoons instant coffee, dissolved in ¼ cup (2 fluid ounces / 59 milliliters) of water, for the liqueur.

Mohn (Poppy-Seed) Strip

Some years ago, a young woman came into the bakery, pointed to several trays on the counter that contained long poppy-seed strips, and asked, "Isn't there another name for these?" I told her they were called *mohn strips*. "*Mohn*," she repeated; "that's it!" Then she burst into tears. Between sobs, she managed to blurt out, "*Mohn*. That's what my mother called it. She was Polish. She made it when I was a little girl and seeing it now reminds me of my mama."

1 (18-ounce / 500-gram) portion
Babka Dough (page 68)

1½ cups (16.5 ounces / 470 grams)
Poppy Butter (Mohn) Filling (page 38),
or more to taste, at room temperature

1 egg

1 tablespoon water

Grease a half-sheet pan or line with parchment paper or greased wax paper.

On a floured work surface, roll out the Babka dough into a ⅛-inch-thick rectangle about 18 inches long and 12 inches wide, with the long side facing you. Spread the poppy butter ¼ inch thick over the dough, leaving a ½-inch border at the top.

> **ဆ Baker's Secret:** *An alternative to softening the poppy butter by letting it come to room temperature is to roll out the chilled filling between two sheets of waxed paper until it is ¼ inch thick and the size of the rolled dough. Flip it over onto the rolled dough. You may have to transfer it in sections if it tears. Leave a ½-inch border at the top.*

Lightly beat the egg with the water to make an egg wash. Brush the top uncovered border with egg wash.

Now here comes the trick. Starting at the bottom, gently fold over a 2-inch flap. Try not to stretch the dough. Continue folding loosely for three or four folds, ending with the seam centered on the bottom. The loose folds help to keep the dough from bursting in the oven.

Place the strip onto the prepared baking sheet, leaving space for it to spread. Brush the top with egg wash, and then cut a series of slashes with a sharp blade crosswise down the length of the strip, about 1 inch apart. Set aside in a warm, draft-free area. Let rise until doubled in size. When touched very gently on the side with a fingertip, the dough should be soft and yield readily. With a skewer or pointed tool, punch a hole between each slash down the length of the strip. Brush with egg wash a second time before baking.

Position a rack in the center of the oven and preheat to 375°F/190°C.

Bake for about 35 minutes, or until well browned. The top and sides should feel firm to the touch and spring back when lightly pressed with your fingers. Do not touch any exposed filling as it can cause a burn.

Cool in the pan on a wire rack.

ᔆ Baker's Secret: *Hungarian bakers spread this strudel while it is still warm with a coat of tart raspberry jam and then a thin overlay of Simple Icing, allowing jam and icing to run together. Try it on your Simple Icing (page 41); use the jam straight from the jar.*

Serve warm or at room temperature. Store wrapped in plastic at room temperature for a few days, or up to a week in the refrigerator. It can be frozen for up to 8 weeks

Yield: 1 strip, about 2 pounds (908 grams), serving 8 to 12

Variations

Almond Babka Roll

Substitute Processed Almond-Paste Filling (page 32) for the poppy butter. Top with a handful of chopped nuts.

Hamantaschen

These three-cornered hats are more familiar when made from cookie dough and filled with poppy butter, prune, apricot, or cheese fillings. Quite different are these large 3- to 4-inch pastries made from a yeast-raised dough, the same dough as for babka. Hungarian bakers created the triangular pastries from their richest dough.

There are many differing stories about how these pastries were developed. Hamantaschen have been thought to represent either the tricornered hat worn by Haman, a tyrant in ancient Persia, or the pockets on his clothes; some say they were intended to look like his ears.

Jews celebrate the holiday of Purim each year, recounting the tale of how they were saved from destruction by Queen Esther, and sharing hamantaschen with friends and family.

The traditional use of poppy butter, made with ground poppy seed, honey, sugar, and spice, serves as a reminder that in life, as we celebrate good conquering evil, a bit of bitter always accompanies the sweet.

2 (8-ounce/ 227-gram) portions Babka Dough (page 68)

1 egg

1 tablespoon water

1½ cups (weights vary) Poppy Butter (page 38), Prune Lekvar (page 38), Apricot Lekvar, (page 21), Cream Cheese Filling (page 35), cherry preserves or pie filling, or blueberry preserves or pie filling, or a combination

Poppy seeds (if using poppy butter), granulated sugar (if using prune lekvar), sliced almonds, preferably toasted, or Cinnamon Sugar (page 40), for toppings

Grease two half-sheet pans or line with parchment paper or greased waxed paper.

Cut each piece of dough into six equal pieces to make twelve pieces in total. Roll each into a ball on a surface lightly dusted with flour. Cover and let rest for about 10 minutes. Flatten and roll out each ball into a 4-inch circle. Stretch each circle into a triangular shape. It can be irregular.

Lightly beat the egg with the water to make an egg wash. "Drop out" (see page 36) 2 tablespoons of filling of choice into the center of each triangle. (Note: To identify the pastry's filling, reserve a teaspoon of each filling to top.) Brush the edges with egg wash. With the base toward you, stretch and fold the right and left sides over the filling to form two sides of a triangle, and then bring the bottom up to the center to complete each pastry. Turn the pastries over so that the seams are on the bottom. Roll lightly with the rolling pin to flatten the wedges so that they form nicely shaped triangles.

Place the hamantaschen, evenly spaced, on the two baking sheets. It is not advisable to mix different fillings on the same baking sheet because they may not bake evenly. At this stage, the hamantaschen can be loosely covered with plastic wrap and refrigerated overnight to be baked the following morning. They can also be frozen for a week or more and then thawed slowly overnight in the refrigerator. Brush with egg wash. Set aside and let rise until doubled in volume, 25 to 40 minutes. The sides should be pillowy and yield readily when lightly pressed with a fingertip. Gently brush a second time with egg wash. A dot of topping placed in the center of each pastry will denote which filling is inside.

Position a rack in the center of the oven and preheat to 375°F/190°C.

Bake for 25 to 35 minutes, until evenly browned. If two sheets cannot fit side by side in your oven, bake one at a time. (Alternately, place the racks to divide the oven into thirds. Rotate the baking pans from top to bottom half way into baking time.)

Carefully lift a piece or two with the edge of a spatula to ensure that the bottoms are baked before removing from the oven. Cool in the pan on a wire rack. Serve warm or at room temperature. They will keep for 24 to 48 hours, tightly covered. Freeze baked hamantaschen for up to 8 weeks.

Yield: 12 hamantaschen

CHAPTER 5

Strudel

Traditional strudel is delicate and layered, similar to Middle Eastern baklava. In the bakery, I always made cheese and apple strudel.

No baker can make strudel dough as gossamer light as the village ladies who were taught by their Hungarian grannies. Years ago the best strudel makers in New York were employed in several well-known Hungarian pastry shops and all were, without exception, women. This extraordinary Hungarian pastry has long narrow strips of dough with a lacquered, mahogany sheen and a crackled finish. It's an elegant pastry, with a hint of Old World mystery, something that might have been prepared for a midnight Magyar ball.

I recall a time my father took me along to visit Mrs. Herbst's Bakery, which was the gold standard of Hungarian bakeries in New York. It was a short walk from the el, the elevated subway, on Third Avenue in Manhattan. I remember the elegant Hungarian cakes and pastries on display, rivaling the best that Europe had to offer. An elegant Louis XIV desk and chair were set aside in the sales area for handsomely coiffured ladies placing orders. A chauffeur, in purple livery with long polished boots, stood patiently, waiting to pick up madam's pastries for the evening's dinner party.

I still remember my surprise, when Dad took me into the kitchen, at seeing women bakers working at maple work benches, pulling, rolling, and filling tray upon tray of strudel dough to be set aside and baked as needed. Until that time, I had only seen men working as bakers in bakeries.

Both Mrs. Herbst's Bakery and the el are gone now. But I like to think that somewhere, perhaps with Bartok playing softly in the background, those ladies are still pulling strudel dough and happily chatting away.

Strudel Dough

Strudel is pulled with the back of the hands, stretched so thin that you can see through it. I could never get it as light as those ladies did. The dough is then rolled up around a filling (the most popular being apple), until there appears to be hundreds of paper thin layers to bite through.

These days, in both bakeries and home kitchens, most bakers purchase prepared strudel or phyllo dough, which makes strudel baking quite simple and quick. (Instructions for the use of prepared phyllo follow.) There is a difference; strudel dough is wetter and more flexible, while phyllo is brittle and dry. Each has its own unique texture and taste. A bit of fun and a great deal of satisfaction can be derived from becoming a proficient strudel maker. Perhaps it appeals to my Hungarian heritage, but nobody turns down an invitation for coffee and strudel at "Chez George."

2 cups (10 ounces / 284 grams) bread flour or unbleached all-purpose flour

⅛ teaspoon kosher salt

1 egg, lightly beaten

¾ cup water, less 1 teaspoon

1 teaspoon white vinegar

2 tablespoon vegetable oil, plus more as needed

In a large mixing bowl or the bowl of a stand mixer with a flat paddle, combine the flour and salt. Sift lightly with your fingertips. Add the egg, water, vinegar, and 1 tablespoon of the oil. Mix by hand using a sturdy wooden spoon, or by machine on a slow setting, for 8 to 10 minutes (or more as necessary) to develop a soft and elastic dough. If additional water is needed, add 1 tablespoon at a time. The dough must be well kneaded to develop the gluten in the flour and enough elasticity to be stretched. Mix until the dough comes away from the sides of the bowl, stretches easily, and has a satiny sheen. Some-

times little bubbles of air will show under the skin, which is not a problem.

Place the dough in a small oiled loaf pan or a bowl, and brush with the remaining tablespoon of oil. Cover with a cloth or plastic wrap and let rest for at least 30 minutes and up to 2 hours.

Knead the dough by hand on a kitchen counter or use the dough hook in the stand mixer until the oil is absorbed. Cover and let rest for an additional 30 minutes or up to 2 hours.

At this point, the dough can be refrigerated overnight. Brush the dough with oil and cover it tightly with plastic wrap. Let it come to room temperature before continuing.

Rub a cloth with flour and spread it over your work surface. I recommend covering a large table, at least 30 by 48 inches, with a cotton or linen tablecloth. Sprinkle extra flour in the center of the cloth and place the strudel dough on the flour. Roll out the dough lengthwise until it is 16 to 20 inches long and then roll out the width until it is 16 to 20 inches long. Sprinkle with additional flour as necessary. Continue rolling to extend the dough as much as possible,

PREPARED PHYLLO SHEETS

The quality of prepared phyllo, which is used by most home bakers, can be excellent. My Greek and Armenian friends all use prepared phyllo for their pastries. Prepared phyllo dough can be used for any of the strudel recipes in this chapter, if you don't have the time or are not up for the adventure of making your own strudel dough.

Phyllo dough is delicate and requires proper storage and handling. When shopping, look for a source such as a busy Middle Eastern or Greek food shop where a lot of phyllo is sold. If you cannot find it fresh, buy it frozen. I sometimes find it frozen in Middle Eastern stores. If frozen, thaw phyllo overnight in the refrigerator or follow the manufacturer's directions. The phyllo should be at room temperature when you use it.

Phyllo dries out very quickly when exposed to the air. To prevent crumbling and cracking, always keep phyllo sheets covered with a moist cloth as you work. Leftover phyllo can be refrigerated in a tightly closed plastic bag for several days or frozen for later use.

alternating length and width, until it becomes difficult to roll any further. Cover with a moist cloth so that it does not dry out. Let stand about 10 minutes or so, until the dough relaxes and becomes elastic once more.

The dough will now be stretched until the ends hang over the edge of the table. At this point, continue to stretch the dough by draping it over the backs of your hands and gently pulling them apart. This is important to prevent tearing once the dough has become very thin. Be patient and keep moving, pulling and gradually elongating the dough as you work your way around the table. Tears can be patched with small pieces of dough. Keep stretching until the dough becomes tissue-paper thin and translucent. The thick ends may hang over the edge of the table if the dough stretches that far. Note: This can be a bit messy and was often a time when my wife Adele would leave the room and hope the mess would disappear before she came back to the kitchen!

Your first attempts are certain to result in tears and patches. Don't become frustrated or give up. The patched dough will taste fine. With practice, you will become surprisingly proficient.

Trim away the thick edges with kitchen scissors to form a large rectangle. Allow the dough to dry. An electric fan can be used to speed drying. The dried dough will be used in the recipes that follow. This dough must be used within the next few hours.

Yield: Dough weighs 18.75 ounces or 532 grams. Baked, makes 2 strips, each serving 6 to 8

Apple Strudel

My Aunt Anna was very particular. As a child I often accompanied her on excursions to buy groceries. We walked extra blocks to her favorite purveyors. She showed me how to select the best fruit and vegetables from what was available at the least expense. She loved apples and she loved strudel. She told me stories about the home they left behind in Russia and the apple trees in the garden. I think of her whenever I see Apple Strudel.

1 cup (8 ounces / 227 grams) unsalted butter, melted and cooled (or use ½ butter, ½ vegetable oil, for easier spreading)

1 (18.75-ounce / 532-gram) recipe Strudel Dough (page 98)

2 cups (7 ounces / 198 grams) cake crumbs (see page 42) or bread crumbs, preferably fresh

½ cup sugar (3.5 ounces / 100 grams) mixed with 1½ teaspoons ground cinnamon

3 cups (1 pound / 454 grams) Apple Filling (page 33)

Confectioners' sugar, for topping (optional)

Line a half-sheet pan with parchment paper or greased waxed paper.

Brush melted butter over the dough.

Spread crumbs over the bottom third of the dough. Sprinkle the crumbs with cinnamon sugar. Mound the apple filling in a line about 3 inches wide along the bottom edge of the dough. Roll up the strudel, jelly-roll style, by slowly lifting the bottom edge of the cloth and rolling the strudel away from you. Lift and continue rolling until the end is reached and the seam is centered on the bottom. Brush the top with melted butter.

Using the baking sheet as a guide, cut the strudel into long strips the length of the baking sheet. Carefully lift the strudels onto the prepared baking sheet, keeping them equally spaced. At this point, the strudel can be refrigerated and baked the following day, or it can be frozen for up to a week, but the apples tend to weep when thawed. Thaw slowly overnight in the refrigerator when you are ready to bake.

Position a rack in the center of the oven and preheat to 375°F/190°C.

Bake for 25 to 35 minutes, or until the strudels are lightly browned and the dough feels crisp to the touch. Remove from the oven and brush with additional butter. Cool in the pan on a wire rack, then dust with confectioners' sugar, if using. These are best eaten the same day.

Yield: 2 strudels, each serving 6 to 8

Variation

Phyllo Dough Apple Strudel

Melt ½ cup (4 ounces / 113 grams) unsalted butter. Place a sheet of phyllo dough on top of a clean kitchen towel. Brush with melted butter. Layer another sheet on top, brush again with butter, and repeat four more times, using a total of six phyllo sheets. Mound the apple filling in a line about 3 inches wide along the bottom edge of the dough. Roll up the strudel, as above. Cover with a towel and repeat to make a second strudel. Bake as above.

Apple Strudel à la Mode

For a gala dessert, serve warm apple strudel with a scoop of ice cream and a few fresh berries on the side. Vanilla tastes great, but try cinnamon-flavored ice cream for something really special. To make this, allow rich vanilla ice cream to soften. Blend in ground cinnamon, about ¼ teaspoon cinnamon (or to taste) for each cup of ice cream. Return to the freezer until firm. Scoop out and serve immediately. Chocolate aficionados can prepare chocolate-cinnamon ice cream in the same manner with the addition of ¼ cup (2 ounces / 56 grams) chopped bitter-sweet chocolate.

Note: For a nondairy recipe, substitute margarine for the butter.

ဢ Baker's Secret: *A number of options are available to create crisp dough. Some bakers like to baste the top of the strudel several times over the course of baking with melted butter. Others brush the strudel top with egg wash (1 egg beaten with 1 tablespoon water) prior to baking. In place of brushing with additional butter or an egg wash, the pros often bake strudel with steam in the oven.*

To create steam in the oven, place a heavy roasting pan on the floor of the oven for 5 minutes before baking. Place the strudel in the oven and quickly pour a cupful of boiling water or toss 6 to 8 ice cubes into the hot pan. Use caution as the burst of steam can scald. Keep your hand covered with a cloth and your face away from the door. Bake for 10 minutes before opening the oven door. For an electric oven, use a spray bottle of water to mist the oven interior. Aim the spray away from the oven light because the bulb might burst from a direct spray. Mist at least twice, 5 minutes apart.

Raisin and Nut Strudel

This is a heavy, sweet, Jewish-style strudel. Some think it too sweet and cloying; the flavor clings to the palate. Those who love heavy sweets or have acquired a taste for this type of pastry think of it as manna from heaven.

1 (18.75-ounce / 532-gram) recipe Strudel Dough (page 98)

¼ cup (2 ounces / 57 grams) unsalted butter, melted

1 cup Apricot Butter (page 33) (or substitute thickened apricot jam)

1 cup (3.6 ounces /102 grams) cake crumbs (see page 42) or bread crumbs, preferably fresh

2½ cups (10 ounces / 284 grams) walnuts, preferably toasted (page 31), chopped

1½ cups (7.5 ounces / 213 grams) raisins

½ cup (2.5 ounces / 71 grams) candied orange peel, chopped (optional)

¼ cup (2 ounces / 56 grams) Cinnamon Sugar (page 40)

Line a half-sheet pan with parchment paper or greased waxed paper.

Brush the strudel dough with melted butter. Thin the apricot butter with enough water to spread easily and spread it over the bottom third of the dough. Spread carefully to avoid tearing the dough. Sprinkle the cake crumbs, walnuts, raisins, orange peel, and cinnamon sugar over the apricot butter. Roll up the strudel, jelly-roll style, until the seam is centered on the bottom.

Using the baking sheet as a guide, cut the strudel into two long rolls the length of the baking sheet. Carefully lift them onto the prepared baking sheet, keeping the strudels equally spaced apart. At this point, the strudel can be refrigerated for baking the following day. It can be frozen for up to a week. Thaw strudel slowly overnight in the refrigerator when you are ready to bake.

Position a rack in the center of the oven and preheat to 375°F/190°C.

Bake for 25 to 35 minutes, or until the strudel is lightly browned and the dough feels crisp to the touch. Remove from the oven and brush with additional butter. Cool in the pan on a wire rack. This is best eaten the same day it is baked.

Yield: 2 strudels, each serving 6 to 8

LUNGEN STRUDEL

If the Raisin and Nut Strudel seems a bit too much, read on. The old-time bakers recounted stories of their mothers' recipes for Lungen strudel (stewed lung), and I remember my own grandmother and aunts preparing lungen stew with lung and spleen. This offal was a normal part of the diet for many Europeans and poor immigrant families and still is considered a delicacy in many ethnic European and Asian cuisines. Lungen strudel, as the bakers recount, was prepared with cooked lung, goose grieben (skin cracklings), and hard-cooked eggs—a cholesterol cocktail! For your health, the recipe is not included.

Variation

Phyllo Dough Raisin and Nut Strudel
Melt ½ cup (4 ounces / 113 grams) unsalted butter. Place a sheet of phyllo dough on top of a clean kitchen towel. Brush with melted butter. Add another layer on top, brush with melted butter, and repeat four more times, using a total of six phyllo sheets. Thin the apricot butter with enough water to spread easily and spread it over the bottom third of the dough. Spread carefully to avoid tearing the phyllo. Sprinkle the cake crumbs, walnuts, raisins, orange peel, and cinnamon sugar over the apricot butter. Roll up the strudel as above. Cover with a towel and repeat to make a second strudel. Bake as above.

Cheese Strudel

The cheese strudel may be second to apple strudel in popularity, but it is the favorite in my own family.

1 (18.75-ounce / 532-gram) recipe Strudel Dough (page 98)

¼ cup (2 ounces / 57 grams) unsalted butter, melted

1 cup (1 ounce / 28 grams) crushed corn flakes or cake crumbs (see page 42)

¼ cup (2 ounces / 56 grams) Cinnamon Sugar (page 40), plus additional for topping

1½ cups (12 ounces / 340 grams) Cream Cheese Filling (page 35)

Line a half-sheet pan with parchment paper or greased waxed paper.

Brush the strudel dough with melted butter. Sprinkle the bottom third with the crumbs and the cinnamon sugar. Spread a 3-inch band of the cheese filling along the bottom edge. Roll up the strudel, jelly-roll style, leaving the seam centered on the bottom.

Using the baking sheet as a guide, cut the strudel into two long strips the length of the baking sheet. Carefully lift them onto the prepared baking sheet, equally spaced apart.

Brush the tops with melted butter. Sprinkle a thin line of cinnamon sugar down the entire length. At this point, the strudel can be refrigerated for baking the following day.

Position a rack in the center of the oven and preheat to 375°F/190°C.

Bake for 25 to 35 minutes, until lightly browned and the dough feels crisp to the touch. Remove from the oven and brush with additional butter.

Cool in the pan on a wire rack.

Covered, this strudel keeps well for 1 or 2 days at room temperature or for a week or more in the refrigerator. Reheat at 325°F/165°C for 10 minutes, or until crisp and warm to the touch, before serving.

Yield: 2 strudels, each serving 6 to 8

a jewish baker's pastry secrets

Variations

Phyllo Dough Cheese Strudel

Melt ½ cup (4 ounces / 113 grams) unsalted butter. Place a sheet of phyllo dough on top of a clean kitchen towel. Brush with melted butter. Layer another sheet on top, brush with butter, and repeat four more times, using a total of six phyllo sheets. Sprinkle the bottom third with the crumbs and the cinnamon sugar. Spread a 3-inch band of the cheese filling along the bottom edge. Roll up the strudel as above. Cover with a towel and repeat to make a second strudel. Bake as above.

Fruited Cheese Strudel

Spread a thin layer of preserves or fruit filling over the cheese prior to rolling.

Cherry Strudel

Cherries have always been a favorite fruit of mine. When sour cherries are in season, I make this strudel. Once I start, I cannot stop eating this strudel. Add a bit of pastry cream on the side, and I might not leave the table until it is all gone.

4 cups (1½ pounds / 680 grams) sour or tart cherries, stemmed and pitted, or canned sour pitted cherries, drained

¾ cup (5.25 ounces / 150 grams) sugar

1 teaspoon finely grated lemon zest

½ teaspoon pure vanilla extract

1 tablespoon dark rum (optional)

¼ cup (2 ounces / 57 grams) unsalted butter, melted

1 (18.75-ounce / 532-gram) recipe Strudel Dough (page 98)

2 cups (7 ounces / 198 grams) cake crumbs (see page 42) or bread crumbs, preferably fresh

Line a half-sheet pan with parchment paper or greased waxed paper.

In a mixing bowl, combine the cherries, sugar, lemon zest, vanilla extract, and rum.

Brush or drizzle melted butter over the dough. Spread the crumbs over the bottom third of the dough. Spread a 2- to 3-inch band of cherry mixture along the bottom edge. Roll up the strudel, jelly-roll style, by slowly lifting the bottom edge of the cloth and rolling the strudel away from you. Lift and continue rolling until the end is reached, and the seam is centered on the bottom.

Using the baking sheet as a guide, cut the strudel into two strips the length of the baking sheet. Carefully lift them onto the prepared baking sheet, keeping the rolls equally spaced apart.

Brush the tops with melted butter. At this point, the strudel can be refrigerated and baked the following day.

Position a rack in the center of the oven and preheat to 375°F/190°C.

Bake for 25 to 35 minutes, until the strudels are lightly browned and the dough feels crisp to the touch. Remove from the oven and brush with additional butter. Cool in the pan on a wire rack.

This strudel is best eaten the same day. Covered, it keeps well for 1 or 2 days at room temperature.

Yield: 2 strudels, each serving 6 to 8

Variation

Phyllo Dough Cherry Strudel

Make the cherry filling as above. Melt ½ cup
(4 ounces / 113 grams) unsalted butter. Place a
sheet of phyllo dough on top of a clean kitchen
towel. Brush with melted butter. Layer another
sheet on top, brush with melted butter, and
repeat four more times, using a total of six
phyllo sheets. Sprinkle the bottom third with
the crumbs. Spread a 2- to 3-inch band of cherry
mixture along the bottom edge. Roll up the
strudel as above. Cover with a towel and repeat
to make a second strudel. Bake as above.

Cabbage Strudel

My father, Louie, came to New York from Hungary in 1924. My mother, Sylvia, came from Russia with her parents, grandparents, and three sisters in 1922. Dad was often asked to make his cabbage strudel for the family get togethers. Everyone agreed this Hungarian addition was a keeper, both Louie and the strudel! My father always reminded us that his grandmother's was better. I am sorry I never got to taste her recipe, but this one is great.

1 medium head green cabbage

1 tablespoon kosher salt

¼ cup (2 ounces / 60 grams) unsalted butter or margarine

¼ cup (2 ounces / 59 milliliters) vegetable oil

1 tablespoon sugar

2 tablespoons crushed caraway seeds (see Baker's Secret)

1 (18.75-ounce / 532-gram) recipe Strudel Dough (page 98)

½ cup (1.5 ounces / 45 grams) bread crumbs, preferably fresh

1 egg

1 tablespoon water

Line a half-sheet pan with parchment paper or greased waxed paper.

Remove the outer leaves of the cabbage and discard. Core and shred the cabbage. Place it in a colander and toss with the salt. Invert a plate over the cabbage and place a weight on top. Let it drain for at least 1 hour. Squeeze out the excess water.

Melt the butter and stir in the oil. Set aside half. Pour the remaining butter-oil mixture into a 10-inch or larger sauté pan over medium-high heat. Add the sugar and stir until it dissolves. Add the cabbage, toss, and sauté over medium to medium-low heat until lightly browned (like browning onions). Add the caraway. Remove from the heat and cool. You should have about 3 cups (19 ounces / 540 grams) of cabbage. At this point the cabbage mixture can be kept covered in the refrigerator for 1 to 2 days.

Brush or drizzle some of the melted butter-oil mixture, reserving some for later, over the strudel dough. Sprinkle the crumbs over the bottom third of the dough. Spread the cabbage in a 3½- to 4-inch band along the bottom edge. Roll up the strudel, jelly-roll style, slowly lifting the bottom edge of the cloth and rolling the strudel away from you. Lift and continue rolling until the end is reached and the seam is centered on the bottom. Brush the top with the remaining melted butter-oil mixture.

a jewish baker's pastry secrets

Using the baking sheet as a guide, cut the strudel into long strips about the length of the baking sheet. Carefully lift them onto the prepared baking sheet, keeping the strudels equally spaced apart. Lightly beat the egg with the water to make an egg wash. Brush the strudel with the egg wash.

At this point, the strudel can be refrigerated for baking the following day. It can be frozen for up to a week. Thaw slowly overnight in the refrigerator when you are ready to bake.

Position a rack in the center of the oven and preheat to 375°F/190°C.

Bake for 25 to 35 minutes, or until the strudel is lightly browned and the dough feels crisp to the touch. Remove from the oven and brush with additional butter or butter-oil mixture. Cool in the pan on a wire rack.

This is best eaten the day it is baked, but it can be refrigerated for up to a week. Reheat at 325°F/165°C for 10 minutes, or until crisp and warm to the touch before serving.

Yield: 2 strudels, each serving 6 to 8

ʂɔ Baker's Secret: *Crush caraway seeds with the edge of a heavy rolling pin or grind in a food processor, blender, or coffee grinder.*

Variation

Phyllo Dough Cabbage Strudel

Prepare the butter-oil mixture and cabbage filling as above. Place a sheet of phyllo dough on top of a clean kitchen towel. Brush with the butter-oil mixture. Layer another sheet on top, brush with the butter-oil mixture, and repeat four more times, using a total of six phyllo sheets. Sprinkle the crumbs over the bottom third of the dough. Spread the cabbage in a 3½- to 4-inch band along the bottom edge. Roll up the strudel as above. Cover with a towel and repeat to make a second strudel. Bake as above.

Gugelhopf and Portuguese Sweet Bread

Pronounced KOO-Gloaf, Gugelhopf is a delicate coffee cake that is simple and elegant. Austrian in origin, the name translates as "high cake." It is perfect with a cup of espresso, but you might also try it with a Viennese roast served with whipped cream (or, in German, *mit Schlag*).

Portuguese sweet bread, *massa sovada*, is a traditional recipe from the Azores that is a standard in Portuguese bakeries. This bread is most popular at Easter, but I enjoy it year-round. I like to have mine for breakfast with a little butter on it.

Gugelhopf is baked in large decorative tube pans (similar to Bundt pans, which can be used). The smaller forms run 6 to 9 inches in diameter, with a tapered cone rising in the center. Gugelhopf forms generally have decorative fluted sides all around. The bottoms are rounded, beginning at the broad base of the tube, and curve gracefully upward, giving the finished confection a turban-like appearance when the cake is baked. The larger pans, 10 to 12 inches or more in diameter and 5 to 6 inches high, make a striking dessert.

—Master Recipe—
Gugelhopf Dough

Gugelhopf is a soft yeasty cake with raisins, nuts, and dried fruit originally made in Austria, Germany, Switzerland, and Alsace. Legend is that "hupf" is a variation of yeast and might come from the word "hupfen," which means jump, which is what this cake does—jump out of the pan.

Sponge

4 scant tablespoons (4 packets / 28 grams) active dry yeast

¼ cup (2 fluid ounces / 59 milliliters) warm milk 95°F to 115°F / 35°C to 46°C

½ cup (4 fluid ounces / 118 milliliters) milk, room temperature

1¾ cups (8 ounces / 227 grams) bread flour

Dough

½ cup (4 ounces / 113 grams) sugar

½ cup (4 ounces / 113 grams) unsalted butter, at room temperature

¼ cup (2 ounces / 59 grams) sour cream (or substitute yogurt)

2 eggs

1 egg yolk

2⅔ cups (13 ounces / 368 grams) bread flour, plus more as needed

2 teaspoons kosher salt

1½ teaspoons pure vanilla extract

Finely grated zest and juice of ½ lemon

⅛ teaspoon ground nutmeg, preferably freshly ground

a jewish baker's pastry secrets

Flour a half-sheet pan.

To make the sponge, in the mixing bowl of a stand mixer fitted with a flat paddle, sprinkle the yeast over the warm milk to soften. Add the rest of the milk and the flour. Mix at low speed until blended. Continue to mix for 8 to 10 minutes. The dough should come away from the sides of the bowl. If not, continue for a few minutes at medium speed. Remove the paddle and cover the bowl with a cloth. Let stand until doubled in volume, 20 to 30 minutes.

To make the dough, use a dough hook, if available, or the flat paddle. Beat the sponge down with a few turns of the dough hook. Add the sugar, butter, sour cream, eggs, egg yolk, flour, salt, vanilla, lemon zest and juice, and nutmeg. Pulse with the on/off switch until the flour is absorbed so it does not fly out of the bowl.

Mix for 8 to 10 minutes at slow speed. Increase to medium speed and mix for several minutes to allow the dough to develop gluten and come away from the sides of the bowl. If necessary, add additional flour, 1 tablespoon at a time. The dough should remain soft and a little sticky.

On a floured work surface, turn the dough out. Punch down, pressing out all of the air, and then tighten the dough by folding the top over bottom, then fold the sides over each other in thirds, as if folding a letter.

Cut the dough into three equal pieces. Roll up each piece, jelly-roll style, and then press down into a rectangular shape. Place on the prepared baking sheet, cover, and refrigerate for an hour or more to chill. At this point, the dough can be used in one of the recipes below or refrigerated overnight for use within 24 hours. The dough can be frozen for up to a week or longer if well wrapped.

Yield: 2.75 pounds or 1.25 kilograms of dough, enough for 3 small or 2 large cakes

Gugelhopf with Walnut Filling

Lena was the lead front of the house staff at the bakery. No matter the weather, Lena was at the bakery 5 days a week at 6 a.m. to prepare the store for customers. She knew the regular customers' orders and how to fit our many products in the store front. I could not have run the bakery without her.

Lena grew up in Germany. When we made this cake, she would box one up for herself before she put any of the others in the store. She told me it reminded her of home.

1¼ cups (7.2 ounces / 204 grams) Walnut Sugar (page 40)

¼ cup (3.5 ounces / 100 grams) granulated sugar

1 teaspoon ground cinnamon

1 (21-ounce / 612-gram) portion Gugelhopf Dough (page 112)

¼ cup (2 ounces / 57 grams) unsalted butter, melted

1 cup (4 ounces / 227 grams) toasted, chopped walnuts

Confectioners' sugar, for dusting (optional)

Grease a 9-inch gugelhopf or Bundt pan.

In a mixing bowl, combine the walnut sugar, granulated sugar, and cinnamon. Set aside.

On a floured work surface, roll out the dough into a rectangle about ¼ inch thick and measuring 12 inches long and about 8 inches wide. Brush off any excess flour. Brush with melted butter, leaving a ½-inch border along the top of the short side. Sprinkle the sugar mixture over the dough, leaving the top border clear. Spread the walnuts over the sugar.

Beginning at the bottom, roll up, jelly-roll fashion. Pinch the seam shut with your fingers. Twist into a rope by rolling the ends with your palms in opposite directions (upward with the right hand, downward with the left). Avoid stretching the rope while twisting. Bring the ends together to form a circle. Slip about an inch of one end inside of the other to form a ring. Carefully lift into the prepared pan.

Set aside, cover, and allow the dough to rise until doubled in volume, about 1 hour (will vary with temperature and humidity). When touched very gently on the side with a fingertip, the dough should be soft and yield readily.

Position a rack in the lower third of the oven and preheat to 375°F/190°C.

Place the pan in the oven and reduce the oven temperature to 350°F/175°C. Bake for 25 to 35 minutes, until lightly and evenly browned. This is a tall cake; if the top begins to brown too quickly, cover with a tent made from aluminum foil or a brown paper bag. When baked, the top and edge should feel firm to the touch and spring back when lightly pressed with the fingers.

Invert the pan onto a baking sheet. Carefully remove the pan and check the sides and bottom of the cake for even baking. If baking is uneven, return cake to pan right-side up and cover with foil and return to the oven for 5 to 10 minutes longer.

Return cake to pan and cool, uncovered, in the pan on a wire rack.

Slide the Gugelhopf onto a flat dish or cardboard cake circle. Dust lightly with confectioners' sugar before serving. Well wrapped, the cake keeps well at room temperature for several days. It can be refrigerated for up to a week or frozen for up to 8 weeks. Thaw overnight in the refrigerator. Serve warm or at room temperature.

Yield: One 9-inch cake, serving 10 to 12

Variations

Nut-Filled Gugelhopf
Replace the walnuts with any other nut. Try hazelnuts, pistachios, or almonds. Replace Walnut Sugar with another nut sugar if desired. Roll up and proceed as for Walnut Gugelhopf.

Raisin-Nut Gugelhop
Sprinkle ¾ cup (3.75 ounces / 105 grams) raisins over the nut mixture before rolling. Roll up and proceed as for Walnut Gugelhopf.

Sour Cream Gugelhopf
Mix ½ cup (3.5 ounces / 100 grams) granulated sugar with 2 teaspoons ground cinnamon. Roll out the dough as above. Spread with ½ cup (4.25 ounces / 121 grams) sour cream in place of the melted butter, leaving a ½-inch border along the top edge. Sprinkle with ¾ cup (3.75 ounces / 105 grams) raisins to cover, if desired. Cover with the cinnamon sugar. Roll up and proceed as for Walnut Gugelhopf.

Double Chocolate Gugelhopf
Melt 4 ounces (113 grams) semisweet chocolate with 1 tablespoon unsalted butter. Spread the rolled out gugelhopf dough with the melted chocolate, leaving a ½-inch border along the top. Sprinkle 1 tablespoon orange-based liqueur (try Grand Marnier or Triple Sec, 1 cup (4 ounces / 227 grams) walnuts or pecans, toasted (see page 31) and chopped, and 2 ounces (57 grams) semisweet or bittersweet chocolate bits or bar chocolate, chopped or coarsely ground or grated over the dough. Roll up, twist, and proceed as for Walnut Gugelhopf.

> ✎ **Baker's Secret:** *In place of liqueur, you can substitute 1 teaspoon orange extract.*

Susi's Hungarian Coffee Cake

Susi Effross, who held a faculty position at Rutgers University, is an unabashed foodie. As a hobby, Susi teaches baking for sheer joy and for the pleasure she brings to her family, friends, and students. The following is an excerpt from a letter that Susi wrote about Gugelhopf, which she calls Austro-Hungarian Coffee Cake, a cake for which she gives credit to her grandmother and mother. Surprisingly her recipe is so similar to the one I used in the bakery that it makes me suspect that her grandma must have had a close alliance with a Hungarian baker. All of the other similarities aside, as soon as I see sour cream included in a yeast-cake recipe, I think, *Hungarian*. Susi writes about using professional quality high-gluten flour:

> "The taste and texture of this coffee cake was the ultimate test of a baker's expertise in my grandmother's and mother's time. In the leisurely days before television, Viennese families would gather for afternoon coffee and cake. Each weekend the cake was judged: as good as last week's, not so good, better, or best ever! The ladies used to worry about the rise that the yeast would give, the quality of the flour, and the subtle-tasting blend of the filling. The first time that I baked this cake with this new [high-gluten] flour (last fall), my family pronounced it "Best ever, bar none!" and I had been making it for some 35 years quite successfully."

Susi's method of preparation is both interesting and unorthodox. The following is adapted from her recipe.

½ cup (3.5 ounces/100 grams) sugar

2 teaspoons cinnamon

4 ounces (113 grams) semi sweet chocolate

1 tablespoon unsalted butter

½ portion (1 pound 5.6 ounces / 612 grams) Gugelhopf dough (page 112)

½ cup apricot jam, thickened

1 tablespoon orange–based liqueur (optional)

1 cup (4 ounces / 227 grams) walnuts chopped, preferably toasted

¾ cup (3.75 ounces / 105 grams) raisins

½ cup (4.25 ounces / 121 grams) sour cream

Confectioners' sugar

Grease a 9-inch guglehopf or Bundt pan.

In a small bowl combine sugar and cinnamon. Set aside. Melt chocolate with butter. Set aside as well.

On a floured work surface, roll out the dough into a rectangle about ¼ inch thick and measuring 12 inches long and about 8 inches wide. Brush off any excess flour. Spread the rolled out gugelhopf dough with a thin layer of apricot jam from edge to edge. Then spread the melted chocolate, leaving a ½ inch border. Sprinkle the liqueur (try Grand Marnier or Triple Sec), walnuts, raisins, and cinnamon sugar over the dough. Press down lightly with hands or rolling pin. Spread sour cream over filling.

Roll up jelly-roll style. Cut into twelve pieces. Place four pieces, cut side up, equally spaced around the bottom of the pan. Fill with two additional layers, four pieces to each layer, staggering the layers. Set aside, cover, and allow the dough to rise until doubled in volume, about 1 hour (will vary with temperature and humidity). When touched very gently on the side with a fingertip, the dough should be soft and yield readily.

Position a rack in the center of the oven and preheat to 350°F/175°C.

Bake for about 40 minutes until the dough is lightly and evenly browned. The baked dough should feel firm to the touch and spring back when lightly pressed with the fingers.

Cool in the pan on a wire rack for 10 to 15 minutes. Using oven pads or gloves to protect fingers, invert onto the wire rack and gently remove the pan. This is best when served warm or at room temperature. Dust lightly with confectioners' sugar before serving. Well wrapped, the cake keeps well at room temperature for several days. It can be refrigerated for up to a week or frozen for up to 8 weeks. Thaw overnight in the refrigerator.

Yield: 1 cake, serving 8

Portuguese Sweet Bread

Portuguese immigrants arrived in New Bedford, Massachusetts, to work in the whaling industry in the early 1800s. The whaling ships are gone, but Portuguese flavors can still be found.

Every summer Adele and I go to Martha's Vineyard. Our favorite road stop is a bakery in New Bedford where we buy a few loaves of Portuguese sweet bread. One of the loaves is usually gone by the time we get off the ferry. It is a fabulous treat dunked in coffee.

Sponge

2 scant tablespoons (2 packets / 14 grams) active dry yeast

¼ cup (2 fluid ounces / 59 milliliters) warm water 95° to 115°F / 35° to 46°C

1 cup (8 fluid ounces / 237 milliliters) milk, room temperature

2 cups (10 ounces / 242 grams) unbleached all-purpose flour

Dough

½ cup plus 2 tablespoons (4.4 ounces / 125 grams) sugar

¼ cup (2 ounces / 57 grams) unsalted butter, softened

2 eggs

1 egg, separated

2½ cups (14 ounces / 397 grams) unbleached all-purpose flour, plus more as needed

2 teaspoons kosher salt, preferably sea salt

¼ teaspoon ground mace

1 teaspoon vegetable oil

1 tablespoon water

Grease two 7-inch or one 9-inch round layer cake pans with 2-inch sides.

To make the sponge, in the mixing bowl of a stand mixer fitted with a flat paddle, sprinkle the yeast over the warm water to soften. Add the milk and flour. Mix at low speed until blended. Continue to mix at a slow speed for 8 to 10 minutes, until the dough comes away from the sides of the bowl. If necessary, continue for a few minutes at medium speed. Remove the bowl from the mixer and cover the dough with a cloth. Let stand until doubled in volume, 30 to 45 minutes.

To make the dough, use a dough hook, if available, or the paddle. Beat the sponge down with a few turns of the hook. Add the sugar, butter, eggs, egg yolk, 2 cups of the flour, salt, and mace. Mix by pulsing with the on/off switch until the flour is absorbed so that it does not fly out of the bowl.

Mix for 10 to 12 minutes at slow speed. Increase to medium speed for several minutes to allow the dough to develop enough gluten and come away from the sides of the bowl. If necessary, add additional flour, 1 tablespoon at a time. The dough should remain soft and sticky.

With the machine running, dribble the vegetable oil down the sides of the bowl. Use care, keeping your fingers clear of the bowl. Remove the hook and turn the dough around and from top to bottom to coat with oil. Cover the bowl with a cloth or plastic wrap. Let stand until doubled in volume, about 45 minutes.

Brush a small amount of oil on a cookie sheet. Turn the dough out onto the oiled surface. Punch down and flatten out the dough. Cut in half (or leave whole for one large bread). Knead into a tight ball. Place in the prepared pan(s). At this point, the dough can be prepared for baking or refrigerated for several hours or overnight on the coldest shelf in the refrigerator. Or the dough can be frozen for up to a week or longer if well wrapped.

Lightly beat the reserved egg white with 1 tablespoon of water to make an egg wash. When you are ready to bake, brush the top with egg wash, taking care to avoid letting the egg drip down the sides of the dough. Set aside and let rise until doubled in volume, about 45 minutes. (Refrigerated dough may have risen fully and can be taken from refrigerator to oven.) When pressed very gently on the side with a fingertip, the dough should be soft and yield easily.

Using a delicate touch, carefully brush a second time with the egg wash for a high sheen. Let dry for a few minutes.

Position a rack in the center of the oven and preheat to 375°F/190°C. Bake for 10 minutes. If the top has begun to brown, cover with a tent cut from aluminum foil or a brown paper bag. Reduce the oven temperature to 350°F/175°C and bake for 25 to 35 minutes, until browned. The top should feel firm to the touch and spring back when lightly pressed with your fingers.

Remove the bread from the oven. Tip over, using a towel to prevent your fingers from getting burned, and check the color of the bottom. If necessary, set the baking pan aside and return the bread to the oven set directly on the oven rack for 5 minutes to allow the bottom to brown. Cool on a wire rack. Serve warm or at room temperature. This keeps well at room temperature in a plastic bag for several days. It can be frozen for 6 to 8 weeks. Thaw overnight in the refrigerator.

Yield: Two 7-inch breads or one 9-inch bread, serving 10 to 12

CHAPTER 7

Stollen and Polish Kolacz

Every December in the bakery, I made rack loads of stollen and kolacz. Both these pastries were popular seasonal treats. They both are variations of a large filled turnover, perfect with tea or a nip of brandy.

Stollen (pronounced SHTULL-en) is a German yeast-raised fruitcake usually baked at Thanksgiving and Yule time. After baking, these loaves are soaked with butter to enrich them in a dazzling fashion. All the same, these holiday treats avoid the cloying sweetness of most traditional American holiday fruit cakes.

Polish *kolacz* (pronounced KO-watz) is an eggy and light peasant bread. It is a traditional Polish pastry originally made as a wedding cake. It has become a favorite in American homes as a holiday treat. It is a lot like challah, but closer to babka, only less rich. It is similar to the Czech *kolach*. Pile it with ice cream and fruit for dessert or spread it with butter and jam for breakfast.

In Europe, bakers begin preparing these loaves in September to assure an adequate supply for the holidays. Because they are so rich, they keep well for long periods of time. Each region in Germany prepares stollen in a distinct fashion, generally using specific fillings and flavors that define the area where the cakes are baked. The best known of the stollen in the United States is Dresden stollen. Many of these stollen are imported from Germany for sale in confectionery and gourmet shops.

Stollen with Triple Butter

This sweet yeast dough is packed with fruit. It is heavenly—and great with a cup of coffee. Splashes of rum are optional in the recipe and also optional in your coffee.

Sponge

1 cup (8 fluid ounces / 237 milliliters) warm water, 95° to 115°F / 35° to 46°C

4 scant tablespoons (4 packets / 28 grams) active dry yeast

3 cups (1 pound / 454 grams) unbleached all-purpose flour

¾ cup (5.25 ounces / 149 grams) sugar

2 tablespoons nonfat dry milk powder

Dough

10 egg yolks

1 tablespoon malt syrup (optional)

2 cups (11 ounces / 311 grams) unbleached all-purpose flour

1 cup (5.25 ounces / 149 grams) cake flour

2 teaspoons kosher salt, preferably sea salt

Finely grated zest and juice of ½ lemon

1 tablespoon pure vanilla extract

½ teaspoon ground mace

¼ cup (2 fluid ounces / 59 milliliters) dark rum

¼ cup (2 fluid ounces / 59 milliliters) brandy (see Baker's Secret)

2 cups (1 pound / 454 grams) unsalted butter, melted

1⅓ cups (8 ounces / 227 grams) citron, cut into ¼-inch dice

3 cups (1 pound / 454 grams) golden raisins

3 cups (12 ounces / 340 grams) walnuts, chopped, preferably toasted

½ cup (6.5 ounces / 180 grams) finely diced candied ginger (optional)

2½ cups (1 pound / 454 grams) glacé cherries

1 cup (7.2 ounces / 200 grams) Cinnamon Sugar (page 40)

Confectioners' sugar, for dusting (optional)

Grease two half-sheet pans.

To make the sponge, in the mixing bowl of a stand mixer fitted with flat paddle, sprinkle the yeast over warm water to soften. Add the flour, sugar, and milk powder. Mix at slow speed for 8 to 10 minutes. Increase to medium speed for the last few minutes if the dough does not come away from the sides of the bowl. Remove the paddle, cover the bowl, and let rise until the dough doubles in volume, 20 to 30 minutes.

Beat the sponge down with a few turns of the hook. To make the dough, add the egg yolks, malt syrup, all-purpose flour, cake flour, and salt to the sponge. Stir lightly with your fingertips to combine. Add the lemon zest and juice, vanilla, mace, rum, and brandy. Using the dough hook, pulse at slow speed with the on/off switch until the flour is absorbed and does not fly out of the bowl. With the machine running, slowly blend in 1¼ cups of the melted butter.

Mix at slow speed for 8 to 10 minutes to develop enough gluten in the dough. Add the citron, raisins, walnuts, and ginger, if using. Mix only long enough to distribute; you may have to mix in the fruits and nuts by hand with the hook removed. Cover the dough and allow to rise until doubled in volume, 30 to 45 minutes.

On a floured work surface, turn out the dough. Knead for a few minutes to punch out all of the air. Cut into six equal pieces, about 20 ounces each. Flatten each piece, fold the ends in toward the center, and roll from the bottom up, jelly-roll style, to flatten slightly into a rectangle. Cover and let rest for about 10 minutes.

While dough is resting, rinse the glacé cherries in cold water, drain, and set aside.

Roll out each piece of dough into a 1-inch-thick rectangle about 8 inches long and 5 inches wide, with the long edge facing you. With a rolling pin or a thick dowel, press down, lengthwise across the center of each, using a slight back and forth motion, until you've created a valley, leaving the top and bottom edges untouched and forming a thick lip on top and bottom.

Brush off any excess flour. Brush melted butter along the valleys, leaving the ridges dry with a trickle of butter glistening down the centers. Sprinkle with a little cinnamon sugar down the centers. Place the glacé cherries in a line over the cinnamon sugar. When baked and sliced each serving will have a cherry snuggled in the center.

Carefully fold the top over the bottom of each stollen so the upper edge rests about ¼-inch shy of the bottom edge. With your palms outstretched, press the back edge of the dough down with the heel of your hands, leaving the lips of the dough thick and untouched. Place three stollen, spaced evenly apart, on each baking sheet. Brush with melted butter.

At this point, if the oven cannot accommodate both pans on one shelf, place one pan in the refrigerator, covered with plastic wrap. Set the other stollen aside and let rise until doubled in volume, about 45 minutes. When pressed very gently on the side with a fingertip, the dough should be soft and yield readily.

Position a rack in the center of the oven and preheat to 375°F/190°C.

Bake for 35 to 45 minutes, or until well browned. The top should feel firm to the touch and spring back when lightly pressed with the fingers.

Immediately after removing from the oven, stipple a series of holes throughout the top with a skewer or fork. Brush with melted butter. Place the pan on a wire rack and allow the butter to be absorbed. Brush with butter a second time.

When the butter is absorbed and while the stollens are still warm, sprinkle the tops with a dusting of cinnamon sugar. Cool in the pan on wire rack. Sprinkle any wet spots with additional cinnamon sugar. Alternatively, when cooled, omit the cinnamon sugar and dust with confectioners' sugar.

When completely cooled, wrap in plastic wrap. If you can wait, it tastes best the next day. The stollens keep for a week or more at room temperature. Freeze at Thanksgiving until Christmas or New Year's Eve and thaw in the refrigerator. Unbaked stollen may be wrapped tightly in plastic and frozen for up to 8 weeks. Defrost in the refrigerator and let rise as described above.

Yield: Six 20-ounce loaves, each serving 6 to 8

Variations

Dresden Stollen
Make the dough using ½ cup (5 ounces / 142 grams) citron, finely diced, 1½ cups (8 ounces / 227 grams) golden raisins, 1½ cups (9 ounces / 255 grams) dark raisins, ½ cup (3 ounces / 85 grams) currants, 2 cups (8 ounces / 227 grams) almonds (chopped, preferably toasted) and 3 tablespoons glazed or candied orange peel, chopped. Omit the walnuts and cherries. Bake as above and dust with confectioners' sugar after baking.

Almond Stollen
Make the dough and roll out as above. Omit citron, golden raisins, walnuts, and cherries. Substitute with the 5 cups (1 pound / 454 grams) almonds (chopped, preferably toasted) and 1 ounce (28 grams) bitter almonds, chopped (optional) and desirable if available (bitter almonds are hard to find). Dust with confectioners' sugar after baking.

Polish Kolacz
(Country Polish Bread)

Babe Kruk is, in her own words, a wife, mother, baker, cook, maid, chauffeur, and so on. "A few traditions we should keep, and more than a few if we can!" she says.

Ms. Kruk is of Slovenian descent, and her husband, T.J., is Polish. T.J. says the correct Polish spelling for this bread is *kolac*. Ms. Kruk likes to form four loaves from one recipe. T.J.'s mother and aunt both made the same recipe into one large round bread. This is an adaptation of the Kruk's kolacz.

Sponge

2 scant tablespoons (2 packets / 14 grams) active dry yeast

½ cup (4 fluid ounces / 118 milliliters) warm water, 95° to 115°F / 35° to 46°C

1½ cups (12 fluid ounces / 355 milliliters) evaporated milk

3⅓ cups (1 pound / 454 grams) bread flour

Dough

¾ cup (5.25 ounces / 150 grams) sugar

1 cup (8 ounces / 227 grams) unsalted butter, melted and cooled

4 eggs, beaten

3⅓ cups (1 pound / 454 grams) bread flour, plus more as needed

1 tablespoon kosher salt

½ cup (2.5 ounces / 70 grams) golden raisins, or more to taste

Filling

½ cup (4 ounces / 113 grams) cream cheese

1 tablespoon sugar

1 egg, beaten

½ teaspoon pure vanilla extract

Egg Wash

1 egg

1 tablespoon water

Grease four 8-inch loaf pans.

To make the sponge, in the mixing bowl of a stand mixer fitted with a flat paddle, sprinkle the yeast over the warm water to soften. Add the evaporated milk and 3 cups of the flour. Mix at slow speed for 8 to 10 minutes. The dough should come away from the sides of the bowl. If necessary, allow additional mixing time or mix at medium speed for a few minutes.

Cover and let rise until doubled in volume, 25 to 40 minutes.

To make the dough, stir or mix the sponge with a dough hook to punch it down. Add the sugar, butter, eggs, flour, and salt. Pulse the dough with the on/off switch until the flour is absorbed so that it does not fly out of the bowl. Mix at slow speed for 8 to 10 minutes. The dough should come away from the sides of the bowl. If necessary, mix at medium speed for a few minutes. Additional flour can be added at slow speed, 1 tablespoon at a time, as necessary. Keep the dough fairly soft.

Add the raisins and stir only for a few turns to avoid crushing them or knead in by hand. Cover with a cloth or plastic wrap and let rise until puffy, about 20 minutes.

While the dough is rising, prepare the filling and egg wash. Mix or mash the cream cheese to soften; then add the sugar and mix until smooth. Blend in the egg and vanilla. Set aside. To prepare the egg wash, lightly beat the egg with the water. Set aside.

Flour the work surface. When the dough is fully risen, turn out onto work surface. Punch down. Divide into four equal pieces for loaves.

Roll up individual pieces jelly-roll style into a rectangular shape, flatten slightly. Cover and let rest for about 10 minutes. Flatten slightly and then roll again, jelly-roll style earlier. Place in the prepared pans, seam down. With your fingertips, make a deep depression down the center of each loaf along its entire length. Brush the loaves with the egg wash and then, using a pastry bag or a tablespoon, make a line of the cream cheese filling over the depression.

Let rise until doubled in volume and rising above the rim of the pans, about 45 minutes. When touched very gently on the side with a fingertip, the dough should be soft and yield readily. Delicately brush once more with the egg wash and let dry.

Position a rack in the center of the oven and preheat to 350°F/175°C.

Bake for 20 minutes. Reduce the oven temperature to 325°F/165°C and bake for 15 to 20 minutes more, until the top is evenly baked and the center springs back when lightly touched with the fingertips. Carefully remove from the pans to test sides and bottom. The sides should feel firm. The bread may be returned to the oven without the pans, placed directly on the oven rack for 5 minutes longer, if needed.

Cool on a wire rack. Tightly covered, the bread keeps well at room temperature for several days; keep for a week or more in the refrigerator. The bread is good toasted. It can be frozen for up to 8 weeks.

Yield: 4 loaves, each serving 6 to 8, or 1 large round, serving 25

Large Round Polish Kolacz

Grease one 10-inch round springform pan and line a half sheet pan with parchment paper, lightly greased. Prepare the dough and fillings and let dough rise as above.

Flour the work surface. When the dough is fully risen, turn out onto work surface. Punch down. Using all of the dough, roll the large piece up, jelly-roll style, into a rectangular shape and flatten slightly. Cover and let rest for about 10 minutes. Flatten slightly and then roll again, jelly-roll style, into a round loaf. Place into the prepared pan, seam down.

With your fingertips, make a depression in the shape of a ring two inches in from the edge of the loaf. Brush the loaf with the egg wash and then, using a pastry bag or a tablespoon, make a line of the cream cheese filling over the depression. Let rise again and preheat oven as above.

Bake for about 30 minutes at 350°F/175°C and then 15 to 20 minutes at 325°F/160°C, until the top is evenly baked and the center springs back when lightly touched with the fingertips.

Finish, cool, and store as above.

CHAPTER 8

Puff Pastry

In French, puff pastry is called *millefeuille*, the pastry of a thousand leaves. This delicate flaky pastry, which contains no added sugar and no leavening, is a miracle of the baker's art. A simple, tender dough is rolled out, studded with sweet dairy butter, rolled, folded, and rolled again, until hundreds of layers are created by the fat having been worked into the pastry layers. Puff pastry, when rolled out into a thin sheet no more than ⅛ inch in thickness, can spring up tenfold in height when placed in the oven.

Puff pastry is used for both savory and sweet baked goods. Two of the most popular items in the bakery made of puff pastry were Napoleons and apple turnovers. Savory tarts can be filled with meats, vegetables, or many other interesting fillings. Puff pastry is used universally, from Asia, through the Americas, and across the Atlantic to the countries of the European continent.

Before World War II, bakery ovens were huge affairs, manufactured from steel and tile and lined with brick. Fueled with wood or coal, temperatures were difficult to control. Fires had to be banked during the hours that the bakery remained idle. At the beginning of each work day, the oven heat was highest. One couldn't raise or lower the heat at will.

The order of the day necessitated first preparing and baking items requiring the highest heat. The full oven, when loaded with goods, drew off more heat than the oven could quickly replace. Subsequently, the temperature began to drop. If higher heat was needed for the next baking, the oven had to rest while empty until the temperature slowly rose. If temperatures were too high, the baker lowered it quickly by filling the oven with baked goods. Bakers refer to this as "baking down" the oven. If all went well, the oven was allowed to bake down throughout the day, and each successive baking required a lower heat.

Puff pastries required the lowest temperature of the day, and the ovens had to be fully baked down for them. When the oven was filled with puff pastry, the bakers were finishing their last task and preparing to go home.

Today prepared frozen puff pastry is available in sheets, ready to thaw and use. There is great satisfaction, however, in making one's own.

Preparation Methods

Two methods of preparation are commonly used in the modern bakery: the Belgian method and the classic French method. Louis Daniel, wine connoisseur, former proprietor of a well-known midtown Manhattan French restaurant, Le Chambertin, once asked me if I used *le methode Belgique* for my pastry dough. I shook my head, admitting that I was unfamiliar with the term. He described the method to me. It turned out that I had been using it in the bakery for years but had no idea of the origin or the name. It had been taught to me when I began working and was the commonly used method in bakeries at the time.

BELGIAN METHOD

A single-stage version in which chilled bits of butter and a touch of cream of tartar or lemon are blended directly into the dough, which is then rolled and folded as described below. When placed in the oven, the bits of butter burst in the heat and force the dough to rise.

CLASSIC FRENCH METHOD

Requires the pastry to be prepared in two stages, similar to that for croissants and Danish pastry. Dough is mixed and rolled out. Butter is spread on top and then the dough is folded and rolled so that the butter is layered in the dough. Multiple layers of dough and butter are created. Many bakers feel that this dough has a better rise, is more tender, and leaves a more delicate aftertaste on the palate. In the last few years, many professional bakers, myself included, have reverted to this method.

Try it both ways to decide upon your personal preference. Both recipes follow.

Belgian-Method Puff Pastry Dough

Adele, my wife, groans and plans a day of shopping when she sees me getting ready to make a batch of this dough. After more than forty years of marriage, she knows to avoid the stress of seeing the kitchen while I make puff pastry.

3 cups (1½ pounds / 680 grams) unsalted butter, chilled and cut into small dice

5 cups (1½ pounds / 680 grams) unbleached all-purpose flour, plus more for dusting

1½ teaspoons kosher salt

⅛ teaspoon cream of tartar

Juice of ½ lemon

1⅓ cups (10.4 fluid ounces / 306 milliliters) ice water

Vegetable oil or melted butter, for brushing

Flour a half-sheet pan.

In the mixing bowl of a stand mixer, preferably fitted with a dough hook, stir the butter and flour together with your fingers. Add the salt, cream of tartar, lemon juice, and water. Mix at low speed until the water is absorbed. Increase speed slightly and mix for 5 minutes or until the dough comes away from the sides of the bowl and forms a shaggy dough, which may be sticky and may have some small bits of butter visible. Further kneading is not necessary; the dough will become properly developed during the rolling and folding that follows.

On a floured work surface, turn out the dough. Dust with flour and shape into a rectangle about 1 inch thick, 10 inches wide, and 6 inches long. Cover with a cloth or plastic wrap and let rest for 20 minutes.

FIRST ROLL

On a floured work surface, roll out the dough into a rectangle about 24 inches by 8 inches. Brush off any excess flour. Fold the short ends in to meet at the center. Line up the corners, stretching carefully if necessary to keep them even. Brush off any flour on top and fold over as if closing a book. You now have four layers, called a four-fold. With a fingertip, make an indentation in one corner to denote the first fold. Cover and refrigerate on the prepared pan for 35 minutes.

SECOND ROLL

On a floured work surface, turn the dough lengthwise. Roll out as before into a rectangle measuring 24 by 8 inches. Brush off any excess flour. Fold the short ends in to meet at the center. Line up the corners, stretching carefully if necessary to keep them even. Brush off any flour on top and fold over as if closing a book. Make two indentations in a corner, cover, and refrigerate on the prepared pan for at least 35 minutes and up to overnight. If left overnight, allow the dough to rest at room temperature for 20 to 30 minutes before rolling.

THIRD AND FOURTH ROLL

Continue rolling, folding two more times and marking the rolls with an indentation for each four-fold. It is important to mark with indentations; it is easy to become distracted and forget how many rolls have been completed. Continue until 4 four-folds have been completed. There should be four indentations in the dough. Place on the floured pan. Roll or gently press to conform to the size of the pan.

Brush the top with vegetable oil or melted butter. Cover with plastic wrap and refrigerate for at least 3 hours, preferably overnight.

Instead of chilling, the dough can be cut in half and frozen at this point and kept for 10 to 14 days (or longer) if well wrapped. Wrap each half separately. Allow the dough to thaw overnight in the refrigerator before using.

Yield: One 18 by 12-inch sheet (3.75 pounds / 1.7 kilograms)

Classic-Method Puff Pastry Dough

A family friend, Lucy, is an accomplished home baker and a traditionalist. She insists this method creates a flakier puff pastry. You be the judge.

3 cups (1½ pounds / 680 grams) unsalted butter, chilled

5 cups (1½ pounds / 680 grams) unbleached all-purpose flour, plus more for dusting

1½ teaspoons kosher salt

⅛ teaspoon cream of tartar

Juice of ½ lemon

1⅓ cups (10.4 fluid ounces / 305 milliliters) ice water

Vegetable oil or melted butter, for brushing

Dust a half-sheet pan with flour.

Set aside ¼ cup (2 ounces / 57 grams) of butter for the dough. Cut the rest of the butter into strips measuring ¾ by ¾ by 5 inches. Arrange the strips, in a rectangular shape, on lightly floured waxed paper. Dust the tops with additional flour and cover with another sheet of waxed paper. Roll out the butter or pound it between the sheets of waxed paper into an 11 by 9-inch rectangle. Chill for about 20 minutes.

Meanwhile, in the mixing bowl of a stand mixer, fitted, preferably, with a dough hook, combine the remaining butter, 2¾ cups flour, salt, cream of tartar, lemon juice, and water. Mix at low speed for 5 minutes, or until the dough comes away from the sides of the bowl. Further mixing is not necessary; the dough will become fully developed as it is rolled. The dough should be shaggy and a bit sticky. Place on the prepared baking sheet. Roll out or press lightly to roughly the dimensions of the pan. It's okay if it's a bit short. Cover and chill for 30 minutes.

Remove the butter from the refrigerator 10 minutes before folding in. The goal is to have the roll-in butter and the dough at the same consistency to ease rolling. The butter should still be chilled but remain plastic enough to allow it to be rolled without tearing the dough. If the butter is too stiff, wait a few minutes until it can be rolled, or soften by pounding lightly with the rolling pin, first lengthwise and then crosswise.

PRELIMINARY ROLL-IN

Leave the dough in the floured pan. Brush off any excess flour and place the roll-in butter on top of the dough so that it covers two-thirds of the dough. Leave a ½-inch space along the edges to prevent the butter from oozing out while rolling. As if folding a letter in thirds, fold the non-buttered section over half the buttered section. Brush away any excess flour. Fold the remaining third over. Pat down the dough.

FIRST ROLL

Transfer the dough from the pan to a floured work surface, roll out the dough into a rectangle about 24 by 8 inches. Brush off any excess flour. Fold in the short ends to meet at the center. Line up the corners, stretching carefully if necessary to keep them even. Brush off any flour on top and fold over as if closing a book. You now have four layers, called a four-fold. With a fingertip, make an indentation in one corner to denote the first fold. Cover and refrigerate on the prepared pan for 35 minutes.

SECOND ROLL

On a floured work surface, turn the dough lengthwise. Roll out as before to a rectangle measuring 24 by 8 inches. Fold in the short ends to meet at the center. Line up the corners, stretching carefully if necessary to keep them even. Brush off any flour on top and fold over as if closing a book. Return dough to prepared pan. Make two indentations in a corner, cover, and refrigerate for at least 35 minutes and up to overnight. If left overnight, allow the dough to rest at room temperature for 20 to 30 minutes before rolling.

THIRD AND FOURTH ROLL

Continue rolling, folding two more times and marking the rolls with an indentation for each four-fold. It is important to mark with indentations; it is easy to become distracted and forget how many rolls have been completed. Continue until 4 four-folds have been completed. There should be four indentations in the dough. Place on the floured pan. Roll or gently press to conform to the size of the pan.

Brush the top with vegetable oil or melted butter. Cover with plastic wrap and refrigerate for at least 3 hours, preferably overnight.

Instead of chilling, the dough can be cut in half and frozen at this point and kept for 10 to 14 days (or longer) if well wrapped. Wrap each half separately. Allow the dough to thaw overnight in the refrigerator before using.

Yield: One 18 by 12-inch sheet (3.75 pounds / 1.7 kilograms)

Note: Some bakers roll out as many as 5 four-folds. Among the professional bakers with whom I worked, the general consensus is to roll 4 four-folds. However, this varies throughout the food world. Feel free to try additional rolls and make the decision for yourself.

Apple Turnovers

"The Apple Turnover Man" bought a turnover every weekday at 8 a.m. for many years. We made sure they were out of the oven and ready for him. One day they were not ready. Reluctantly he accepted a cheese Danish as a replacement. Next day he was back for the Apple Turnover.

I wish I knew his name to send him a copy of this recipe.

About ½ sheet (1 pound, 14 ounces / 850 grams) puff pastry dough (pages 130–33)

1 egg

1 tablespoon water

1 cup (3.6 ounces / 90 grams) cake crumbs (see page 42) or bread crumbs, preferably fresh

6 cups (1½ pounds / 680 grams) Apple Filling (page 33)

Baker's Danish Glaze (page 41) (optional)

Simple Icing (page 41) warm (optional)

Line two half-sheet pans with parchment paper or greased waxed paper.

On a floured work surface, roll out the pastry dough into a rectangle about 26 by 20 inches. Shrink down the dough by holding one corner of the bottom edge with each hand, lift gently, and give a little shake, like smoothing out a tablecloth. The dough should now be about 24 by 18 inches. If it's too short, gently roll to size, working from the center out to the edges.

Using a pizza wheel, sharp blade, or bench knife, trim the edges to form straight lines. Using a yardstick or a bench knife along the length as a gauge, measure off 6-inch squares (four squares by three squares). Cut with the pizza wheel or a sharp blade into twelve squares.

Lightly beat the egg with the water to make an egg wash.

Brush a thin line of the egg wash around the edges of the squares. Sprinkle a generous tablespoon of cake crumbs in the center of each square. "Drop out" (see page 36) ¼ cup of the apple filling, mounding it on the cake crumbs. Keep the filling away from the brushed line of egg wash.

Bring a corner up and over the filling to the opposite corner to form a triangle. Press down along all edges to seal. Seal once again and remove any indentations from finger marks with a tap from the side of the hand on both sides of the turnover.

a jewish baker's pastry secrets

Pierce the center of each turnover with a fork or a corner of the bench knife to allow the steam to vent while baking. Brush the tops with the egg wash, taking care not to let the egg drip down the sides of the dough. Place the turnovers, equally spaced, on the prepared baking sheets. At this point, the turnovers can be wrapped and refrigerated overnight for baking the next day or frozen for up to 4 weeks. Frozen turnovers can be taken directly from the freezer to the oven for baking.

Using a delicate touch, carefully brush the tops a second time with the egg wash. Let dry for a few minutes.

Position a rack in the center of the oven and preheat to 400°F/200°C.

Put the turnovers in the oven and reduce the oven temperature to 375°F/190°C. Bake for 35 to 45 minutes, until evenly browned. If two sheets cannot fit side by side in your oven, bake one at a time. (Alternately, place the racks to divide the oven into thirds. Rotate the baking pans from top to bottom half way into baking time.)

Brush the tops with the Danish glaze. Set on a wire rack to cool. When cool, drizzle with the warm icing. Serve warm or at room temperature. Loosely covered, the turnovers keep well for a day or two. Refrigeration or freezing is not recommended: the apples tend to weep.

Yield: 12 turnovers

Variations

Fruit Turnovers
For fruit turnovers, substitute your favorite fruit fillings or thickened jam (see page 37) for the apples.

Half Moons
With a 3-inch or 4-inch fluted (or plain edged) cookie cutter, cut out rounds from the rolled-out pastry dough. Place a tablespoon of applesauce or your favorite fruit filling or thickened jam (see page 37) in the center. Brush the edges with the egg wash. Fold the top over and seal. Brush with the egg wash. Bake as above.

Cheese Pockets

When a piece of baking equipment malfunctioned in the bakery, it was a possible disaster. Relationships with repairmen were sacred. Morris, our beloved refrigerator repairman, would answer my calls at all hours of the day or night and in any weather. I remember a particular morning standing in the back doorway watching the sunrise with Morris. Coffee in hand, Morris proclaimed Cheese Pockets the best breakfast ever.

½ sheet (1 pound, 14 ounces / 850 grams) puff pastry dough, (pages 130–33)

1½ cups (15 ounces / 425 grams) Cream Cheese Filling (page 35)

1 egg

1 tablespoon water

2½ cups (24 ounces / 680 grams) Butter Streusel (page 40)

Confectioners' sugar, for topping (optional)

Line two half-sheet pans with parchment paper or greased waxed paper.

On a floured work surface, roll out the pastry dough into a rectangle about 26 by 20 inches. Shrink down the dough by holding one corner of the bottom edge with each hand; lift gently and give a little shake, like smoothing out a tablecloth. The dough should now be about 24 by 18 inches. If it's too short, gently roll to size, working from the center out to the edges.

With a pizza wheel, sharp blade, or bench knife, trim the edges to form straight lines. Using a yardstick or the bench knife along its length as a gauge, measure off 6-inch squares (four squares by three squares). Cut with the pizza wheel or a sharp blade into twelve squares.

"Drop out" (see page 36) 2 tablespoons of the cream cheese filling in the center of each square. To form a pocket, lift one corner of the dough, bringing it over until just past the filling. Press with the thumb to seal. Bring the opposite end over in the same manner and press down to seal. You now have an open pocket. Turn the pastry one-quarter turn. Bring one corner over the filling and seal. Repeat with the opposite corner. This results in a closed pocket. Proceed with the rest of the pockets.

Lightly beat the egg with the water to make an egg wash. Brush the tops with the egg wash, taking care not to let the egg drip down the sides of the dough.

Spread a layer of the butter streusel on the work surface or in a clean baking sheet. Invert the cheese pockets and place them on top of the streusel, pressing lightly to make the crumbs adhere.

Place the pockets, streusel side up and equally spaced, on the prepared baking sheets. Pierce the centers with a fork or the tip of a knife to allow the steam to vent in the oven.

Let the pastry rest for 15 to 20 minutes to reduce shrinkage in the oven. At this point, the pockets can be wrapped and refrigerated overnight for baking the next day or can be frozen for up to 4 weeks. Frozen pockets can be taken directly from freezer to oven for baking.

Position a rack in the center of the oven and preheat to 400°F/200°C.

Put the pockets in the oven and reduce the temperature to 375°F/190°C. Bake for 35 to 45 minutes, or until evenly browned. If two sheets cannot fit side by side in your oven, bake one at a time. (Alternately, place the racks to divide the oven into thirds. Rotate the baking pans from top to bottom half way into baking time.)

Cool in the pan on a wire rack.

When cool, sift a light coating of confectioners' sugar over the tops. Serve warm or at room temperature. Loosely covered, the pastries keep well for several days at room temperature. They can be refrigerated or frozen for up to 4 weeks but may become soggy.

Yield: 12 pastries

Variations

Prune Pockets

Substitute Prune Lekvar (page 38) for the cheese filling.

Almond Pockets

Replace the cheese filling with Frangipane (page 36) or Processed Almond-Paste Filling (page 32). Omit the streusel, brush the tops twice with the egg wash, and sprinkle with sliced almonds before baking. If desired, brush the tops with Baker's Danish Glaze (page 41) after baking.

Palmiers
(Palm Leaves)

Bakers call these pastries palm leaves, elephant ears, sow's ears, or pig ears. The French name sounds more refined. But call it what you please: a rose by any other name tastes just as sweet.

½ sheet (1 pound, 14 ounces / 850 grams) puff pastry dough (pages 130–33)

2 to 3 cups (14 to 21 ounces / 400 to 600 grams) sugar

Set out three half-sheet pans. Leave them unlined and ungreased.

In place of dusting flour, spread 1 cup (more if necessary) granulated sugar over the work surface. Place the pastry on the work surface and sprinkle the top with a generous coating of sugar. Roll out the dough lengthwise until it is 20 inches long and then roll out the width to 18 inches. Dust with sugar as necessary to prevent sticking.

Shrink down the dough by folding the dough in half, opening it and folding again from the opposite side. The dough should now measure about 18 by 16 inches. If it's too short, roll very gently from the center out. Trim the edges to form straight lines. Bring the bottom edge up halfway and the top one down, both meeting at the center.

Even off the ends of the dough, stretching the corners slightly, if needed. Fold over once more, bottom edge up halfway, top down, forming a four-fold, the top and bottom edges meeting at the center. Now fold over, top over bottom, completing the palmier shaped log.

a jewish baker's pastry secrets

Trim the ends of the log to form straight lines. Cut crosswise into eighteen 1-inch strips. Place on the baking sheets, cut side up so that the pieces fan open. Space evenly, in two staggered rows, six palmiers per sheet. Set aside and let rest for 20 minutes or more to prevent shrinkage in the oven. At this point, the palmiers can be frozen for up to 4 weeks. Frozen ones can be taken directly from the freezer to the oven for baking.

Position a rack in the center of the oven and preheat the oven to 400°F/200°C.

Put the palmiers in the oven and reduce the temperature to 375°F/190°C. Bake for 15 to 20 minutes, until bottoms begin to brown lightly. If two sheets cannot fit side by side in your oven, bake one at a time. (Alternately, place the racks to divide the oven into thirds. Rotate the baking pans from top to bottom half way into baking time.)

Using oven pads or mitts, remove the pan(s) from the oven temporarily. With a metal spatula, carefully flip each palmier over, as if turning pancakes. Use care not to get burned, especially by the sugar that has been caramelized on the bottom.

Return to the oven and continue baking for 20 minutes, or until browned.. Check the bottoms by gently lifting one or two pieces with the tip of the spatula.

Remove from pan and cool on a wire rack. The pastries keep well in a closed container at room temperature for a week or longer. Do not refrigerate or freeze.

Yield: 18 pastries

❧ **Baker's Secret:** *German bakers like to make their "sow's ears" larger and thinner for additional caramelization. To accomplish this, after cutting the folded pastry into 1-inch slices as above, spill a layer of granulated sugar on the work surface. Lay down two pastries at a time on top of the sugar, placing them on a diagonal about 2 inches apart. Sprinkle with sugar. With a rolling pin, roll out and enlarge the pastries until about ½ inch thick. Place on the baking pans as above, using additional baking sheets if necessary. Bake as above. A shorter baking time may be required. Keep close watch.*

Raspberry Bars

Raspberry bars are very popular with children and those of us with a sweet tooth. These never lasted very long on the bakery shelves or in our home kitchen.

½ sheet (1 pound, 14 ounces / 850 grams) puff pastry dough (pages 130–33)

1 cup (10.5 ounces / 300 grams) thickened raspberry jam, or more to cover

1 egg

1 tablespoon water

2½ cups (24 ounces / 680 grams) Butter Streusel (page 40)

Confectioners' sugar, for topping (optional)

Grease the bottom and sides of a half-sheet pan. Line with parchment paper or waxed paper and then grease the paper.

Cut the dough into two halves. On a floured work surface, roll each piece out until about 1 inch wider than the baking sheet. Shrink down the dough by holding one corner of the bottom edge with each hand, lifting gently, and giving a little shake, like smoothing out a tablecloth. Roll out again if necessary. Let rest for 5 minutes.

Brush off any excess flour. Gently fold one sheet of the dough into quarters, lift onto a prepared pan, and open. Spread with your fingers from the center out if the dough does not cover the bottom of the pan.

Spread the raspberry jam over the dough from edge to edge. Fold the remaining sheet of dough into quarters and place on top, covering the raspberry jam, and then open it. Trim any excess from the edges. Prick the dough all over with a fork.

Lightly beat the egg with the water to make an egg wash. Brush the top with the egg wash, taking care not to let the egg drip down the sides of the dough.

a jewish baker's pastry secrets

Spread a generous layer of the streusel over the top, covering completely. Press down lightly with hands or rolling pin. With a bench knife or chef's knife, score off sixteen 4 by 4-inch bars and then cut straight down through the dough. Allow the pastry to rest for 15 to 20 minutes. At this point, the pastry can be refrigerated overnight for baking the next day or it can be frozen for up to 4 weeks. Frozen pastries can go directly from the freezer to the oven.

Position a rack in the center of the oven and preheat the oven to 400°F/200°C.

Put the raspberry bars in the oven and reduce the temperature to 375°F/190°C. Bake for 35 to 45 minutes, or until evenly browned. Cool in the pan on a wire rack. Cut through the bars again before removing from pan.

When cool, dust the top with confectioners' sugar. Serve warm or at room temperature. Loosely covered, the pastries keep well at room temperature for up to a week. They can be frozen for up to 4 weeks but may become soggy.

Yield: 16 bars

Variation

Fruit Bars

Replace the raspberry jam with thickened blueberry, cherry, or apricot preserves (page 37).

Cream Horns

Pastry horns are formed on tapered, tinned-steel tubes we call "Lady Locks." Picture a metal hair curler, made expressly for this purpose. They're available in gourmet food and kitchen stores, ask for stainless steel cream horn molds. I suggest purchasing at least eight, which will allow the horns to be baked in two batches. You can substitute cannoli tubes, although they lack the taper for the classic shape.

½ sheet (1 pound, 14 ounces / 850 grams) puff pastry dough (pages 130–33)

1 egg

1 tablespoon water

Granulated sugar or confectioners' sugar, for topping

1 cup (8 fluid ounces / 237 milliliters) whipping cream, preferably not ultra-pasteurized

½ teaspoon pure vanilla extract

Grease eight to sixteen 5-inch pastry horn molds. Line two half-sheet pans with greased parchment paper or waxed paper.

On a floured work surface, roll out the dough into a rectangle about ⅛ inch thick, measuring 16 inches long by 18 inches wide.

Brush off any excess flour and any flour that remains on the work surface. With a 4-inch pizza wheel, bench knife, or a sharp blade and a yardstick, trim the edges to form straight lines. With a fork, prick the dough all over to prevent it from cracking in the oven. Cut crosswise into strips ¾ inch wide.

Place the narrow edge of a tube horizontally along the bottom of the first strip. Leave the end of the tube protruding by at least ¼ inch. Roll up allowing each new turn to overlap half of the previous one. Do not stretch, but wind loosely so that the horns do not burst in the oven.

Lightly beat the egg with the water to make an egg wash. Brush the tops and sides of the horns with the egg wash and then roll them in granulated sugar so that three-quarters of the cylinder are coated. Set on the baking sheet with the uncoated area down. Repeat until all of the dough is used.

Position a rack in the center of the oven and preheat to 400°F/200°C.

Bake while still frozen. Place in the oven, reduce the oven temperature to 375°F/190°C, and bake for 25 to 35 minutes, or until evenly light brown. If two sheets cannot fit side by side in your oven, bake one at a time. (Alternately, place the racks to divide the oven into thirds. Rotate the baking pans from top to bottom half way into baking time.)

Cool for 5 minutes on the baking sheet. Carefully, to avoid getting burned, remove the horns from the metal tubes. Generally a light tap of the end of the tube on a wooden board will free them. Return the pastries to the baking sheet to finish baking for 5 to 10 minutes, until the inside is browned lightly. Let cool completely.

If not using immediately, store the horns at room temperature in a covered container for up to several days. When you are ready to serve, whip the cream with the vanilla extract until they yield soft peaks. A small amount of sugar can be added, but it is not necessary. Fill with whipped cream. Use a pastry bag or make a parchment paper cone for filling. Filled horns should be eaten as soon as possible, before they become soggy.

Yield: About 16 horns

Variations

Cannoli Horns
Substitute 2 cups (1¼ pounds / 580 grams) Cannoli Filling (page 33) for the whipped cream.

Custard Cream Horns
Substitute 2 cups (18 ounces / 510 grams) Pastry Cream (page 37) for the whipped cream.

Whipped Custard Horns
Make whipped cream using ½ cup (4 fluid ounces / 118 milliliters) of whipping cream and fold into 2 cups (18 ounces / 510 grams) Pastry Cream (page 37). Substitute for the whipped cream.

Almond Bars

Another almond pastry? What can I say: almonds are wonderful.

½ sheet (1 pound, 14 ounces / 850 grams) puff pastry dough (pages 130–33)

2 cups (20 ounces / 566 grams) Processed Almond-Paste filling (page 32)

1 egg

1 tablespoon water

Sliced almonds, preferably toasted, for topping

Baker's Danish Glaze (page 41) (optional)

Line a half-sheet pan with parchment paper or greased waxed paper.

On a floured work surface, roll out the dough into a rectangle about 24 by 12 inches. If necessary, continue rolling the length until about ⅛ inch thick. Dust with flour as necessary to prevent sticking. Shrink down the dough by folding it in quarters and reopening. If necessary, roll gently from the center outward to maintain the 12-inch width.

Brush off any excess flour. Trim the edges with a pizza wheel, sharp blade, or bench knife, and yardstick to form straight lines. Cut lengthwise into three strips, each about 4 inches wide. Apply a 1-inch-tall by 1-inch-wide mound of almond filling along the bottom edge of each strip.

Lightly beat the egg with the water to make an egg wash.

Brush a 1-inch line of the egg wash across the top edge of each strip. Roll the dough up, jelly-roll style. Roll the seam underneath so that it does not open during baking. Cut each strip into four equal pieces.

Brush the tops with the egg wash, taking care not to let the egg drip down the sides of the dough. Sprinkle with the sliced almonds. Place them seam side down on the prepared baking sheet, equally spaced in three rows, four pastries to each row. Set aside and let rest for 20 minutes or more to prevent shrinkage in the oven. At this point, the pastries can be refrigerated overnight for baking the next day; to keep for a week or more, freeze. Frozen pastries can be taken directly from the freezer to the oven for baking.

Position a rack in the center of the oven and preheat to 400°F/200°C.

Place the pan in the oven and reduce the oven temperature to 375°F/190°C. Bake for 35 to 45 minutes, until evenly browned. Brush the tops with Danish glaze.

Cool on a wire rack. Loosely covered, the pastries keep well for several days at room temperature. Freezing is not recommended.

Yield: 12 bars

Variations

Apple Sticks
Substitute Apple Filling (page 33) for the almond filling.

Apple–Frangipane Sticks
Spread rolled dough strips with a thin layer of Frangipane (page 36) instead of the almond filling and then top with apples, as above.

Cock's Combs
(Bear's Claws)

Cock's Comb or Bear Claws became popular in the 1920s. As the dough rises, the shape looks like a bear claw or cock's comb.

½ sheet (1 pound, 14 ounces / 850 grams) puff pastry dough (pages 130–33)

2 cups (20 ounces / 566 grams) Processed Almond-Paste filling (page 32)

1 egg

1 tablespoon water

2½ cups (24 ounces / 680 grams) Butter Streusel (page 40), for topping

Confectioners' sugar, for topping (optional)

Line two half-sheet pans with parchment paper or greased waxed paper.

On a floured work surface, roll out the dough into a ¼-inch-thick rectangle about 18 inches long and 12 inches wide. Dust with flour as necessary to prevent sticking. Continue rolling the length until the dough is about ⅛ inch thick. Shrink down the dough by holding one corner of the bottom edge with each hand, lifting gently, and giving a little shake, like smoothing out a tablecloth. Brush off any excess flour.

Using a pastry bag with a ¾- to 1-inch-wide opening, pipe a 1-inch strip of the almond filling along the bottom edge and down the entire length of the 12-inch side. Lift the dough over and around the filling. Turn one-quarter turn to ensure that the filling is entirely enclosed. Cut along the entire length with a pizza wheel or sharp blade, severing the filled roll from the dough. Turn the roll so that the seam lies on the bottom. Reach over the severed roll and continue with another roll. Fill and cut as before, carefully snuggling it up to the previous roll. Repeat until all of the dough is used up. Brush away any excess flour.

> ɞ **Baker's Secret:** *If you don't want to use a pastry bag to pipe out the almond filling, roll out the filling by the handful into 1-inch ropes on a floured work surface. Place along the bottom edge of the pastry and continue rolling, butting each piece against the end of the previous one.*

Lightly beat the egg with the water to make an egg wash. Brush the tops with the egg wash. Smother with the butter streusel. Cover thoroughly, allowing it to spill over onto the work surface.

Beginning at the left, cut crosswise into pieces about 5 inches long. Preferably with a bench knife, cut a series of notches crosswise through the bottom edge, about ½ inch deep, every ½ inch along the entire length.

Curve the ends of each cock's comb in a semicircular shape (the notches on the outer edge) as you place them, equally spaced, on the baking sheets. Set aside and let rest for 20 minutes or more to prevent shrinkage in the oven. At this point, the pastries can be refrigerated overnight for baking the next day, or they can be frozen for up to 4 weeks. Frozen pastries can be taken directly from the freezer to the oven for baking.

Position a rack in the center of the oven and preheat to 400°F/200°C.

If two sheets cannot fit side by side in your oven, bake one at a time. (Alternately, place the racks to divide the oven into thirds. Rotate the baking pans from top to bottom half way into baking time.)

Place the baking sheet in the oven and then reduce the oven temperature to 375°F/190°C. Bake for 35 to 45 minutes, or until evenly browned. Dust with confectioners sugar, if using.

Place on a wire rack until cool. Loosely covered, the pastries keep for a week at room temperature. Freezing not recommended.

Yield: 12 pastries

Variation

Fruit Claws

Prepare the pastry dough as for the Cock's Combs. Substitute any fruit filling or thickened fruit preserves (cherry, blueberry, pineapple, and so on) for the almond filling. Omit the streusel and top with 1 cup (8.7 ounces / 236 grams) coarse sugar. Fill and cut into individual pastries for Cock's Combs, but don't cut the notches in the bottom and don't shape into a curve when placing pastries on baking sheet. Stipple the tops with a fork before baking as above.

Napoleon Pastry Sheets

The perfect Napoleon starts with baked sheets of pastry, pastry that is notorious for shrinking in the oven. This causes excessive trimming when baked and a corresponding loss in size for the finished pastries. To remedy this, bakers often nest a second baking sheet on top of the pastry dough. They then place an ovenproof weight (such as a brick or a saucepan with a heatproof handle, half-filled with water) in the center of the top pan. The weight prevents the Napoleon sheet from shrinking as usual, permitting the finished Napoleon to be trimmed and served properly.

Cooked pastry cream sandwiched between thin layers of many leafed puff pastry represents the most classic form of this French pastry. When I was a kid in the Bronx, a Napoleon was a 5-cent pastry that I brought home in a paper sack.

⅓ sheet (1 pounds, 4 ounces / 567 grams) puff pastry dough (pages 130–33)

> ✑ **Baker's Secret:** *Over the years I discovered the secret for preventing excessive shrinkage. By inverting the baking sheet and placing it in the oven upside down, the weight of the dough hanging over the rim plus the weight on top reduces shrinkage. Proceed with the directions below, baking with the pans in the inverted position and weighted on top. When baked and cooled, flip the double pans over, right side up, before removing the top pan.*

Line the top of an upside-down half-sheet baking pan with parchment paper or greased wax paper. Set out a second half-sheet pan.

On floured work surface, roll out the pastry dough until it is about 2 inches longer and wider than the prepared baking sheet. Brush off any excess flour. Shrink down the dough by folding over in quarters. Open and measure against the baking sheet. There should be enough of an overhang to rise up along the sides of the pan by about 1 inch. Adjust, if necessary, by rolling the entire dough gently from the center out. Allow to rest for 5 minutes.

Fold in quarters once more, lift onto the prepared pan, and open. If the dough does not fill the pan and rise up the sides, press gently from the center outward to fill. It's okay if the sides are somewhat uneven; they will be trimmed before they are used.

Prick the dough all over with a fork. Let the pastry rest for 30 to 60 minutes (or as long as overnight in the refrigerator) to help prevent shrinkage in the oven.

Position a rack in the center of the oven and preheat to 400°F/200°C. Place the second baking sheet on top of the dough right-side up so the pastry is between the bottoms of both pans. Invert both pans together (so the top pan is now on the bottom) and proceed as described above.

Place the doubled sheets in the oven, top with a weight, and reduce the oven temperature to 375°F/190°C. Bake for 25 to 35 minutes, until browned. With oven pads or mitts, remove the weight and top baking sheet for the last 5 minutes to aid browning. Use caution when removing the top pan and the pan with hot water (or the brick) from the oven. Invert pan and cool in pan on wire rack.

When cool, remove from pan, trim any uneven edges and put aside. The trimmings can be used later for topping; they keeps well for a week or more if lightly covered. Store in a cool, dry area. In the bakery, I kept the sheets unwrapped, stacked two or three deep in a closed cabinet called a "dry box."

Yield: 1 sheet, enough for 12 pastries

> **Baker's Secret:** *On a floured work surface, with a 4-inch round cookie cutter, plain or fluted, cut out rounds of puff pastry from thinly rolled dough. Brush with the egg wash for gloss. Bake as for the Napoleon sheets. Use to make round Napoleons, as a topping for other cakes or pastries, or as a base for fruits, sorbet, or ice cream. Use in savory dishes as a cover for casseroles, pot pie, and as many other variations as your imagination prompts you to create.*

Napoleon: The Pastry

Napoleons are best when freshly assembled and served within a few hours. In the refrigerator, they will keep well for 24 hours. However, the longer they are held, the more likely they are to absorb moisture and lose their crisp quality. The sheets can be prepared well ahead. Pastry cream can be made 1 or 2 days in advance. Assembly is best done no more than an hour or two before serving.

1 Napoleon Pastry Sheet, baked (page 148)

3 cups (22.3 ounces / 630 grams) Pastry Cream (page 37)

½ cup (2.2 ounces / 62 grams) confectioners' sugar

Carefully place the pastry sheet on a work surface, handling with care to avoid cracking. With the point of a sharp knife, trim any uneven edges. Using a sharp serrated knife, cut crosswise into three strips, each measuring 12 by 6 inches. Lifting gently so that the sheet does not break, place the bottom strip on top of a clean, inverted baking sheet.

> **ɞ Baker's Secret:** *Cut a 6 by 12-inch piece of cardboard from a corrugated carton. Use this to lift the cut strip and gently slide it onto the baking sheet.*

Spread the pastry strip with a layer of the pastry cream about ¼ inch thick. Lift another strip onto the cardboard and slide on top of the pastry cream. Gently adjust the strip until the edges are even. Spread with a layer of the pastry cream about ¼ inch thick. Carefully slide the remaining strip onto the corrugated board. Slide it on top of the pastry cream, to form the third layer. Adjust the edges, if necessary. Place the empty baking sheet (inverted) on top of the Napoleon strips. Using the palms of your hands and applying firm, even pressure, press down on the strips with just enough pressure to sandwich all three layers together. This assures an even, level surface over the tops, preventing the finished pastries from appearing lopsided. Remove inverted pan before continuing.

> ℘ **Baker's Secret:** *Place in the refrigerator or freezer to chill for several hours. Napoleons are easier to cut when nearly frozen.*

Dust the tops with confectioners' sugar. I like to cut and serve the Napoleans at the table. If you prefer less drama, cut after filling. Dust tops with confectioners' sugar before serving. Best eaten the day they are made. Will keep refrigerated for a day.

Yield: 4 Napoleons, each serving 3 to 4

Variation

Berry Napoleon

Add berries to the top of the pastry cream. Raspberries or strawberries cut in half are particularly good.

Pastry Pillows with Berries 'n' Cream

These pastries easily adapt to many variations, some of which follow below. Think of these as a good base with which to experiment. Consider it an opportunity to let your imagination run wild.

Pastry

About ¼ sheet (15 ounces / 425 grams) puff pastry dough (pages 130–33)

1 egg

1 tablespoon water

1 cup (3 ounces / 85 grams) sliced almonds, preferably toasted, for topping

1 cup (7 ounces / 198 grams) sugar, for topping

Filling

2 tablespoons sugar, or more, to taste

1 pint (or more) fresh berries in season (try mixed berries)

2 tablespoons Kirsch or any fruit liqueur (optional)

2 cups (16 fluid ounces / 473 milliliters) whipping cream, preferably not ultra-pasteurized

½ teaspoon pure vanilla extract

Line a half-sheet pan with parchment paper or greased wax paper.

To make the pastry, on a floured work surface, roll out the dough until it is about 1 inch wider than the prepared baking sheet. Shrink down the dough by folding in quarters and reopening. Roll again, very gently working from the center out. Brush off any excess flour.

Fold the sheet of dough over in quarters, lift onto the prepared pan and open. Spread with your fingers from the center out, if the dough does not cover the bottom of the pan. Trim any excess from the edges.

Prick the dough all over with a fork. Let stand for 20 to 30 minutes to minimize shrinkage.

With a bench knife or chef's knife, score to mark off twelve pieces, each measuring 3⅓ by 4 inches. Then cut straight down through the dough.

Lightly beat the egg with the water to make an egg wash. Brush the pastry with the egg wash, taking care to not let the egg drip down the sides of the dough. Sprinkle with the sliced almonds, and then with the sugar.

Allow the pastry to rest for 15 to 20 minutes.

Position a rack in the center of the oven and preheat to 400°F/200°C.

Place the sheet pan in the oven and reduce the oven temperature to 350°F/175°C. Bake for 25 to 35 minutes, until lightly browned.

When cool, cut through all of the previously cut lines. The pillows can be baked ahead of time and stored for a week or longer in a closed container at room temperature.

To make the filling, sprinkle sugar to taste over the berries. The amount of sugar will vary with the sweetness of the berries. Sprinkle with the Kirsch. Let macerate for about 30 minutes.

Whip the cream with the vanilla extract. A small amount of sugar can be added, but it is not necessary. Both the whipped cream and berries can be prepared and refrigerated for an hour before assembling.

To assemble, split each pillow horizontally and place on 12 individual dessert plates or a serving platter that holds them all. Spoon out a portion of berries with their syrup on the bottom half of the pastries. "Drop out" (see page 36) a mound of whipped cream or pipe with a pastry bag fitted with a #8 star tip. Cover with the pastry lid and pipe a line of whipped cream on top or "drop out" (see page 36) a dollop of cream with a spoon and serve.

Yield: 12 pastries

Variations

Berries 'n' Ice Cream

Omit whipped cream in the recipe above. Top the berries with 2 scoops of ice cream or sorbet, softened for 10 to 20 minutes at room temperature. Cover with the pastry lid. Serve immediately.

Cannoli Pillows

Substitute 2 cups (1¼ pounds / 580 grams) Cannoli Filling (page 33) for the whipped cream.

Cream–Custard Pillows

Substitute 2 cups (15 ounces / 210 grams) Pastry Cream (page 37) for the whipped cream.

Savory Pillows

Prepare the pastry pillows as above, but omit the topping of sugar and sliced nuts. Try one of the following options.

1. Stuff with fillings of your choice: seafood, vegetables, or stews. Serve either warm or cold.
2. Fill with a favorite cheese and warm in the oven or toaster oven to melt.
3. Sandwich ripe brie and creamed mushrooms within the pastry pillow. Heat in a 325°F/165°C oven until the cheese has melted, about 10 minutes.

Glazed Fruit Strips

Dress up your table and dazzle your guests with these eye-catching desserts. Puff pastry strips can be prepared 1 or 2 days in advance. Pastry cream can be made 24 hours ahead. Assemble no more than an hour or two before serving.

Pastry

About ½ sheet (1 pound, 14 ounces / 850 grams) puff pastry dough (pages 130–33)

1 egg

1 tablespoon water

Filling

2 tablespoons dark rum (optional) (try Myer's dark)

1½ cups (11.1 ounces / 315 grams) Pastry Cream (page 37), chilled

Assorted fresh fruits and berries, such as strawberries, raspberries, blackberries, blueberries, kiwifruit, banana, grapes, cherries, and/or pineapple slices

Apricot Glaze (page 41), warmed

Line a half-sheet pan with parchment paper or greased waxed paper.

On a floured work surface, roll out the dough about 1 inch wider than the baking sheet. Shrink down the dough by folding in quarters and reopening. Roll again, working gently from the center out. Brush off any excess flour. Invert a baking sheet over the dough. Using the baking sheet as a guide, trim the edges to form straight lines with a pizza wheel knife or sharp blade. Set the trimmings aside. Cut the dough crosswise into four equal strips, each measuring 4 by 12 inches. Prick all over with a fork. Take one of the strips and cut six ½-inch strips from the long edge.

Carefully place one or more of the three remaining strips on the prepared baking sheet. Lightly beat the egg with the water to make an egg wash. Brush a thin line of the egg wash along the long edges of each strip. Lay one of the ½-inch strips on top of each painted edge, to form a rim.

At this point, you can bake all three strips or bake one and freeze the rest on a separate sheet. Wrap well if freezing. The frozen pastry can be kept for several months. (Baked strips can be kept in a covered container for 1 to 2 weeks at room temperature. Leftovers can be crumbled for topping.)

Position a rack in the center of the oven and preheat to 400°F/200°C.

Place the sheet pan in the oven and reduce the oven temperature to 375°F/190°C. Bake for 25 to 35 minutes, until lightly browned. Cool the pastry on a wire rack.

Mix rum into pastry cream if using. Prepare the fruit. Clean, hull, or pit the fruit as necessary. Canned fruits should be drained. Spread the pastry cream over the pastry strips and place the fruit on top, creating attractive combinations or designs. Brush the top with warm apricot glaze.

> **℘ Baker's Secret:** *When glaze is dry, brush it a second time to create a thicker layer that will enhance the appearance and extend the shelf life of the fresh fruit.*
>
> *Be imaginative in your fruit toppings. Here are a few ideas:*
>
> 1. *Cover one strip entirely with strawberries. You can use whole strawberries standing upright in rows. Alternately, slice strawberries in half and place them all face down or all face up in overlapping rows.*
> 2. *Alternate rows of fruit, such as strawberry halves, kiwifruit slices, round or diagonal slices of banana, and so forth.*
> 3. *Experiment with tropical fruits, such as star fruit or lychees.*

The pastries are best served the day they are made, but they can be kept at room temperature for a day or two.

Yield: 3 pastries, each serving 4 to 8

> **℘ Baker's Secret:** *Bake the reserved trimmings until brown. Cool them and then crunch into flakes. Sprinkle the flakes on top of the finished pastry if your fruit is not as attractive as you hoped.*

Almond Horseshoe

I bought flour and other dry goods from David Rosen. Over the years David was there for me with advice—business and personal, sometimes the loan of a machine or a shoulder to cry on. His advice was always on the mark. In the early 1970s, he told me to buy a building in the then nonfashionable part of Manhattan now called Soho. I should have listened to him. We always sent him back to his office with a coffee cake; this was his favorite.

⅓ sheet (1 pound, 4 ounces / 567 grams) Puff Pastry Dough (pages 130–33)

2 cups (1¼ pounds / 566 grams) Processed Almond-Paste filling (page 32)

1 cup (4 ounces / 113 grams) walnuts or pecans, chopped, preferably toasted

1 cup (3.6 ounces / 90 grams) cake crumbs (see page 42) or bread crumbs, preferably fresh

2 tablespoons Cinnamon Sugar (page 40)

1 egg

1 tablespoon water

Sliced or chopped almonds, preferably toasted (optional)

Baker's Danish Glaze (page 41) (optional)

Simple Icing (page 41), warm (optional)

Line two half-sheet pans with parchment paper or greased wax paper.

On a floured work surface, cut the dough crosswise into two strips. Roll out each strip into a rectangle about 16 inches long and 8 to 10 inches wide, rolling the length first and then the width. Brush away any excess flour and place the strips with the length parallel to the edge of the work surface.

Spread the almond filling over the entire surface of each strip, leaving a 1-inch border along the top edges for sealing. Sprinkle half the walnuts on each strip. Cover with half of the cake crumbs and sprinkle half of the cinnamon sugar on top of each. Press down lightly with the palms of your hands.

Lightly beat the egg with the water to make an egg wash. Brush the egg wash over the border along the top edges. Fold over the bottom edge of the dough on each to form a 2-inch flap; then carefully roll up the strips, strudel style. Avoid stretching the dough as you roll. End with the seams centered on the bottoms.

In one continuous motion, lifting the strip by the ends and stretching gently, place on the prepared baking sheet in a crescent shape. Fit the second horseshoe on the same pan.

With a fork, pierce a series of holes along the center line of each to allow the steam to vent while baking. At this point, the pastries can be refrigerated overnight for baking the next day or they can be frozen for up to 4 weeks. Thaw overnight in the refrigerator before baking.

Brush the tops with the egg wash, taking care not to let the egg drip down the sides of the dough. Let the pastries rest for 15 to 20 minutes before baking to reduce shrinkage in the oven.

Using a delicate touch, carefully paint a second time with the egg wash. Sprinkle the tops with the almonds. Let dry for a few minutes.

Position a rack in the center of the oven and preheat to 400°F/200°C.

Place the baking sheet in the oven and reduce the oven temperature to 375°F/190°C. Bake for 35 to 45 minutes, until evenly browned. Immediately brush the tops with Danish glaze. Place on a wire rack to cool.

When cool, drizzle with the warm icing. Serve warm or at room temperature. Loosely covered, the pastries keep for up to a week at room temperature.

Yield: 2 horseshoes, each serving 6 to 10

Variation

Chocolate Walnut Horn

Melt 4 ounces (113 grams) best-quality semi-sweet or bittersweet chocolate with 2 tablespoons unsalted butter. Prepare as for Almond Horseshoe, spreading the almond filling over the pastry. Reserve half the melted chocolate and spread the remainder over the almond filling. Sprinkle 1 cup (4 ounces / 113 grams) walnuts, chopped, preferably toasted (see page 31) over the chocolate. Proceed to roll up, shape, and bake as above. When baked and cool, dust the top with confectioners' sugar, if desired, and drizzle with the reserved melted chocolate.

CHAPTER 9

Charlotte Dough

Rich short pastry dough when made with eggs was called Charlotte dough or *Mürbe* by the German and Jewish bakers. Over the years, a pastry evolved that combined rich pastry dough rolled into puff pastry, creating a new and unusual taste. This amalgam combined the flakiness of puff pastry with the cookie-like texture of the short dough, resulting in a dough that lends itself easily to shaping like puff pastry and emulates the richness of a tender cookie. The resulting pastry is tender rather then crumbly but has a long shelf life.

Sunday was the busiest day at the bakery. Customers would line up out the door to buy cake, pastries, and bread. They were always amazed and delighted that there were so many tastes and textures to choose from because we stocked a wide assortment. Lena was the matron of organization and flow. I remain mystified to this day that she was able to display the full assortment of baked goods we made in our small bake shop. I used many different doughs, but when combined with similar fillings, the results were different.

This charlotte dough was one of the variations in the "Danish and Coffee Cake" section. Add it to your repertoire.

In the bakery, we called this apple charlotte dough or just plain charlotte dough (named for the strudel-like pastry I made with it). Some of the European bakers began calling it Mürbe, causing some confusion. But all's well that ends well. Try this pastry, and you will understand what I mean.

Rich Sugar Dough

This is the sugar dough that you will combine with puff pastry to create the unique flavor of the charlotte dough. Use a floured cloth for rolling this dough when combining with the puff pastry.

¾ cup (6 ounces / 170 grams) sugar

1½ cups (12 ounces / 340 grams) unsalted butter

4½ cups (1½ pounds / 680 grams) unbleached all-purpose flour

1 teaspoon kosher salt

2 eggs

1 egg yolk

Flour a half-sheet pan.

In the mixing bowl of a stand mixer fitted with a paddle, lightly cream the sugar and butter, using a medium speed, until lighter in color and density. Mix together the flour and salt. Add the eggs, yolk, and flour mixture to the sugar and butter. Mix at slow speed only until combined.

Scoop the dough out onto a floured work surface and knead lightly.

> **๑ Baker's Secret:** *Don't worry if the dough is not entirely smooth; the ingredients will blend when the dough is rolled out. Sugar dough, like pie crust, becomes tough when overworked.*

Place the dough on the prepared baking pan; press or roll out until dough fills the pan evenly. Cover with plastic wrap or a cloth and refrigerate for several hours. The dough can be prepared up to 48 hours in advance. Soften it at room temperature just long enough to allow it to be rolled (about 20 minutes).

> ✂ **Baker's Secret:** *The dough is easier to work with if it remains partially chilled*

Sugar dough can be frozen, tightly wrapped, for up to 6 months. Divide dough into quarters, wrap, and freeze each section individually. Thaw as needed in the refrigerator overnight.

Yield: About 3 pounds of dough

Variation

Rich Chocolate Sugar Dough
Decrease the flour to 4¼ cups (23 ounces / 650 grams) and add ⅓ cup (1 ounce / 33 grams) Dutch-process cocoa powder. Proceed as above.

Apple Charlotte

The hint of apricot that overlays the flavor of the apples is enough to make the taste of the apple charlotte outstanding. Adding raisins, walnuts, or both might be construed as gilding the lily. But raisins and walnuts always complement apples, so see how well it suits you. The pastries go very well with vanilla ice cream.

¼ sheet (15 ounces / 425 grams) puff pastry dough (pages 130–33)

1 egg

1 tablespoon water

⅓ portion (1 pound /453 grams) Rich Sugar Dough (page 160)

1½ to 2 cups (15 to 20 ounces / 425 to 566 grams) Apricot Butter (page 33) or thickened apricot jam (page 37)

2 cups (7.2 ounces / 180 grams) cake crumbs (see page 42) or bread crumbs, preferably fresh

1 cup (5 ounces / 140 grams) raisins, preferably golden raisins (optional)

1 cup (4 ounces / 113 grams) walnuts, chopped, preferably toasted (optional)

6 cups (1½ pounds / 680 grams) Apple Filling (page 33)

Coarse sugar, for topping

Line a half-sheet pan with parchment paper or greased waxed paper. Flour a pastry cloth.

On a floured surface, roll the puff pastry into a long rectangle about ½ inch thick. Fold the short ends into the middle so that they meet at the center of the dough. Next, fold over the dough, as if closing the cover of a book. Roll lightly. This is called a four-fold (see page 30). Cut the puff pastry in half lengthwise. Place the halves on top of each other and roll into a long rectangle. Lightly beat the egg with the water to make an egg wash. Brush lightly with the egg wash.

On the floured cloth, roll the sugar dough out to slightly less than half the dimensions of the puff pastry. Set it on top of the puff pastry by rolling it up onto a rolling pin and unrolling over half of the dough. Tears can be mended by pressing small pieces together. Leave a ½-inch border all around.

Fold the opposite half of the puff pastry over (closing the book) and press to seal the edges so that the sugar dough will not be squeezed out while rolling. Turn the dough a quarter turn so the dough lies lengthwise with what would be the opening facing you and parallel with the edge of the work surface.

a jewish baker's pastry secrets

Dust with flour and roll the dough out into a ⅛-inch-thick rectangle measuring 18 by 12 inches. Brush away any excess flour and trim the edges to form straight lines. (A yardstick and pizza wheel work well for this. See page 13.)

Spread the entire sheet from edge to edge with a thin layer of the apricot butter. Sprinkle lightly with the cake crumbs.

In a small bowl, mix the raisins and nuts into the apple filling. Place a line of the apple filling about 2 to 2½ inches wide and 1 inch high along the bottom edge of the dough. Without stretching, carefully roll the bottom edge of the dough over the apples, tucking it slightly underneath the filling, forming a filled charlotte. With a pizza wheel or sharp blade, cut the charlotte from the rest of the dough, leaving a ½-inch tail attached. Roll the charlotte over so that the tail is underneath and the seam is centered on the bottom. Continue filling and rolling until the dough is all used up. If enough excess remains, it can often be pieced together to form an extra charlotte.

Lifting the filled strips, one hand on each end, quickly place on the prepared baking sheet, leaving at least 2 inches between each strip to assure even baking.

Brush the tops with the egg wash, taking care not to allow the egg to drip down onto the pan. Sprinkle a thin line of the coarse sugar through your fingertips down the length of the strips.

With a bench knife or chef's knife, cut each strip crosswise, into six equal pieces, without separating the cut pieces from each other.

> **℘ Baker's Secret:** *Cut by pressing the blade straight down through the dough.*

At this point, the apple charlottes can be refrigerated overnight for baking the next day, or they can be frozen for up to 2 months. Place the pan in the freezer until the charlottes are firm, remove each from the pan, and then wrap well. Frozen charlottes can be taken directly from the freezer to the oven for baking; baking time may have to be extended.

Position a rack in the center of the oven and preheat to 350°F/175°C.

Bake for 35 to 45 minutes, until well browned.

Cool the charlottes on the baking sheet on a wire rack. When cool, cut through each piece once more so that they are completely severed from each other. The pastries keep well in a covered container at room temperature for at least 2 days. They can be frozen, but the apples may weep slightly when thawed. Serve warm or at room temperature.

Yield: 12 to 16 pastries

Almond Sticks

Almond Paste Filling and Charlotte dough are a perfect combination—even more perfect with a cup of tea.

¼ sheet (15 ounces / 425 grams) puff pastry dough (pages 130–33)

1 egg

1 tablespoon water

⅓ portion (1 pound / 453 grams) Rich Sugar Dough (page 160)

1½ to 2 cups (15 to 20 ounces / 425 to 566 grams) Frangipane (page 36) or Processed Almond-Paste filling (page 32)

1 cup (4 ounces / 113 grams) walnuts, finely chopped and preferably toasted (optional)

1 to 2 cups (3.6 to 7.2 ounces / 90 to 180 grams) cake crumbs (see page 42) or bread crumbs, preferably fresh

Sliced almonds, for topping, preferably toasted

Baker's Danish Glaze (page 41)

Line a half-sheet pan with parchment paper or greased wax paper. Flour a pastry cloth.

On a floured surface, roll the puff pastry into a long rectangle, about ½ inch thick. Fold the short ends into the middle, so that they meet at the center of the dough.

Next, fold over the dough, as if closing the cover of a book. Roll lightly. This is called a four-fold.

Next, cut the puff pastry in half lengthwise. Place the halves on top of each other and roll into a long rectangle. Lightly beat the egg with the water to make an egg wash. Brush lightly with the egg wash.

On the floured cloth, roll the sugar dough out to slightly less than half the dimensions of puff pastry. Set it on top of the puff pastry by rolling it up onto a rolling pin and unrolling over half of the dough. Tears can be mended by pressing small pieces together. Leave a ½-inch border all around.

Fold the opposite half of the puff pastry over (closing the book) and press to seal the edges so that the sugar dough will not be squeezed out while rolling. Turn the dough a quarter turn so the dough lies lengthwise with what would be the opening facing you and parallel with the edge of the work surface.

a jewish baker's pastry secrets

Roll out the dough into a ⅛-inch-thick rectangle about 24 inches long and 12 inches wide. Dust with flour as necessary to prevent sticking.

With a pizza wheel or a sharp blade, trim the edges to form straight lines. Set the scraps aside for reuse. Spread a thin band (about 1-inch wide) of frangipane along the bottom edge of the dough from end to end. Sprinkle about ⅓ of the walnuts sparingly over the frangipane. Sprinkle the filling lightly with crumbs. Brush away any spilled filling or flour that remains on the work surface.

Fold a flap of about ½ inch over the bottom edge. Without stretching, carefully roll the bottom edge of the dough over the frangipane, tucking it slightly underneath the filling, forming a filled charlotte. With a pizza wheel or sharp blade, cut the filled roll from the rest of the dough leaving a ½-inch tail attached. Roll the pastry over so that the tail is underneath and the seam is centered on the bottom. Continue filling and rolling until the dough is all used up. If enough excess dough remains, it can often be pieced together to form an extra roll. With a little practice, it is possible to gauge the thickness of the rolls so that all of the dough is utilized.

Line up the strips vertically so that they touch one another. Trim the ends so that all are even.

Brush lightly with the egg wash, taking care to not let the egg drip down the sides of the dough. Sprinkle lightly with the sliced almonds. With a bench knife or chef's knife, cut each strip into four equal pieces. Cut straight down through the strips. Place on the prepared baking sheet in three rows, four pastries to each row. Set aside and let rest for about 20 minutes before baking.

Position a rack in the center of the oven and preheat to 375°F/190°C.

Bake for about 10 minutes. Reduce the temperature to 350°F/175°C and continue to bake for 35 to 45 minutes longer until evenly browned. Lift the edge of a pastry and check to see that the bottom has color. Remove from the oven and brush with the Danish Baker's glaze while still hot.

Cool in the pan on a wire rack for 10 to 15 minutes; then remove the pastries from the pan. The pastries keep well at room temperature for as much as a week in a closed container. They can be frozen for 6 to 8 weeks. Thaw overnight in the refrigerator. If necessary, crisp in a 325°F/165°C oven for about 15 minutes before serving.

Yield: 12 pastries

Variations

Apple Charlotte Sticks
Substitute 2 cups (8 ounces / 227 grams) Apple Filling (page 33) for the frangipane.

Prune Sticks
Substitute Prune Lekvar (page 38) for the frangipane.

Cigars

These cigar-shaped pastries were a favorite with our customers. Warning: They are habit forming.

¼ sheet (15 ounces / 425 grams) puff pastry dough (pages 130–33)

1 egg

1 tablespoon water

⅓ portion (1 pound / 453 grams) Rich Sugar Dough (page 160)

1½ cups (21 ounces / 595 grams) Processed Almond-Paste filling (page 32), or more, to cover

1 cup (4 ounces / 113 grams) walnuts or almonds, chopped and preferably toasted (optional)

2 cups (7.2 ounces / 200 grams) cake crumbs (see page 42) or bread crumbs, preferably fresh

1 cup (7.2 ounces / 200 grams) Cinnamon Sugar (page 40)

Sliced almonds, for topping, preferably toasted

Baker's Danish Glaze (page 41)

Line a half-sheet pan with parchment paper or greased wax paper.

On a floured surface, roll the puff pastry into a long rectangle, about ½ inch thick. Fold the short ends into the middle so that they meet at the center of the dough.

Next, fold over the dough, as if closing the cover of a book. Roll lightly. This is called a four-fold.

Next, cut the puff pastry in half lengthwise. Place the halves on top of each other and roll into a long rectangle. Lightly beat the egg with the water to make an egg wash. Brush lightly with the egg wash.

On the floured cloth, roll the sugar dough out to slightly less than half the dimensions of the puff pastry. Set it on top of the puff pastry by first rolling it up onto a rolling pin and then unrolling it over half of the dough. Tears can be mended by pressing small pieces together. Leave a ½-inch border all around.

Fold the opposite half of the puff pastry over (closing the book) and press to seal the edges so that the sugar dough will not be squeezed out while rolling. Turn the dough a quarter turn so the dough lies lengthwise with what would be the opening facing you and parallel with the edge of the work surface.

Roll out the dough into a ⅛-inch-thick rectangle about 18 inches long and 12 inches wide; dust with flour as necessary to prevent sticking.

Brush off excess flour. Spread the top of the dough from edge to edge with the almond filling. Sprinkle the walnuts over the top and cover well with crumbs. Press down lightly with

a jewish baker's pastry secrets

your hands or a rolling pin and then sprinkle with the cinnamon sugar. Roll out and lengthen the dough somewhat to help make the fillings adhere. Brush away any spilled filling or flour that remains on the work surface.

With a 4-inch pizza wheel or a sharp blade, trim the edges to form straight lines. Set the scraps aside for reuse. Cut crosswise into strips about 1½ inches wide. (Measure with your thumb, approximately from the tip to the last fold on the knuckle, or use a yardstick.)

Cigars are rolled on a diagonal. Starting with the first strip from the left, fold the right-hand corner of the bottom edge over to the left, forming a 45-degree angle. Take a small bit of scrap from the trimmings and place it on the edge to give the first roll some thickness. Begin to roll slowly, at about a 45-degree angle. Wind up, allowing each turn to overlap half of the previous one. Avoid stretching. A wee bit of practice will result in perfect cigars.

Roll until the cigar reaches about 6 inches in length (the width of a standard bench knife). The cigar should be about an inch thick and 4½ to 5 inches long. Cut off the first cigar at 4½ to 5 inches, leaving behind an inch with which to begin the next roll. You can unravel the inch and add a small piece of scrap to use it up. Continue rolling. When the last inch of the strip is reached, join by placing the bottom of the next strip on top and pressing to seal. Continue rolling as if it were one continuous strip.

As you work, line up the cigars in horizontal rows, each touching the one below. When all are finished and aligned, trim the edges so that all are the same length.

Brush the tops with the egg wash, taking care to not let the egg drip down the sides of the dough. Sprinkle with the sliced almonds. Place on the prepared baking sheet, equally spaced in three rows, four pastries to each row.

Set aside and let rest for 20 minutes or more to prevent shrinkage in the oven. At this point, the cigars can be refrigerated overnight for baking the next day, or they can be frozen for 6 to 8 weeks. Frozen cigars can be taken directly from freezer to oven for baking; baking time may have to be adjusted.

Position a rack in the center of the oven and preheat to 350°F/175°C.

Bake for 35 to 45 minutes, or until well browned. Cool on a wire rack and brush the tops with the Baker's Danish Glaze (page 41). Well wrapped, the pastries keep well at room temperature for a week or more. They can also be frozen for 6 to 8 weeks.

Yield: 12 pastries

Variations

Chocolate Cigars

Prepare Rich Chocolate Sugar Dough (page 161) and incorporate a ⅓ portion into puff pastry as above. Melt 4 ounces dark semisweet or bittersweet chocolate with 2 tablespoons unsalted butter. Spread over the almond filling. Omit the sliced almonds. Finish as above.

Bear Claws

Bears?!!! Should we run? Yes, for the hot cocoa to drink with these, or dare I say, "Dunk!"

¼ sheet (15 ounces / 425 grams)
puff pastry dough (pages 130–33)

1 egg

1 tablespoon water

⅓ portion (1 pound / 453 grams)
Rich Sugar Dough (page 160)

1½ cups (21 ounces / 595 grams)
Processed Almond-Paste filling (page 32)

2½ cups (24 ounces / 680 grams)
Butter Streusel (page 40), for topping

Confectioners' sugar, for dusting
(optional)

Line a half-sheet pan with parchment paper or greased wax paper.

On a floured surface, roll the puff pastry into a long rectangle, about ½ inch thick. Fold the short ends into the middle so that they meet at the center of the dough.

Next, fold over the dough as if closing the cover of a book. Roll lightly. This is called a four-fold.

Next, cut the puff pastry in half lengthwise. Place the halves on top of each other and roll into a long rectangle. Lightly beat the egg with the water to make an egg wash. Brush lightly on the pastry.

On the floured cloth, roll the sugar dough out to slightly less than half the dimensions of the puff pastry. Set it on top of the puff pastry by rolling it up onto a rolling pin and unrolling over half of the dough. Tears can be mended by pressing small pieces together. Leave a ½-inch border all around.

Fold the opposite half of the puff pastry over (closing the book), and press to seal the edges so that the sugar dough will not be squeezed out while rolling. Turn the dough a quarter turn so the dough lies lengthwise with what would be the opening facing you and parallel with the edge of the work surface.

Roll out the dough into a ¼-inch-thick rectangle about 18 inches long and 12 inches wide; dust with flour as necessary to prevent sticking. Continue rolling in the length and then the width, until the dough is about ⅛ inch thick. Brush off excess flour.

Along the bottom edge, pipe ("bag out") a 1-inch strip of the almond filling down the entire length. Alternatively, on a heavily floured work surface, roll out by the handful 1-inch ropes of filling. Place along the bottom edge, butting each piece against the end of the previous one.

Lift the dough over and around the filling. Cut along the entire length with a pizza wheel or sharp blade, leaving a ½-inch tail. Then sever the roll from the dough. Give the roll a one-half turn so that the seam lies on the bottom. Continue filling and cut as before, until all of the dough is used up. Brush away any excess flour. Line up the strips, parallel to and touching each other.

Brush the tops with the egg wash, taking care not to let it drip. Smother with butter streusel and trim the ends so that they are even. Beginning at the left, cut vertically into pieces about 5 inches long. Cutting straight down with a bench knife or a chef's knife, cut crosswise through all of the rows. Again, cut a series of notches, crosswise, through the bottom edge, about ½ inch deep every ½ inch along the entire length.

Curve the ends of each Bear Claw into a semicircular shape, notched ends to the outside as you place them, equally spaced, on the baking sheet. Set aside and let rest for 20 minutes or more to prevent shrinkage in the oven. At this point, the pastries can be refrigerated overnight for baking the next day. To keep for a week or more, they can be frozen, wrapped in plastic for up to 8 weeks. Freeze until solid on the baking sheet then remove and wrap for easier storage. Thaw overnight in the refrigerator before baking.

Position a rack in the center of the oven and preheat to 350°F/175°C.

Bake for 35 to 45 minutes, or until browned. Transfer to a wire rack to cool. Dust with confectioners' sugar, if using.

The pastries keep well at room temperature in a closed container for several days. They can be refrigerated for up to a week or frozen for up to 6 weeks but may become soggy.

Yield: About 12 pastries

Raspberry Horns

As much as I wish it was not true, my body is on baker's time. I am usually up hours before the sun. Sometimes I use this time to bake a morning treat for my wife, Adele. She loves raspberries. I surprised her one morning with these raspberry horns topped with fresh berries. She was delighted and perhaps less annoyed by the mess I left in the kitchen than usual.

¼ sheet (15 ounces / 425 grams) puff pastry dough (pages 130–33)

1 egg

1 tablespoon water

⅓ portion (1 pound / 453 grams) Rich Sugar Dough (page 160)

1 cup (11.2 ounces / 320 grams) thickened raspberry jam (page 37), or more, to cover

¼ cup (1.25 ounces / 36 grams) poppy seeds, preferably Dutch blue (optional)

½ cup (3 ounces/ 100 grams) Cinnamon Sugar (page 40)

2 cups (7.2 ounces / 200 grams) cake crumbs (see page 42) or bread crumbs, preferably fresh

Baker's Danish Glaze (page 41)

Simple Icing (page 41), warm (optional)

Line two half-sheet pans with parchment paper or greased wax paper.

On a floured surface, roll the puff pastry into a long rectangle, about ½ inch thick. Fold the short ends into the middle so that they meet at the center of the dough.

Next, fold over the dough as if closing the cover of a book. Roll lightly. This is called a four-fold.

Next, cut the puff pastry in half lengthwise. Place the halves on top of each other and roll into a long rectangle. Lightly beat the egg with the water to make an egg wash. Brush lightly on the pastry.

On the floured cloth, roll the sugar dough out to slightly less than half the dimensions of puff pastry. Set it on top of the puff pastry by rolling it up onto a rolling pin and unrolling over half of the dough. Tears can be mended by pressing small pieces together. Leave a ½-inch border all around.

Fold the opposite half of the puff pastry over (closing the book), and press to seal the edges so that the sugar dough will not be squeezed out while rolling. Turn the dough a quarter turn so the dough lies lengthwise with what would be the opening facing you and parallel with the edge of the work surface.

Roll out the dough into a ¼-inch-thick rectangle about 12 by 18 inches. Dust with flour to prevent sticking. Let rest for 5 minutes to relax the dough.

Brush away any excess flour. With a pizza wheel or a sharp blade and a yardstick, trim the edges to form straight lines. Spread a thin layer of the raspberry jam from edge to edge. Sprinkle lightly with the poppy seeds and cinnamon sugar; cover with the cake crumbs. Press down with your hands or a rolling pin to make it adhere. Using the blade of a bench knife along its length, or a yardstick and a blade, trim the edges to form straight lines. Cut lengthwise into two strips and then cut crosswise to make four strips. Next make two crosswise cuts midway between the center cut. You will have eight squares of equal size. Cut each square on the diagonal to make a grid of 16 triangles.

Cut a ½-inch notch through the center of each triangle base. When rolling up the triangle, the cut allows the base to expand and become a bit more elongated.

Begin to roll up, loosely, from the base, first folding over a ½-inch flap.

Proceed to roll up the triangle into a horn. Seal the tip by pressing with a fingertip. Roll the horn over so that the tip lies on the bottom. It's okay if some of the filling appears to be seeping out. Continue working until all of the horns are formed.

Lightly beat the egg with the water to make an egg wash.

Brush the tops with the wash, taking care not to let the egg drip down the sides of the dough. Place the horns equally spaced apart on the two prepared baking sheets. Allow the pastries to rest for 15 to 20 minutes before baking to reduce shrinkage in the oven. If two baking sheets cannot fit side by side in your oven, bake one and refrigerate or freeze the other. At this point, the pastries can be wrapped in plastic and refrigerated overnight for baking the next day.

Frozen horns can be taken directly from freezer to oven for baking, but the baking time may have to be extended slightly.

Position a rack in the center of the oven and preheat to 350°F/175°C.

Bake for 35 to 40 minutes, until well browned. Transfer to a wire rack to cool.

Brush the tops with the Danish Baker's glaze. Drizzle with icing. Serve warm or at room temperature. The pastries keep well at room temperature in a closed container for several days. They can be refrigerated for up to week or frozen for up to 6 weeks but may become soggy.

Yield: 16 pastries

Variations

Lemon Poppy–Seed Horns
Substitute lemon marmalade or lemon curd for the raspberry jam. Proceed as for raspberry horns.

Prune Horns
Omit the raspberry jam and poppy seeds. Spread with Prune Lekvar (page 38). Proceed as for raspberry horns.

Chocolate Horns
Melt 6 ounces (170 grams) semisweet or bittersweet chocolate with 2 tablespoons unsalted butter. Cool and reserve about ¼ cup (2 ounces / 57 grams). Spread 1½ cups (21 ounces / 595 grams) of Almond Paste filling on the dough and then spread the melted chocolate on top. Sprinkle with ½ cup (3.6 ounces / 100 grams) Cinnamon Sugar (page 40). Proceed to cut, shape, and bake as for raspberry horns. When baked and cool, drizzle with the reserved melted chocolate.

CHAPTER 10

Danish Pastries

Two hundred and sixteen alternating layers of butter make this dough so rich. They make a Danish Pastry that is tender and flaky, with a scent of sweet dairy butter.

Danish pastry has been accorded the recognition attained by bagels and pizza. "Danish" has given up its ethnicity and is universal, a citizen of the world, so to speak. Although Americans regard this pastry as Danish in origin, in Denmark they call it Viennese pastry. In France, it's *viennoiserie*. I always thought that Danish pastry was Jewish.

I don't miss waking up hours before sunrise to get to the bakery at 3 a.m. I don't miss the emergency calls about freezers not working or ovens not keeping their temperatures. What I do miss is a good cheese Danish. Many bakeries today use croissant dough or Bundt dough and call it a Danish. You need Danish pastry dough to make a Danish. Anything else is something else. If you don't know what I am talking about, you must make this dough. Your life will change. Since we closed Cheesecake King, the only place Adele and I can find a good cheese Danish is at Royal Crown Bakery in Staten Island. I have been known to drive almost an hour for an early morning breakfast. I leave with my belly full and a box of cheese Danish for my freezer.

When prepared from real Danish dough, there is no comparison with any quick dough, no matter how rich. Layering is what distinguishes Danish pastry from all other yeast-raised baked goods. It offers a light, unique bite and a taste that lingers on the palate. It cannot be duplicated.

There is some effort involved, and one can be forgiven for speculating that this is where the expression "Repaid a hundredfold" originated. Certainly it is apropos. In any case, you will be repaid a hundredfold and will be beaming with delight at the results of your work. Beware: after your first bite, you will never enjoy a faux cheese Danish again!

Also included in this chapter is Pressburger, a type of Danish made with a less rich dough but that fits in the Danish section of the bakery and this book.

—Master Recipe—
Danish Pastry Dough

Some bakers use half butter and half vegetable shortening for a flakier pastry, but I suggest all butter. Mix by hand or with a paddle in a stand mixer.

3 scant tablespoons (3 packets / 21 grams) active dry yeast

½ cup (4 fluid ounces / 118 milliliters) warm water 95° to 115°F / 35° to 46°C

1 cup (8 fluid ounces / 237 milliliters) cold milk

7 eggs

¾ cup (5.25 ounces / 150 grams) sugar

6 tablespoons (3 ounces / 85 grams) unsalted butter, softened, plus 2 cups (1 pound / 454 grams) unsalted butter, for roll-in

⅓ cup (1.33 ounces / 38 grams) nonfat dry milk powder

5¾ cups (32 ounces / 925 grams) unbleached all-purpose flour, plus additional flour as needed

1½ cups (8 ounces / 227 grams) cake flour

1 tablespoon kosher salt

Finely grated zest and juice of ½ orange

Vegetable oil, for brushing

Flour a half-sheet pan. In the mixing bowl of a stand mixer fitted with a paddle, sprinkle the yeast over the warm water to soften. Add the milk, eggs, sugar, 6 tablespoons softened butter, milk powder, all-purpose flour, cake flour, salt, and orange zest and juice. Mix at slow speed, pulsing with the on/off switch so that the flour does not fly out of the bowl. When the flour is fully incorporated, stop and scrape all of the ingredients clinging to the bottom and sides using a plastic scraper or rubber spatula.

Mix for 10 to 15 minutes at slow speed. After 10 minutes, if the dough has not come away from the sides of the bowl, use medium speed for a few minutes, adding more flour, ¼ cup at a time, if necessary. It is important to keep the dough soft. Don't add flour unnecessarily. Remove and scrape down the paddle, cover the bowl with a cloth or plastic wrap, and let the dough rise until doubled in volume, 45 to 60 minutes.

Punch down and turn out onto the prepared baking sheet. Cover loosely with a floured cloth or plastic wrap and refrigerate for 30 to 45 minutes, or until chilled.

ROLL-IN
Before removing the dough from the refrigerator, allow the remaining 2 cups of roll-in butter to soften slightly and then cut it into 1-inch cubes. Put the butter in the mixing bowl of a

stand mixer fitted with the flat paddle. Pulse the butter with the on/off switch to break up the cubes. Work fast: the butter should remain cool.

> 🔖 **Baker's Secret:** *Add a tennis ball–size chunk of Danish dough to the butter while softening the butter to make the roll-in more plastic and easier to roll.*

Remove the butter from the mixer. The butter should remain cool to the touch. Don't worry if some lumps remain. They will blend in when the dough is rolled. The goal is to try to have the roll-in and the dough at the same rolling consistency. If necessary, refrigerate the roll-in to achieve rolling consistency.

On a floured work surface, roll out the Danish dough into a 1-inch-thick rectangle measuring 24 inches long by 12 inches wide. First roll the length gently from the center outward to the edge, dusting with sufficient flour to keep the dough from adhering to the rolling pin. Then roll the width. Try not to tear the dough, but if you do, holes can be repaired by pressing in a little piece of dough. Use the dusting flour generously. If the dough sticks to the work surface, flip half the dough over on itself. Scrape the work surface clean wherever the dough has adhered, dust well with more flour, and flip it back. Repeat with the other half. Brush off excess flour from the top of the dough.

To roll-in, dot the butter over two-thirds of the dough, leaving a 1-inch border so that the butter does not ooze out while rolling. As if folding a letter in thirds, fold the nonbuttered third over the center. The goal is to form alternate layers of butter and dough. Brush off the flour and then fold over once more.

FIRST ROLL: THREE-FOLD
Turn the dough a quarter turn so that the seam is facing you, and dust with flour, top and bottom. Roll the dough along the length to about 24 inches and then roll to about 18 inches wide (about the length of your baking sheet).

> 🔖 **Baker's Secret:** *Use your baking sheet to measure.*

After brushing off excess flour, fold in thirds. Gently lift or flip over onto the well-floured baking sheet. Make an indentation in one corner of the dough with your finger. This signifies that the dough has received one roll. Cover with a cloth or plastic wrap and allow to rest in the refrigerator for 30 to 45 minutes.

SECOND ROLL: THREE-FOLD
Repeat as in the first roll, above. Make two indentations and refrigerate. The indentations mark the number of rolls.

THIRD ROLL: FOUR-FOLD
Roll out as for the first two rolls, but this time roll the dough longer and thinner, to about 32 by 18 inches. Brush off the flour. Fold the

short ends in to meet at the center. Brush off excess flour and then flip one end over the other (like closing a book), producing a four-fold.

> **℘ Baker's Secret:** *Before the final flip of the four-fold, sprinkle one side of the dough with cinnamon sugar. This will add extra flavor to the pastry when baked. It also makes it easier for the baker to reopen the final fold later to add fillings.*

Place the dough on the well-floured baking sheet. Gently roll and press the top down with the rolling pin so that the dough fills the pan evenly. Brush off any excess flour from the top and brush with vegetable oil to prevent a crust from forming. Mark with three indentations with your finger tip in the corner of the dough. Cover with a cloth or plastic wrap so that the top does not dry out and place on the lowest shelf of your refrigerator. Refrigerate overnight on the baking sheet until properly aged and well chilled. Cut the dough in quarters, wrapping each section tightly with plastic. Sections can be frozen and thawed in the refrigerator as needed.

Yield: About 6 pounds of dough

> **℘ Baker's Secret:** *Freeze the dough for 30 minutes before refrigerating to slow down the initial rise. Bear in mind that even while frozen, in a home freezer, the dough will continue to age slowly and will lose some strength and consequently some flavor. Remember: never refreeze dough. Thaw frozen dough overnight in the refrigerator.*

a jewish baker's pastry secrets

Prune Danish Pockets

A few of our elderly customers always included at least one prune Danish with their purchase. I never asked if it was preference or medicinal. Either way, they taste fabulous if you like prunes, or, as some call them, "dried plums."

¼ portion (1½ pounds / 680 grams) Danish Pastry Dough (page 174)

1½ cups (12 ounces / 340 grams) Prune Lekvar (page 38)

1 egg

1 tablespoon water

Granulated sugar, for topping

Baker's Danish Glaze (page 41)

Line two half-sheet pans with parchment paper or greased waxed paper.

On a floured work surface, roll out the dough into a rectangle about 18 inches long by 14 inches wide. Shrink down the dough by holding one corner of the bottom edge with each hand, lifting gently, and giving a little shake, like smoothing out a tablecloth. The dough should now be at least 16 inches long by 12 inches wide. If it's too short, gently roll to size, working from the center out to the edges.

With a pizza wheel or a sharp blade and a yardstick, trim the edges to form straight lines. Scraps can be set aside for reuse. Brush off any excess flour. With the knife, make an indentation to mark every 4 inches.

With a yardstick as a guide, cut twelve squares, each 4 by 3 inches (about 2 ounces each). "Drop out" (see page 36) a rounded tablespoon of prune lekvar in the center of each square. Lightly beat the egg with the water to make an egg wash. Brush all of the edges with the egg wash. Grasp two corners diagonally opposite each other. Stretching slightly, bring one end over and just beyond the filling. Press down hard to seal. Bring the other end over and seal once more. Do not be afraid to press hard; if you don't, they may open while baking. A bit of prune should peek out at the top and bottom of the closure.

Finish all of the pieces. Line them up in a row. Brush with the egg wash, taking care to keep excess egg from running down the sides. A dot of granulated sugar spilled in the center of each pastry serves to mark the pastry as prune filled. Place six to a pan, equally spaced on the prepared baking sheets.

Set aside and let rise until doubled in volume, about 45 minutes. When pressed very gently on the side with a fingertip, the dough should be soft and yield readily. Using a delicate touch, carefully brush a second time with the egg wash. Let dry a few minutes.

Position a rack in the center of the oven and preheat to 375°F/190°C.

Bake for 30 to 45 minutes, until well browned. If two sheets cannot fit side by side in your oven, bake one at a time. The top should feel firm to the touch and spring back when lightly pressed with the fingers. Remove from the oven and brush with the Danish glaze while still hot.

Cool in the pan on a wire rack. Serve warm or at room temperature. Tightly covered, the pastries keep for several days at room temperature. They can be frozen for 4 to 8 weeks. Thaw overnight in the refrigerator.

Yield: 12 pastries

Variation

Fruit Pockets
Fill the pockets with fruit fillings or various thickened fruit preserves, (page 37) of your choice.

Cheese Danish

Cheese Danish were so popular that they were always first to be sold out in the bakery. Eventually I instituted a system allowing us to have freshly baked cheese Danish on hand at all times.

I prepared extra pans of pastries that were kept unbaked and frozen. One or two thawed pans were always kept in the refrigerator, retarding the rising and allowing us to have fresh, hot-from-the-oven Danish with about a 1-hour lead time—the time required to allow the dough to rise and be baked.

Pans that remained unused in the refrigerator were perfect for the first baking early on the following morning. A similar system can be adapted in the home by the astute baker who wishes to maintain a reserve of fresh baked goods.

¼ portion (1½ pounds / 680 grams) Danish Pastry Dough (page 174)

1 egg

1 tablespoon water, for egg wash

1½ cups (15 ounces / 425 grams) Cheese Filling (page 35) or Cream Cheese Filling (page 35)

Sliced almonds, for topping, preferably toasted (optional)

Baker's Danish Glaze (page 41)

Line two half-sheet pans with parchment paper or greased waxed paper.

Follow the direction for Prune Danish Pockets, substituting a cheese filling for the prune, and sprinkle the tops with almonds after the egg wash is applied.

Yield: 12 pastries

Variation

Custard-Filled Pockets
Fill with Pastry Cream (page 37) in place of the cheese.

Cinnamon Danish
(Snails or Schnecken)

This is my personal favorite. There are two mindsets as to how these Danish should be eaten. Some people pop out the center, the tastiest part, and devour it first. Some people nibble or cut with knife and fork around the edges, slowly working toward the best part. It all depends on whether you are impatient to consume the best part first or prefer to linger, savoring the sweetest part for last. Any way you eat it, it tastes just as good. If crumbs are not available, you can make your pastry even more luxurious by substituting streusel.

¼ portion (1½ pounds / 680 grams) **Danish Pastry Dough** (page 174)

1½ cups (12 ounces / 340 grams) **Processed Almond-Paste filling** (page 32)

2 tablespoons ground cinnamon

½ cup (1.8 ounces / 51 grams) cake crumbs (see page 42) or bread crumbs, preferably fresh, plus more if needed to cover

¼ cup (2 ounces / 56 grams) unsalted butter, melted

½ cup (3.6 ounce / 100 grams) **Cinnamon Sugar** (page 40)

1 egg

1 tablespoon water

Baker's Danish Glaze (page 41)

Line two half-sheet pans with parchment paper or greased waxed paper.

On a floured work surface, roll out the dough into a ¼-inch-thick rectangle about 18 inches long by 12 inches wide. Dust with flour as necessary to prevent sticking.

Brush off any excess flour. Spread the top of the dough with the almond filling, leaving a ½-inch border along the top. Dust lightly with the cinnamon. Cover with the crumbs. Press down lightly with your hands or a rolling pin. Drizzle with half of the melted butter. Reserve 2 tablespoons of the cinnamon sugar but sprinkle on the rest.

Lightly beat the egg with the water to make an egg wash. Brush the border with the egg wash.

Starting at the bottom edge, fold over a flap, about 2 inches wide. Fold over again. Keep folding or rolling until the end is reached. Turn so that the seam is centered along the bottom.

Brush the top with the remaining melted butter. Cut into twelve equal pieces, each about 1½ inches wide. Place cut side up, evenly spaced, on the prepared baking sheets. If the ends do not appear to be well sealed, tuck them under the edge of the dough.

a jewish baker's pastry secrets

Brush the tops with the egg wash, taking care not to let the egg drip down the sides of the dough. Set aside and let rise until doubled in volume, about 45 minutes. When pressed very gently on the side with a fingertip, the dough should be soft and yield readily. Carefully brush a second time with the egg wash. Let dry a few minutes and then sprinkle a pinch of cinnamon sugar on top of the center of each piece.

Position a rack in the center of the oven and preheat to 375°F/190°C.

Bake for 30 to 40 minutes, until evenly browned. If two sheets cannot fit side by side in your oven, bake one at a time. (Alternately, place the racks to divide the oven into thirds. Rotate the baking pans from top to bottom half way into baking time.)

The top should feel firm to the touch and spring back when lightly pressed with your fingers. Remove from the oven and brush with the Danish glaze while still hot.

Cool on a wire rack for 10 to 15 minutes before removing from the pan. Serve warm or at room temperature. Tightly covered, the pastries keep for several days at room temperature. They can be frozen for 4 to 8 weeks. Thaw overnight in the refrigerator.

Yield: 12 pastries

Variations

Fruit Schnecken

Prepare as above. When fully risen, press an indentation into the center of each piece with your thumb. Fill with a tablespoon of a fruit filling or thickened jam (page 37). Bake as above.

Pecan Schnecken

Prepare as for Cinnamon Danish. Sprinkle 1 cup (4 ounces / 113 grams) pecans, toasted (see page 31) and chopped, over the almond filling. Fill, roll, and slice as above. Brush the cut side of the schnecken with the egg wash. Spread 1 cup (4 ounces / 113 grams) pecan halves on the work surface or on a baking sheet. Dip the tops of each piece into the pecans, pressing lightly to make them adhere. Turn right side up on the baking sheet. Do not brush with the egg wash a second time. (If desired, sprinkle with cinnamon sugar.) Let rise and bake as above.

Streusel Schnecken

Prepare as for Cinnamon Danish. Fill, roll, and slice as above. Spread 2½ cups (24 ounce / 680 grams) Butter Streusel (page 40) on the work surface or a baking sheet. Brush the cut side of prepared Cinnamon Danish with the egg wash. Turn, cut side down, on top of the streusel. Press gently to make it adhere. Place on the prepared pan, streusel side up. Let rise and bake as above.

Raspberry Bow Ties

These raspberry pastries with streusel might become your favorite. They are sublime.

¼ portion (1½ pounds / 680 grams) Danish Pastry Dough (page 174)

1½ cups (15 ounces, 425 grams) thickened raspberry jam (page 37)

2 cups (7.2 ounces / 200 grams) cake crumbs (see page 42) or bread crumbs, preferably fresh

½ cup (3.6 ounce, 100 grams) Cinnamon Sugar (page 40)

¼ cup (2 ounces / 56 grams) unsalted butter, melted

1 egg

1 tablespoon water

2½ cups (24 ounces / 680 grams) Butter Streusel (page 40), for topping

Baker's Danish Glaze (page 41)

Confectioners' sugar, for topping (optional)

Line two half-sheet pans with parchment paper or greased waxed paper.

On a floured work surface, roll out the dough into a 1-inch-thick rectangle about 12 inches long by 15 inches wide. Brush off any excess flour.

Spread the bottom two-thirds of the dough with the raspberry jam. Cover with the crumbs, sprinkle with cinnamon sugar, and drizzle with melted butter. Brush the top one-third of the dough with the butter. Fold or flip the top one-third of the dough over half of the raspberry-streusel section. Brush off extra flour from the dough, brush with melted butter, and then fold over remaining raspberry- streusel section. Brush off any excess flour. Lightly beat the egg with the water to make an egg wash. Brush the plain side with the egg wash.

Roll out lengthwise to about 18 inches. Roll the width slightly to even it out and help seal. Cut crosswise into twelve equal pieces, each about 1½ inches wide. Grasping the center of each piece (use both hands), quickly twist twice (two half turns) to form a bow tie shape. Press down with your thumbs just behind the twist to overcome the pastry's tendency to unravel. As the bow ties are formed, line them up in a vertical line, touching each other. Brush the tops with the egg wash. Top with a heavy layer of streusel, pressing down lightly with your palms to make it adhere.

Place six, evenly spaced, on each of the prepared baking sheets. Set aside and let rise until doubled in volume, about 45 minutes. When pressed very gently on the side with a fingertip, the dough should be soft and yield readily.

Position a rack in the center of the oven and preheat to 375°F/190°C.

Bake for 30 to 40 minutes, or until well browned. If two sheets cannot fit side by side in your oven, bake one at a time. (Alternately, place the racks to divide the oven into thirds. Rotate the baking pans from top to bottom half way into baking time.)

The top should feel firm to the touch and spring back when lightly pressed with the fingers. Remove from the oven and brush with the Danish glaze while still hot.

Cool on a wire rack for 10 to 15 minutes before removing from the pan. Dust with confectioners' sugar. Serve warm or at room temperature. Tightly covered, the pastries keep at room temperature for several days. They can be frozen up to 8 weeks. Thaw overnight in the refrigerator.

Yield: 12 pastries

Variations

Chocolate–Raspberry Bow Ties

Melt 6 ounces (170 grams) best-quality semi-sweet or bittersweet chocolate with ¼ cup (2 ounces / 56 grams) unsalted butter. Let cool. Reserve about ¼ cup (2 ounces / 56 grams).

Spread the melted chocolate over the raspberry jam, sprinkle the streusel and the cinnamon sugar and proceed to roll, slice, shape, and bake as above. When baked and cool, drizzle with the reserved melted chocolate instead of the Danish Baker's Glaze and confectioners' sugar.

Almond Bow Ties

Replace the raspberry jam with 1½ to 2 cups (15 to 20 ounces / 425 to 566 grams) Almond Paste Filling (page 31) or Frangipane (page 36). Over the filling, sprinkle the streusel and cinnamon-sugar. Proceed to roll, slice, shape, and bake as above.

Chocolate–Almond Bow Ties

Melt 6 ounces (170 grams) best-quality semi-sweet or bittersweet chocolate with ¼ cup (2 ounces / 56 grams) unsalted butter. Let cool. Reserve about ¼ cup (2 ounces / 56 grams).

Spread the dough with 1½ cups (15 ounces/ 425 grams) Processed Almond-Paste Filling (page 32). Spread the melted chocolate over the almond filling. Over the chocolate, sprinkle the streusel and cinnamon sugar and then proceed to roll, slice, shape, and bake as above. When baked and cool, drizzle with the reserved melted chocolate instead of the Danish Baker's Glaze and the confectioners' sugar.

Braided Rings

Sunday was the busiest day in the bakery. My day began at 4 a.m. Adele and my daughters arrived at 6:30 a.m. We all worked hard—there was a nonstop flow of customers. Many Sundays after our day was complete we would pile into the car and drive an hour to Hong Fat in Chinatown in Manhattan. We would walk past the long line of waiting customers outside and hand the first waiter who met us at the door the coffee cakes we had brought. We never ordered: the dishes arrived at the table. Waiters, plates full of coffee cake in one hand, fork in the other, would visit with us throughout our meal. "Mr. George, best cake! Thank you." The cake assured us a table with no wait. These cakes will assure you gratitude from those who taste them.

Rings baked in a ring pan will rise higher and bake fluffier than those baked directly on a sheet pan. Baking directly on the baking sheet will produce a wider, flatter ring with a chewier consistency. Due to the difference in texture, the two rings will taste different. Savarin pans bake rings with a high, beautifully rounded top. Try them each and prepare to suit your own taste.

⅓ portion (2 pounds / 906 grams) **Danish Pastry Dough (page 174)**

1½ cups (12 ounces / 340 grams) **Processed Almond-Paste filling (page 32)**

2 cups (7 ounces / 200 grams) cake crumbs (see page 42) or bread crumbs, preferably fresh

½ cup (3.6 ounces / 112 grams) **Cinnamon Sugar (page 40)**

1 egg

1 tablespoon water

Baker's Danish Glaze (page 41)

Simple Icing (page 41), warm (optional)

Grease two half-sheet pans or three 10-inch coffee cake ring pans or Savarin pans.

On a floured work surface, carefully pry or cut open the center fold of the Danish pastry dough as you would open the page of a book. This will be easier if you previously sprinkled the four-fold of the Danish dough with cinnamon sugar, as described in the master recipe (page 174).

Turn the dough lengthwise. Spread the almond filling over the bottom half of the opened dough leaving a ½-inch border along both top and bottom. Sprinkle the cake crumbs over the almond filling and then top with the cinnamon sugar. Press down lightly with your hands or a rolling pin to make the crumbs adhere. Brush the top half of the dough with the egg wash and turn or flip the top over the filled half.

Roll out the dough to a ½-inch-thick rectangle measuring 9 inches long and then 6 inches wide. If the dough gets too tough to roll, allow it to rest, covered, for 5 to 10 minutes until it softens; then finish rolling. With a bench

a jewish baker's pastry secrets

knife or pizza wheel, cut crosswise into thirds; each piece should weigh about 12 ounces. Cut each section once again in thirds.

Twist each section into a spiral. With your palms on each end, roll the right end up and away from you, while at the same time rolling the left side down and toward you. When twisted, lengthen into ropes 10 to 11 inches long by rolling gently with your palms working from the center out to the ends.

Braid three ropes together into a three-strand braid. This is the typical pigtail braid. Starting at the top, begin braiding, right over center, left over center, until reaching the end. Do not stretch while working; the braid should remain uniform throughout. Form each braid into a ring with the ends overlapping by about an inch. Seal where the ends cross by pressing with your thumbs or the side of your hand. Fold the resulting flap under.

Place on prepared baking sheets—two on one sheet, one on the other—or place each in a greased coffee cake ring pan or Savarin pan.

Set the rings aside until doubled in size, about 40 minutes. When touched gently with your fingertips, the dough should feel soft and yield to the touch.

Position a rack in the center of the oven and preheat to 375°F/190°C.

Bake for about 35 to 40 minutes, or until nicely browned. The braids should feel firm when lightly pressed with your fingertips. If white lines show between the braids, continue baking for 5 to 10 minutes. When baked directly on the baking sheet, check that the bottoms are browned by slipping a bowl knife or spatula underneath and lifting an edge carefully to sneak a peek. Remove from oven and immediately brush the tops with the Danish glaze. Cool in the pans on wire racks. When cool, remove from the pans and drizzle with the warm icing. Wrapped tightly, they keep for up to a week at room temperature or frozen for up to 6 weeks. Thaw overnight in the refrigerator.

Yield: 3 rings, each serving 8 to 10

Variations

Raisin Braided Ring

Follow the directions for the Braided Ring. Sprinkle 1 cup (5 ounces / 140 grams) of raisins over the almond filling (before the cake crumbs) on one third of the dough.

Pecan Rings

Follow the directions for Braided Rings but after forming the braided rings, lightly brush the top of the rings with 1 egg beaten with 1 tablespoon water. Spread 2 cups (8 ounces / 227 grams) of pecans, chopped and preferably toasted, on a baking sheet or work surface. Press each ring, egg wash side down on the pecans. Place the dough in greased pans or on greased half-sheet pans, pecan side down, and follow directions for baking as above.

Nut Rings

Follow the directions for Braided Rings but after forming the braided rings, lightly brush the tops of the rings with 1 egg beaten with 1 tablespoon water. Spread 2 cups (8 ounces / 227 grams) walnuts, cashews, or other nuts, chopped and preferably toasted, on a baking sheet or work surface. Press each ring, egg wash side down on the nuts. Place the dough in the greased pans or on greased half-sheet pans, nut side down, and follow directions for baking as above.

Streusel Rings

Prepare as for Braided Rings, above, adding nuts if desired. Lightly brush the tops of the rings with 1 egg beaten with 1 tablespoon water. Spread a generous layer of Butter Streusel (page 40) on a baking sheet or work surface. Press each ring, egg wash side down, into the streusel. Place the dough in greased ring pans or on greased half-sheet pans, streusel side up and follow the directions for baking as above. When baked and cooled, drizzle with warm simple icing or dust with confectioners' sugar. The rings can also be left plain.

> ℬ **Baker's Secret:** *Streusel lovers, gently sprinkle additional streusel on top of the ring when fully risen and ready for the oven.*

Fruit Streusel Rings

Prepare as for Braided Rings, above, adding nuts if desired. Lightly brush the tops of the rings with 1 egg beaten with 1 tablespoon water. Spread a generous layer of Butter Streusel (page 40) on a baking sheet or work surface. Press each ring, egg wash side down, into the streusel. Place the dough in the greased ring pans or on greased half-sheet pans streusel side down. Using any fruit filling or thickened jam, place a ring of fruit over the streusel forming a circle along the center of the ring and follow the directions for baking as above. When baked and cooled, drizzle with warm simple icing or dust with confectioners' sugar. The rings can also be left plain. Thickened raspberry jam or apple filling are my favorites.

Fruit Rings

Follow the directions for Braided Rings but after forming the braided rings, with your fingertips, press four to six evenly spaced indentations around the ring. Lightly brush the tops of the rings with 1 egg beaten with 1 tablespoon water. With a tablespoon, drop dots of fruit pie filling or thickened jam (see page 37) into the indentations. Top with sliced almonds, if desired. Follow the directions for baking as above. When baked and cooled, drizzle with warm simple icing or dust with confectioners' sugar. The rings can also be left plain.

Strawberry Chantilly Ring

This ring is best when made from a Danish ring that has been baked one day in advance. This gives the flavors time to marry and makes the ring easier to split open. Although any Danish coffee cake ring will do, I prefer a Pecan Ring (page 185) for this pastry. At home, I always prepared an extra pecan ring that was set aside for a chantilly ring, to be prepared the following day or frozen and filled when desired.

1 baked Danish coffee cake ring (page 184), chilled or at room temperature

1 cup (8 ounces / 227 grams) fresh strawberries, diced or sliced, plus 3 whole berries reserved for garnish

Splash of Kirsch or fruit-flavored liqueur (optional)

1 pint (16 fluid ounces / 473 milliliters) whipping cream, chilled, preferably not ultra-pasteurized

1 tablespoon sugar (optional)

1 teaspoon pure vanilla extract

¼ cup (2.5 ounces / 70 grams) strawberry jam

Confectioners' sugar, for dusting

With a long serrated knife, slice off the top half of the Danish ring by first cutting partially around the circumference of the ring, then slicing through to the center. Set the top aside. Slide the bottom onto a flat serving dish.

Place the sliced or diced strawberries in a bowl; sprinkle with the liqueur. Let macerate until the cream is whipped.

Pour the chilled cream into the chilled mixing bowl of a stand mixer fitted with a whisk attachment and beat at medium speed until the beater forms tracks in the cream. (The cream can be beaten by hand with a balloon whisk.) With the machine running at slow speed, slowly add the sugar and vanilla. Continue whipping at medium speed until the cream begins to fluff. Whip at high speed for about a minute, allowing the cream to aerate and increase in volume. Do not overbeat.

Stir the berries and jam together and spread over the cut side of the ring. Pipe out the cream with a cloth pastry bag fitted with a #8 star or French tip. Alternatively, spoon out the cream. Leave some whipped cream aside for garnish. Gently lift the top half of the ring over the cream with the aid of a spatula. Press very lightly to set the top in place. Pipe six equally spaced rosettes or spoon out dots of the reserved cream on top of the ring. Place the three whole berries on alternate dots or slice the strawberries in half and place on 6 dots. Using a small sieve, dust the top of the finished ring lightly with confectioners' sugar.

Yield: One cake, serving 8 to 10

Scotch Coffee Cake

Scotch coffee cake is neither Scottish in origin, nor is it made with Scotch whiskey. The name refers to the butterscotch filling, a confection made mainly from butter and brown sugar.

¼ portion (1½ pounds / 680 grams) Danish Pastry Dough (page 174), cut into three 8-ounce pieces

1½ cups (15 ounces / 425 grams) thickened raspberry jam (page 37)

1 cup (8 ounces / 240 grams) firmly packed brown sugar, plus more to cover

¾ cup (6 ounces / 170 grams) unsalted butter, melted

1 cup (4 ounces / 113 grams) walnuts, chopped, preferably toasted

1½ cups (14.4 ounces / 408 grams) Butter Streusel (page 40)

Baker's Danish Glaze (page 41)

Simple Icing (page 41), warm

Line two half-sheet pans with parchment paper or greased waxed paper.

On a floured work surface, roll out each piece of dough until ⅛ inch or less in thickness and 12 inches long; then roll the width to 7 inches wide. Be patient and allow the dough to rest when it resists rolling. Set the piece aside and continue with the next two, returning to the first piece when it relaxes.

Position a rack in the center of the oven and preheat the oven to 375°F/190°C.

On each rolled piece, spread a thin layer of the raspberry jam from edge to edge, leaving a ½-inch border along the top. Sprinkle the brown sugar over the raspberry jam. Drizzle generously with ¼ cup of the melted butter. Brush the ½-inch border with water. Starting from the bottom, fold the dough over in thirds. Press the edge down to seal.

Place on the prepared baking sheets. Brush the tops lightly with ¼ cup melted butter. Sprinkle on the walnuts and a layer of the butter streusel, rubbed fine through a sieve.

Drizzle the remaining ¼ cup butter over the top. You want the streusel to melt in the oven and form a crust. Let the dough rest for about 5 minutes until it relaxes. Bake without allowing it to rise.

Bake for 35 to 45 minutes, until browned. The top should feel firm and spring back when lightly pressed with the fingers. If two sheets cannot fit side by side in your oven, bake one at a time. (Alternately, place the racks to divide the oven into thirds. Rotate the baking pans from top to bottom half way into baking time.)

Brush with the Danish glaze immediately upon removal from the oven. Drizzle with icing that has been thinned with a small amount of water before the glaze has time to dry. The heat from the newly baked pastry will melt the icing into a thin white glaze. Cool in the pan on a wire rack. Keep for a few days at room temperature, wrapped in plastic, or freeze for up to 8 weeks.

Yield: 3 coffee cakes, each serving 3 to 4

Pressburger Dough

Traditionally, pressburger is made with one of two fillings: poppy seed (referred to by bakers as poppy butter or *mohn*) or nut, generally made with almonds. In the bakery, I made long strips of this pastry and sold slices of it by the pound. You can also use this dough to make miniature pastries; follow the directions for making rugelach (page 2).

¼ cup (2 fluid ounces / 59 milliliters) warm water, 95° to 115°F / 35° to 46°C

1½ teaspoons (½ packet / 3.5 grams) active dry yeast

¾ cup (6 fluid ounces / 178 milliliters) milk, room temperature (see Note)

½ cup (3.5 ounces / 100 grams) sugar

1 cup (8 ounces / 227 grams) unsalted butter, at room temperature

1 egg yolk

4 cups (17 ounces / 484 grams) unbleached all-purpose flour, plus more as needed

1 tablespoon nonfat dry milk powder

1 teaspoon pure vanilla extract

¼ teaspoon kosher salt

1 egg, separated

Line a half-sheet pan with parchment paper or greased waxed paper.

In the mixing bowl of a stand mixer fitted with a flat paddle, or in a large mixing bowl, sprinkle the yeast over the warm water. Add the milk, sugar, butter, egg yolk, flour, milk powder, and vanilla. Pulse with the on/off switch until blended, making sure that the flour does not fly out of the bowl. Then mix at slow speed for 8 to 10 minutes. The dough should come away from the sides of the bowl and gather up around the paddle. If not, turn the mixer to medium speed for a few minutes. Additional flour can be added, 1 tablespoon at a time, if necessary. Stir with a wooden spoon until the dough comes away from the sides of the bowl. Turn out the dough onto a floured work surface and divide the dough into four pieces. Flatten each into a rectangle and roll each up jelly-roll style into an oblong shape. Cover and let rest for at least 5 and up to 10 minutes. This is not a dough that rises. At this stage, the dough can be covered and refrigerated overnight, or it can be frozen, well wrapped, for a week or more.

Yield: Dough for 4 pressburgers (about 2.4 pounds / 1089 grams)

Note: For a nondairy recipe, replace the milk with water, the butter with margarine, and omit the milk powder.

Almond Pressburger

"Press what?" most customers asked. A slice of Pressburger reveals many layers of pastry with rich almond paste in between each layer. It is sturdy enough to hold the slice in your hand and bite into it like a sandwich. It is indescribably delicious.

10 ounces Pressburger Dough
(page 190)

1 cup (10 ounces / 284 grams) Processed
Almond-Paste filling (page 32)

1 egg, separated

Line a half-sheet pan with parchment paper or greased waxed paper.

On a floured work surface, roll out one piece of dough into ⅛-inch-thick rectangle measuring 12 by 8 inches. Spread with a ¼-inch layer (about 1 cup) of almond filling, leaving a 1-inch border at the bottom along the length and a ½-inch border along the sides and top. Gently and loosely fold over a 1-inch flap along the bottom. Do this about two and a half turns, until the strip is 3 to 4 inches wide with the seam centered along the bottom. Avoid rolling or folding tightly, or the crust may burst in the oven. Fold the ends under and place on the prepared baking sheet.

Lightly beat the egg yolk. Brush the top and sides of the pressburger with the beaten yolk; avoid letting any egg drip onto the baking pan. Let stand until the egg is dry. Refrigerate until well chilled, at least several hours or overnight.

Before baking, beat the reserved egg white lightly and brush onto the dough and let dry. With an ice pick or skewer, stipple the pastry by poking a few holes an inch or two apart along the center of the pastry.

Position a rack in the center of the oven and preheat to 350°F/175°C.

Bake for 25 to 35 minutes, until the crust is browned and feels firm; it should spring back when lightly pressed with a fingertip.

Cool in the pan on a wire rack. Serve at room temperature. Wrapped in plastic, this keeps well for a week; it can be frozen for up to 8 weeks.

Yield: 1 strip, serving 8

Variations

Poppy-Seed (*Mohn*) Pressburger

Substitute Poppy Butter Filling (page 38) for the almond filling.

Walnut Pressburger

Substitute Walnut Filling (page 39) for the almond filling. If desired, scatter ¼ cup (1 ounce / 28 grams) chopped walnuts, preferably toasted, over the walnut filling.

Almond Pressburger Crescents

Crescents were the height of fashion in Vienna in 1793. Austrian bakers celebrated the end of a Turkish attack by making rolled pressburger pastries in the shape of crescents, the design on the Ottoman flag. You will find instructions to make individual pastries and larger cakes, similar to strudel. Any bakery that makes Hungarian pressburgers is sure to display an accompanying tray of pressburger crescents.

1 recipe (2.4 pounds / 1089 grams) Pressburger Dough (page 190)

2 cups (20 ounces / 567 grams) Processed Almond-Paste filling (page 32)

1 egg, separated

Line two half-sheet pans with parchment paper or greased waxed paper.

On floured work surface, roll out the dough into a ⅛-inch-thick rectangle measuring 20 inches long and 12 inches wide. Cut in half lengthwise to make two strips, 20 by 6 inches. Cut each strip into triangles, 5 inches wide at the base and 6 inches long. Press the scrap ends together to form two additional triangles for a total of eighteen.

Spread a tablespoonful of almond filling at the base of each wedge and roll up from the base. Bring the ends around into a crescent shape. Place on the prepared baking sheets, equally spaced apart, nine crescents to each sheet. Lightly beat the egg yolk.

Brush the crescents with the beaten egg yolk; avoid letting any egg drip onto the baking pan. Let stand until the egg wash is dry. Refrigerate until well chilled, at least several hours; overnight is best.

Lightly beat the egg white. Brush the crescents once more with the beaten egg white. Let dry.

Position a rack in the center of the oven and preheat to 350°F/175°C.

Bake for 25 to 35 minutes, or until browned. If two sheets cannot fit side by side in your oven, bake one at a time. (Alternately, place the racks to divide the oven into thirds. Rotate the baking pans from top to bottom half way into baking time.)

The crust should feel firm and spring back when lightly pressed with a fingertip. Cool in the pan on a wire rack. Serve warm or at room temperature. The crescents keep well for a week wrapped in plastic wrap at room temperature; freeze for up to 8 weeks.

Yield: 18 crescents

Variation

An Alternative Way to Make Crescents

As a home baker, you may find this alternative way to make crescents easier.

Cut the dough into three equal pieces, about 13 ounces each. Roll into three balls, cover, and let rest for a few minutes. On a floured surface, roll each ball into a circle about 1/8 inch thick and 10 inches in diameter. Cut each circle into six equal wedges. Arrange the wedges in a line with the bases turned toward you. Roll out each wedge until 8 to 10 inches in length. Brush off any excess flour. Place a spoonful of the filling at the large end of the wedge and roll toward the small end.

Arrange nine pastries on each pan. Brush with the beaten egg yolk, taking care to keep excess egg from running down the sides or onto the baking pan. Let stand until the egg wash has dried. Proceed as above.

a jewish baker's pastry secrets

Apple Swirls

Apples, walnuts, and spice, all rolled up in strudel-like layers of rich dough and then baked into a streusel-topped loaf—what could be more delicious? When sliced, you'll see—and smell—savory cinnamon-scented swirls of fruit and nuts.

½ recipe (1¼ pounds / 544 grams) Pressburger Dough (page 190)

6 cups (1½ pounds / 680 grams) Apple Filling (page 33)

2 cups (8 ounces / 227 grams) walnuts, toasted (page 31) and chopped

3 cups (10.5 ounces / 298 grams) cake crumbs (see page 42) or bread crumbs, preferably fresh

1 tablespoon water

¼ cup (2 ounces / 57 grams) unsalted butter, melted

2 cups (11 ounces / 312 grams) Butter Streusel (page 40), or more, to taste

Grease two 8-inch loaf pans.

Cut the dough into two 10-ounce (284-gram) strips. On a floured work surface, roll out each strip lengthwise until it is ⅛ inch thick and measures 12 by 8 inches. Spread the filling evenly over both strips leaving a 1-inch border at the top and bottom of the short sides. Top with the walnuts and then sprinkle with the cake crumbs. Drizzle the two strips with half of the melted butter. Fold over a 1-inch flap at the bottom. Avoid stretching. Continue folding, jelly-roll style, ending with the seam centered on the bottom.

Place one strip in each loaf pan. Brush the tops with remaining melted butter and sprinkle with large clumps of streusel to cover. With a skewer or an ice pick, stipple by poking a series of holes down the center of each loaf. Let rest until barely beginning to rise, 45 to 60 minutes. At this point, the dough can be refrigerated overnight.

Position a rack in the center of the oven and preheat to 375°F/190°C.

Place the loaf pans on a baking sheet and bake for 35 to 45 minutes, until well browned. The top should feel firm to the touch and spring back when lightly pressed with the fingers. Be careful when pressing because hot streusel can burn.

Cool on a wire rack for 10 to 15 minutes before removing from the pans. Tightly covered, the pastries keep well at room temperature for several days. They can be frozen for up to 8 weeks. Thaw overnight in the refrigerator.

Yield: Two 8-inch loaves, each serving 6 to 8

Afterword

This book was a joint effort. After we rescued it from George's rather complicated computer system and discussed the possibility, we set about testing recipes. We enrolled a few friends to try some recipes as well. Everyone's freezer became full of assorted dough and fillings. After making George's recipes, some of us began mixing and matching the leftover parts. You will find each dough adapts well to new variations. Intermix the fillings, shapes, and dough, and use your common sense about timing. If you do not have almond paste, use another almond filling or replace the almond with a different nut. Be courageous.

We think George would have approved of the coffee cake made out of Danish dough, goat cheese, and apricot filling, with streusel on top. That was a result of being too lazy to go the store, so cream cheese was replaced with goat cheese. The apricot jam was waiting to be used in the refrigerator. The streusel was leftover from another project.

As you become more familiar with the doughs and fillings, feel free to play around. You will be surprised by how easy it is to create your own masterpiece. Remember one of George's rules: Everything is better with chocolate!

George was a large presence at any family gathering and was always supportive of our baking and cooking. One of Isaac's earliest memories was making rugelach with George and his mother, kneeling on a stool to scoop ingredients out of large glass containers. These forays into baking with his grandfather cemented a passion for food that has and will continue to be a large part of his life. More than three decades before, George and Adele provided similar experiences that fostered the same passion in their daughters, Elaine and Julia.

Even after George passed away, we continued to learn from him as we read and edited the early drafts of this book. When the opportunity arose to complete this book we were excited that we could keep his passion for baking alive for both our family and his readers. We hope that as you bake his recipes that you can benefit from his tips and, most importantly, enjoy good pastries.

—Elaine Greenstein, Julia Greenstein, and Isaac Bleicher

Biography

George Greenstein was born on July 1, 1929. His father, Louis, a baker who dreamed of being an opera singer, arrived in New York from Hungary in 1924. His mother, Sylvia, came from Russia in 1922. Sylvia and Louis met on the Lower East Side. George was their only child.

George thought he was going to become an engineer and went to Brooklyn Tech High School. He was a serious student and a Boy Scout. After a couple years of college, and a few other career attempts, George joined the Army. He was stationed in Louisville, Kentucky, during the Korean War. After, he returned to New York to work with his father in the bakery.

In the late 1950s, George moved with his new family and his parents to Long Island. They opened a bakery together, The Cheesecake King. Louis died in 1964 and George kept baking, eventually writing the beloved *Secrets of a Jewish Baker*, which won a James Beard Award in 1994.

Index

a jewish baker's pastry secrets